Android User Interface Development

Beginner's Guide

Quickly design and develop compelling user interfaces for
your Android applications

Jason Morris

[PACKT] open source
PUBLISHING   community experience distilled

BIRMINGHAM - MUMBAI

Android User Interface Development
Beginner's Guide

First published: February 2011

Production Reference: 1160211

Published by Packt Publishing Ltd.
32 Lincoln Road
Olton
Birmingham, B27 6PA, UK.

ISBN 978-1-849514-48-4

www.packtpub.com

Cover Image by Charwak A (charwak86@gmail.com)

Credits

Author

Jason Morris

Reviewers

David J. Groom

Martin Skans

Acquisition Editor

Chaitanya Apte

Development Editor

Reshma Sundaresan

Technical Editor

Harshit Shah

Copy Editor

Neha Shetty

Indexer

Tejal Daruwale

Editorial Team Leader

Akshara Aware

Project Team Leader

Priya Mukherji

Project Coordinator

Shubhanjan Chatterjee

Proofreader

Joel T. Johnson

Graphics

Nilesh R. Mohite

Production Coordinators

Kruthika Bangera

Aparna Bhagat

Cover Work

Kruthika Bangera

About the Author

Jason Morris has worked on software as diverse as fruit tracking systems, insurance systems, and travel search and booking engines. He has been writing software for as long as he can remember. He is currently working as a Software Architect for Travelstart in South Africa. He works on multiple front-end and middleware systems, leveraging a variety of Java based technologies.

The people I'd like to thank most for their direct, or indirect help in writing this book are my wife Caron Morris, my father Mike Morris, my mom Jayne Morris, and the rest of my family for their love and support. I'd also like to thank Wayne, Stuart, Angela, and James, and everyone on my team at Travelstart. Finally a very big thanks to Martin Skans for his invaluable input.

About the Reviewer

Martin Skans graduated from Lund University in Sweden, with a Master's degree in Computer Science. After a couple of years in the online marketing industry, he moved on to become a developer for Travelstart, an online travel agency. He relocated to Cape Town and is currently working on Travelstart's African travel platform which has been recently launched for the mobile market.

www.PacktPub.com

Support files, eBooks, discount offers and more

You might want to visit www.PacktPub.com for support files and downloads related to your book.

Did you know that Packt offers eBook versions of every book published, with PDF and ePub files available? You can upgrade to the eBook version at www.PacktPub.com and as a print book customer, you are entitled to a discount on the eBook copy. Get in touch with us at service@packtpub.com for more details.

At www.PacktPub.com, you can also read a collection of free technical articles, sign up for a range of free newsletters and receive exclusive discounts and offers on Packt books and eBooks.

http://PacktLib.PacktPub.com

Do you need instant solutions to your IT questions? PacktLib is Packt's online digital book library. Here, you can access, read and search across Packt's entire library of books.

Why Subscribe?

- Fully searchable across every book published by Packt
- Copy and paste, print and bookmark content
- On demand and accessible via web browser

Free Access for Packt account holders

If you have an account with Packt at www.PacktPub.com, you can use this to access PacktLib today and view nine entirely free books. Simply use your login credentials for immediate access.

Table of Contents

Preface

On 9th January, 2007, Apple officially launched the iPhone, and the world of user interface design shifted. While tablet PCs had been around for a while, the iPhone was the first device to give so many people a portable touchscreen, and people loved it. Just over a year later, Google and the Open Handset Alliance announced Android which in many ways is the direct competitor to iPhone.

What is it about touchscreen phones that we love? The answer is simple—feedback. Touchscreens offer a way to directly manipulate on-screen objects, which in the past had to be driven through a keyboard, mouse, joystick, or other input device. The touchscreen model of direct manipulation has a large impact on the way we think about our user interfaces as developers, and changes the expectations a user has for the application. Touchscreen devices require us to stop thinking in terms of forms, and start thinking about object-oriented user interfaces.

Android is used as the primary operating system for a rapidly expanding range of consumer electronics, including:

- Smartphones
- Netbooks
- Tablets
- Some desktop systems

While all of these devices have different purposes and specifications, all of them run Android. This is unlike many other operating environments which are almost always have a special purpose. The services and the APIs they provide to developers generally reflect their target hardware. Android on the other hand makes the assumption that a single application may be required to run on many different types of devices, with very different hardware capabilities and specifications, and makes it as easy as possible for developers to handle the differences between these devices simply and elegantly.

New challenges

As Android and the touchscreen devices it powers become increasingly common, they will bring a new set of challenges to user interface design and development:

- You generally don't have a mouse
- You may have more than one pointing device
- You often don't have a keyboard
- Any keyboard that does exist may be a software keyboard
- A software keyboard may consume some of your application's screenspace

The software keyboard reduces the amount of screen space available to your application, and in much the same vein, if there is a hardware keyboard present it may or may not always be exposed to the user. Therefore, not only are different Android devices different, but they may also appear to change features while your application is running.

The rule of finger

Most Android devices have touchscreens (although this is not a requirement). The first restriction placed on any touchscreen user interface is the size of the human forefinger, which of course varies widely from one person to another. If a widget is too small on the screen, it won't be clear what the user is trying to touch. You'll notice that most Android widgets take up plenty of space, and have more than the normal amount of padding around them. On a touchscreen device, you can't rely on pixel-perfect precision. You need to make sure that when the user touches a widget, they make contact, and they don't accidentally touch another widget.

The magic touch

Another impact touchscreens have on user interface design is that an application and all the widgets that it uses must be entirely self-explanatory (even more than usual). Far too often, we substitute good user interface planning and design with a roll-over or tooltip to indicate a widget's function. On a touchscreen device, there is no mouse or pointing device. The first interaction it has with the user is when they touch it, and they will expect something to happen.

A touchy subject

Most Android devices have a touchscreen, but it's not a requirement. The quality of a touchscreen also varies wildly from device to device. The category of touchscreens and their capabilities will also vary from one device to the next, depending on the intended use of the device and often its intended market segment.

A smaller view on the world

Most Android devices are small, and as a result have smaller screens and generally fewer pixels than a normal PC or laptop. This lack of size limits the size of the widgets. Widgets must be big enough to touch safely, but we also need to pack as much information onto the screen as possible. So don't give your users information that they don't want, and also avoid asking them for information you don't need.

Classic user interface principals

Here are some core guidelines which every user interface should follow. These guidelines are what will keep your users happy, and ensure your application is successful. Throughout the rest of the book, we'll be walking through these guidelines with practical examples of improvements that can be made to a user interface.

Consistency

This is the cornerstone of good user interface design. A button should look like a button. Make sure that the layout of each screen has a relationship with every other screen in your application. People often mistake this principle for "stick to the platform look and feel". Look and feel is important, consistency mostly applies to the layout and overall experience of the application, rather than the color scheme.

Recycling your interface

The easiest way to maintain a consistent user interface, is to recycle as much of it as possible. At first glance, this suggestion looks merely like a "good object-oriented" practice. However, a closer look will reveal ways to reuse graphical widgets in ways you hadn't thought of. By changing the visibility of various widgets, or you can reuse an edit screen to view list items of the intended type.

Simplicity

This is especially important in a phone-based application. Often, when a user encounters a new application, it's because they are looking for something. They may not have the time (or more often patience) to learn a new user interface. Make sure that your application asks for as little as possible, and guides the user to the exact information they want in as few steps as possible.

The Zen approach

Generally, when you are using a mobile device, your time is limited. You may also be using an application in less-than-ideal circumstances (perhaps, in a train). The lesser information a user needs to give an application, and the lesser they need to absorb from it, the better. Stripping away options and information also leads to a shorter learning-curve.

Android's hidden menu

A very useful feature of Android is the hidden menu structure. The menu is only visible when the user presses the "Menu" button, which would generally mean, they're looking for something that isn't currently on the screen. Typically, a user shouldn't need to open a menu. However, it's a good way of hiding advanced features until they are needed.

Feedback

Feedback is what makes a touchscreen device exciting. When you drag an object, it sticks to your finger across the screen until you let go of it. When the users puts their finger on your application, they expect some reaction. However, you don't want to get in their way—instead of showing an error message when they touch a button, disable the button until it's valid to use, or don't show it at all.

Location and navigation

When you're in a place you've never been to previously, it's easy to get disoriented, or lost. The same is true for a piece of software. Just because the application makes sense to you, the developer, it doesn't mean it seems logical to your user. Adding transition animations, breadcrumbs, and progress gauges help the user to identify where in the application they are, and what's happening.

The road to recovery

A common way to tell users that something is wrong on a desktop application, or on the web is to open an error dialog. On a mobile device, people want smoother use of an application. While in a normal application you may inform the user that they selected an invalid option, in a mobile application, you generally want to make sure they can't select that option in the first place. Also, don't make them scroll through huge lists of options. Instead, allow them to filter through the list using an auto-complete or something similar.

When something goes wrong, be nice, and be helpful—don't tell the user, "I couldn't find any flights for your search". Instead tell them, "There were no available flights for your search, but if you're prepared to leave a day earlier, here is a list of the available flights". Always make sure your user can take another step forward without having to go "Back" (although the option to go backwards should always exist).

The Android way

The Android platform is in many ways similar to developing applications for the web. There are many devices, made by many manufactures, with different capabilities and specifications. Yet as a developer, you will want your users to have the most consistent experience possible. Unlike a web browser, Android has built-in mechanisms for coping with these differences, and even leveraging them.

We'll be looking at Android from the point of view of a user rather than having a purely development-centric approach. We'll cover topics such as:

♦ What user interface elements Android provides

♦ How an Android application is assembled

♦ Different types of Android layouts

♦ Presenting various types of data to the user

♦ Customising of existing Android widgets

♦ Tricks and tools to keep user interfaces looking great

♦ Integration between applications

We're about to take a jump into building user interfaces for Android devices—all Android devices, from the highest speed CPU to the smallest screen.

What this book covers

Chapter 1, Developing a Simple Activity introduces the basics of building an Android application, starting with a simple user interface. It also covers the various options available to you when implementing your design as code.

Chapter 2, Views With Adapters shows us how to leverage Adapter-based widgets, Android's answer to the Model-View-Controller (MVC) structure. Learn about these widgets, and where they will best serve you.

Chapter 3, Specialized Android Views takes a close look at some of the more specialized widgets that the Android platform provides, and how they relate to the mundane widgets. This chapter covers widgets such as the gallery and rating-bar, and how they can be used and styled.

Chapter 4, Activities and Intents discusses more about how Android runs your application, and from that point-of-view, how best to write its user interfaces. This chapter takes a look at how to make sure that your application will behave the way users expect it to, with minimal effort on your part.

Chapter 5, Non-Linear Layouts takes a look at some of the advanced layout techniques which Android offers. It talks about the best way to present different screens to the user while taking into account the wide discrepancy in the screens on Android devices.

Chapter 6, Input and Validation provides tips regarding taking input from a user, and how to keep this experience as painless as possible. This chapter investigates the different input widgets Android provides and how to configure them best, depending on the situation. Also, when everything else fails, how best to inform your users that what they are doing is wrong.

Chapter 7, Animating Widgets and Layouts will inform the reader as to where, when, why, and how to animate your Android user interfaces. It also sheds light on what kind of animations are provided by default, how to compose them together, and how to build your own. This chapter looks at the importance of animations in a mobile user interface and demonstrates how complex animations are made easy by Android.

Chapter 8, Content-centric Design details how to go about designing the screen layout, when presenting the user with information on the screen. This chapter looks at the pros and cons of some of the different display techniques which Android offers.

Chapter 9, Styling Android Applications shows us how to keep the look of our entire application consistent, in order to make our application easier to use.

Chapter 10, Building an Application Theme looks at the design process, and how application-wide themes can be applied to help your application stand out.

What you need for this book

Please have a look at "System Requirements" mentioned on the Andriod Developers website at http://developer.android.com/sdk/requirements.html.

The code for this book was tested on Ubuntu Linux 10.04 and Mac OS X.

Who this book is for

This book is aimed at developers with at least some Java experience who want to build applications on the Android platform. It will also be of use to people who have developed applications on the Android platform and would like to gain additional knowledge about its user interface design. It will also be a helpful reference for the numerous widgets and resource structures that the Android platform provides.

This book will also be helpful to:

- Java developers learning Android development
- MIDP developers looking to broaden their skill-set
- iPhone developers wanting to port applications
- Entrepreneurial Android developers wanting to widen their user base

Conventions

In this book, you will find several headings appearing frequently.

To give clear instructions of how to complete a procedure or task, we use:

Time for action – heading

1. Open the `res/layout/main.xml` layout resource in an editor or IDE.

2. Remove the default content within the `LinearLayout` element.

Instructions often need some extra explanation so that they make sense, so they are followed with:

What just happened?

This heading explains the working of tasks or instructions that you have just completed.

You will also find some other learning aids in the book, including:

Pop quiz – heading

These are short multiple choice questions intended to help you test your own understanding.

Have a go hero – heading

These set practical challenges and give you ideas for experimenting with what you have learned.

You will also find a number of styles of text that distinguish between different kinds of information. Here are some examples of these styles, and an explanation of their meaning.

Code words in text are shown as follows: "We'll start off by creating a selector `Activity`, and a simple `NewsFeedActivity`".

A block of code is set as follows:

```
<activity
    android:name=".AskQuestionActivity"
    android:label="Ask Question">
    <intent-filter>
        <action android:name="questions.askQuestion"/>
        <category android:name="android.intent.category.DEFAULT"/>
    </intent-filter>
</activity>
```

When we wish to draw your attention to a particular part of a code block, the relevant lines or items are set in bold:

```
<?xml version="1.0" encoding="UTF-8"?>
<FrameLayout
        xmlns:android="http://schemas.android.com/apk/res/android"
        android:layout_width="fill_parent"
        android:layout_height="fill_parent">
    <ViewStub android:id="@+id/review"
            android:inflatedId="@+id/inflated_review"
            android:layout="@layout/review"/>

    <ViewStub android:id="@+id/photos"
            android:inflatedId="@+id/inflated_photos"
            android:layout="@layout/photos"/>

    <ViewStub android:id="@+id/reservations"
            android:inflatedId="@+id/inflated_reservations"
            android:layout="@layout/reservations"/>
</FrameLayout>
```

Any command-line input or output is written as follows:

```
android create project -n AnimationExamples -p AnimationExamples -k com.
packtpub.animations -a AnimationSelector -t 3
```

New terms and **important words** are shown in bold. Words that you see on the screen, in menus or dialog boxes for example, appear in the text like this: "Generally users are more inclined to feel a sense of trust if they pick the **Buy Music** button and are not suddenly whisked off to their web browser".

 Warnings or important notes appear in a box like this.

Tips and tricks appear like this.

Reader feedback

Feedback from our readers is always welcome. Let us know what you think about this book—what you liked or may have disliked. Reader feedback is important for us to develop titles that you really get the most out of.

To send us general feedback, simply send an e-mail to feedback@packtpub.com, and mention the book title via the subject of your message.

If there is a book that you need and would like to see us publish, please send us a note in the **SUGGEST A TITLE** form on www.packtpub.com or e-mail suggest@packtpub.com.

If there is a topic that you have expertise in and you are interested in either writing or contributing to a book, see our author guide on www.packtpub.com/authors.

Customer support

Now that you are the proud owner of a Packt book, we have a number of things to help you to get the most from your purchase.

Downloading the example code for this book

You can download the example code files for all Packt books you have purchased from your account at http://www.PacktPub.com. If you purchased this book elsewhere, you can visit http://www.PacktPub.com/support and register to have the files e-mailed directly to you.

Errata

Although we have taken every care to ensure the accuracy of our content, mistakes do happen. If you find a mistake in one of our books—maybe a mistake in the text or the code—we would be grateful if you would report this to us. By doing so, you can save other readers from frustration and help us improve subsequent versions of this book. If you find any errata, please report them by visiting http://www.packtpub.com/support, selecting your book, clicking on the **errata submission form** link, and entering the details of your errata. Once your errata are verified, your submission will be accepted and the errata will be uploaded on our website, or added to any list of existing errata, under the Errata section of that title. Any existing errata can be viewed by selecting your title from http://www.packtpub.com/support.

Piracy

Piracy of copyright material on the Internet is an ongoing problem across all media. At Packt, we take the protection of our copyright and licenses very seriously. If you come across any illegal copies of our works, in any form, on the Internet, please provide us with the location address or website name immediately so that we can pursue a remedy.

Please contact us at copyright@packtpub.com with a link to the suspected pirated material.

We appreciate your help in protecting our authors, and our ability to bring you valuable content.

Questions

You can contact us at questions@packtpub.com if you are having a problem with any aspect of the book, and we will do our best to address it.

1

Developing a Simple Activity

In the world of Android, an `Activity` *is the point at which you make contact with your users. It's a screen where you capture and present information to the user. You can construct your* `Activity` *screens by using either: XML layout files or hard-coded Java.*

To begin our tour of Android user interfaces, we need a user interface to start with. In this chapter, we will begin with a simple `Activity`. We will:

◆ Create a new Android project

◆ Build the `Activity` layout in an application resource file

◆ Tie the resource file to an `Activity` class

◆ Dynamically populate the `Activity` with a series of multiple-choice questions

Developing our first example

For our first example, we're going to write a multiple-choice question and answer `Activity`. We could use it for applications such as "Who wants to be a millionaire?", or "What type of a monkey are you?". This example will pose questions in order to answer a very important question: "What should I have to eat?" As the user answers the questions, this application will filter a database of food ideas. The user can exit the process at any time to view a list of suggested meals, or just wait until the application runs out of questions to ask them.

Since it's a user interface example, we'll skip building filters and recipe databases. We'll just ask our user food preference-related questions. For each question, we have a list of preset answers which the user can select from (that is, multiple-choice questions). Each answer they give will allow us to narrow the list of suitable recipes.

Creating the project structure

Before we can start writing code, we need a project structure. An Android project is made up of far more than just its Java code—there are also manifest files, resources, icons, and more. In order to keep things easy, we use the default Android toolset and project structure.

You can download the latest version of the Android SDK for your favorite operating system from `http://developer.android.com`. A single Android SDK may be used to develop against any number of target Android versions. You will need to follow the installation instructions on the website at `http://developer.android.com/sdk/installing.html` to install the latest SDK "starter package" and one or more platform targets. Most of the examples in this book will work on Android 1.5 and higher. The Android website also maintains a very useful chart where you can see what the most popular versions of Android are.

Time for action – setting up the Android SDK

Once you have downloaded the Android SDK archive for your operating system, you'll need to install it and then download at least one Android Platform package. Open a command-line or console and complete the following steps:

1. Extract the Android SDK archive.

2. Change directory to the root of the unpackaged Android SDK.

3. Change directory to the `tools` directory of the Android SDK.

4. Update the SDK by running the following command:

   ```
   android update sdk
   ```

5. Create a new Virtual Device by going to the **Virtual Devices** screen and clicking on the **New** button. Name the new Virtual Device **default**.

6. Specify its target as the most recent version of Android downloaded by the SDK. Set the size of the SD Card to **4096 MiB**. Click on the **Create AVD** button.

What just happened?

The above command tells the new Android SDK installation to look for available packages and install them. This includes installing a Platform Package. Each Platform Package that you install can be used to create an **Android Virtual Device (AVD)**. Each AVD you create is much like buying a new device on which tests can be performed, each with its own configuration and data. These are virtual machines that the Android emulator will run your software on when you wish to test.

Time for action – starting a new project

The Android SDK provides a handy command-line tool named android which can be used to generate the skeleton of a new project. You'll find it under the tools directory of your Android SDK. It's capable of creating a basic directory structure and a build.xml file (for Apache Ant) to help get you started with your Android application development. You will need to make sure that the tools directory is in your executable path for this to work. Open a command-line or console.

1. Create a new directory in your home directory or desktop named AndroidUIExamples. You should use this directory for each of the examples in this book.

2. Change the directory to the new AndroidUIExamples.

3. Run the following command:

```
android create project -n KitchenDroid -p KitchenDroid -k com.packtpub.
kitchendroid -a QuestionActivity -t 3
```

What just happened

We just created a skeleton project. In the preceding command line, we used the following options to specify the structure of the new project:

Option	Description
-n	Gives the project a name, in our case, KitchenDroid. This is really just an internal identifier for the project.
-p	Gives the base directory for the project. In this case use the same name as that of the project. The android tool will create this directory for you.
-k	Specifies the root Java package for the application. This is a fairly important concept since it defines our unique namespace on the Android client devices.
-a	Gives the tool a name for a "main" Activity class. This class will be populated with a skeleton layout XML, and serves as a base point to build your application from. The skeleton project will be pre-configured to load this Activity when it's started.

If you run the command android list targets and it presents you with an empty list of possible targets, then you have not downloaded any of the Android Platform packages. You can generally run the android tool by itself and use its graphical interface to download and install Android Platform packages. The previous example uses API Level 3 which corresponds to Android Platform version 1.5.

Examining the Android project layout

A typical Android project has almost as many directories and files as an enterprise Java project. Android is as much of a framework as it is an operating environment. In some ways, you can think of Android as an application container designed for running on phones and other limited devices.

As part of the new project structure, you will have the following important files and directories:

Folder name	Description
bin	Your binary files will be placed in this directory by the compiler.
gen	Source code generated by various Android tools.
res	Application resources go here, to be compiled and packaged with your application.
src	The default Java source code directory, where the build script will look for source code to compile.
AndroidManifest.xml	Your application descriptor, similar to a web.xml file.

Resource Types and Files

Most types of application resources (placed in the res directory) receive special handling by the Android application packager. This means these files consume less space than they usually would (since XML is compiled into a binary format instead of being left as plain text). You access resources in various ways, but always through an Android API (which decodes them into their original form for you).

Each subdirectory of res indicates a different file format. Therefore, you cannot put files directly into the root res directory since the package tool won't know how to handle it (and you'll get a compile error). If you need to access a file in its raw state, put it in the res/raw directory. Files in the raw directory are copied byte-for-byte into your application package.

Time for action – running the example project

The android tool has given us a minimal example of an Android project, basically a "Hello World" application.

1. In your console or command-line, change directory to KitchenDroid.

2. To build and sign the project, run:

    ```
    ant debug
    ```

3. You will need to start the emulator with the default AVD you created earlier:

    ```
    emulator -avd default
    ```

4. Now install your application in the emulator:

```
ant install
```

5. In the emulator, open the **Android** menu and, you should see an icon named **QuestionActivity** in the menu. Click on this icon.

What just happened?

The Android emulator is a full hardware emulator including the ARM CPU, hosting the entire Android operating system stack. This means software running under the emulator will run exactly how it will on bare-metal hardware (although the speed may vary).

When you use Ant to deploy your Android applications, you will need to use the `install` Ant target. The `install` Ant target looks for a running emulator and then installs the application archive on its virtual memory. It's useful to note that Ant will not start the emulator for you. Instead, it will emit an error and the build will fail.

Application Signatures

Every Android application package is digitally signed. The signature is used to identify you as a developer of the application, and establish permissions for the application. It's also used to establish permissions between applications.

You will generally use a self-signed certificate, since Android doesn't require that you use a certificate authority. However, all applications must be signed in order for them to be run by the Android system.

The screen layout

While Android allows you to create a screen layout in either Java code, or by declaring the layout in an XML file, we will declare the screen layout in an XML file. This is an important decision for several reasons. The first is that, using the Android widgets in Java code requires several lines of code for each widget (a declaration/construction line, several lines invoking setters, and finally adding the widget to its parent), while a widget declared in XML takes up only one XML tag.

The second reason for keeping layouts as XML is that it's compacted into a special Android XML format when it's stored in the APK file. Therefore your application uses less space on the device, takes less time to download, and its in-memory size is also smaller since less byte code needs to be loaded. The XML is also validated by the Android resource packing tool during compilation, and so is subject to the same type safety as Java code.

The third reason XML layouts are a "good idea" is that they are subject to the same resource selection process as all the other external resources. This means that a layout can be varied based on any of the defined properties, such as language, screen orientation and size, and even the time of day. This means that you can add new variations on the same layout in the future, simply by adding new XML files, and without the need to change any of your Java code.

The layout XML file

All XML layout files must be placed in the `/res/layout` directory of your Android project in order for the Android packaging tools to find them. Each XML file will result in a resource variable of the same name. For example, if we name our file `/res/layout/main.xml`, then we can access it in Java as `R.layout.main`.

Since we are building the screen layout as a resource file, it will be loaded by the application resource loader (having been compiled by the resource compiler). A resource is subject to a selection process, so while there is only one resource that the application loads, there may be multiple possible versions of the same resource available in the application package. This selection process is also what Android internationalization is built on top of.

If we wanted to build a different version of the user interface layout for several different types of touchscreens, Android defines three different types of touchscreen properties for us: `notouch`, `stylus`, and `finger`. This roughly translates to: no touchscreen, resistive touchscreen, and capacitive touchscreen. If we wanted to define a more keyboard-driven user interface for devices without a touchscreen (`notouch`), we write a new layout XML file named `/res/layout-notouch/main.xml`. When we load the resource in our `Activity` code, the resource selector will pick the `notouch` version of the screen if the device we're running on doesn't have a touchscreen.

Resource selection qualifiers

Here is a list of commonly used qualifiers (property names) that will be taken into account when Android selects a resource file to load. This table is ordered by precedence, with the most important properties at the top.

Name	Description	Examples	API Level

MCC and MNC	The mobile-country-code (MCC) and mobile-network-code (MNC). These can be used to determine which mobile operator and country the SIM card in the device is tied to.
	
	The mobile-network-code optionally follows the mobile-country-code, but cannot be used on its own (you must always specify country-code first).
		`mcc505`
		`mcc505-mnc03`
		`mcc238`
		`mcc238-mnc02`
		`mcc238-mnc20`
			1

Language and region codes	Language and region codes are probably the most commonly used resource properties. This is generally how you localize your application to the user language preferences.
	
	These values are standard ISO language and region codes, and are not case-sensitive. You cannot specify a region without a country code (similar to `java.util.Locale`).
		`en`
		`en-rUS`
		`es`
		`es-rCL`
		`es-rMX`
			1

Screen size	There are only three variations of this property: small, medium, and large. The value is based on the amount of screen space that can be used:
	
	  ◆ Small: QVGA (320×240 pixel) low-density type screens;
	
	  ◆ Medium: WQVGA low-density, HVGA (480x360 pixels) medium-density, and WVGA high-density type screens;
	
	  ◆ Large: VGA (640x480 pixels) or WVGA medium-density type screens
		`small`
		`medium`
		`large`
			4

Screen aspect	This is the aspect type of the screen, based on the way the device would "normally" be used. This value doesn't change based on the orientation of the device.	`long` `notlong`	4
Screen orientation	Used to determine whether the device is currently in portrait (`port`) or landscape (`land`) mode. This is only available on devices that can detect their orientation.	`land` `port`	1
Night mode	This value simply changes with the time of day.	`night` `notnight`	8

Name	Description	Examples	API Level

Screen density (DPI)	The DPI of the device screen. There are four possible values for this property:
	
	◆ `ldpi`: Low-density, approximately 120dpi;
	
	◆ `mdpi`: Medium-density, approximately 160dpi;
	
	◆ `hdpi`: High-density, approximately 240dpi;
	
	◆ `nodpi`: Can be used for `bitmap` resources that shouldn't be scaled to match the screen density
		`ldpi`
		`mdpi`
		`hdpi`
		`nodpi`
			4

Keyboard status	What sort of keyboard is available on this device? This attribute shouldn't be used to determine whether the device has a hardware keyboard, but instead whether a keyboard (or software keyboard) is currently visible to the user.	`keysexposed`
		`keyshidden`
		`keyssoft`
			1

Time for action – setting up the question activity

To kick things off we're going to be working with Android's simplest layout called: `LinearLayout`. Unlike Java AWT or Swing, Android layout managers are defined as specific container types. Thus a `LinearLayout` is much like a `Panel` with a built-in `LayoutManager`. If you've worked with GWT, you'll be quite familiar with this concept. We'll lay out the screen in a simple top-to-bottom structure (which `LinearLayout` is perfect for).

1. Open the file in the `/res/layout` directory of your project named `main.xml` in you favorite IDE or text editor.

2. Delete any template XML code.

3. Copy the following XML code into the file:

```xml
<?xml version="1.0" encoding="UTF-8"?>

<LinearLayout
    xmlns:android="http://schemas.android.com/apk/res/android"
    android:orientation="vertical"
    android:layout_width="fill_parent"
    android:layout_height="wrap_content">

</LinearLayout>
```

What just happened?

We just removed the "Hello World" example, and put in an entirely empty layout structure which will serve as the platform for us to build the rest of the user interface upon. As you can see, Android has a special XML namespace for its resources.

All resource types in Android use the same XML namespace.

We declare our root element as `LinearLayout`. This element corresponds directly to the class `android.widget.LinearLayout`. Each element or attribute prefixed with the Android namespace corresponds to an attribute that is interpreted by the Android resource compiler.

The AAPT (Android Asset Packaging Tool) will generate an `R.java` file into your root (or primary) package. This file contains all of the Java variables used to reference your various application resources. In our case, we have the `main.xml` package in the `/res/layout` directory. This file becomes an `R.layout.main` variable with a constant value assigned as its identification.

Populating a View and a ViewGroup

A widget in Android is called a `View`, while a container (such as `LinearLayout`) is a `ViewGroup`. We have an empty `ViewGroup` now, but we need to start populating it in order to build up our user interface. While it is possible to nest a `ViewGroup` inside another `ViewGroup` object, an `Activity` has only one root `View`—so a layout XML file may have only one root `View`.

Time for action – asking a question

In order to ask our user a question, you will need to add a `TextView` to the top of your layout. A `TextView` is a bit like a `Label` or `JLabel`. It's also the base class for many other Android `View` widgets that display text. We want it to take up all of the available horizontal space, but only enough vertical space for our question to fit. We populate the `TextView` with **Please wait...** as its default text. Later, on we will replace this with a dynamically selected question.

1. Go back to your `main.xml` file.

2. Between the `<LinearLayout...>` and `</LinearLayout>` create a `<TextView />` element, ending it with the empty element `/>` syntax since elements representing `View` objects are not allowed to have child elements.

3. Give the `TextView` element an ID attribute:
   ```
   android:id="@+id/question"
   ```

4. Change the layout width and height attributes to `fill_parent` and `wrap_content` respectively (the same as the `LinearLayout` element):

```
android:layout_width="fill_parent"
android:layout_height="wrap_content"
```

5. Give the `TextView` some placeholder text so we can see it on the screen:

```
android:text="Please wait..."
```

6. Reinstall the application using Apache Ant from your project root folder:

```
ant install
```

7. Run the application again in the emulator and it should look like the following screenshot:

The code for the `TextView` should end up looking something like this:

```
<TextView android:id="@+id/question"
          android:text="Please wait..."
          android:layout_width="fill_parent"
          android:layout_height="wrap_content"/>
```

What just happened

In the preceding example, we used `fill_parent` and `wrap_content` as values for the layout width and height attributes. The `fill_parent` value is a special value that is always equal to the parent size. If it's used as the value for the `android:layout_width` attribute (as in our example), then it's the width of the parent view. If it's used in the `android:layout_height` attribute, it would be equal to the height of the parent view instead.

The value `wrap_content` can be used much like a preferred size in Java AWT or Swing. It says to the `View` object, "Take as much space as you need to, but no more". The only valid place to use these special attribute values is in the `android:layout_width` and `android:layout_height` attributes. Anywhere else will result in a compiler error.

We will need to access this `TextView` in our Java code later, in order to invoke its `setText` method (which directly corresponds to the `android:text` attribute we used for the placeholder text). A Java reference to a resource variable is created by assigning the resource an ID. In this example, the ID is declared here as `@+id/question`. The AAPT will generate an `int` value as an identifier for each resource of `id` as part of your `R` class. The ID attribute is also needed for accessing resources from another resource file.

Time for action – adding a space for answers

While posing a question to the user is all very fine and well, we need to give them some way to answer that question. We have several possibilities at our disposal: We could use a `RadioGroup` with a `RadioButton` for each possible answer, or a `ListView` with an item for each answer. However, to minimize the required interaction, and make things as clear as possible, we use one `Button` for each possible answer. However, this complicates things slightly, since you can't declare a variable number of `Button` objects in your layout XML file. Instead, we will declare a new `LinearLayout` and populate it with `Button` objects in the Java code.

1. Under the `TextView` where we pose our question, you will need to add a `<LinearLayout />` element. While this element would normally have child elements, in our case, the number of possible answers is varied, so we leave it as an empty element.

2. By default, a `LinearLayout` will place its child `View` objects horizontally alongside each other. However, we want each child `View` to be vertically below each other, so you'll need to set the `orientation` attribute of the `LinearLayout`:

   ```
   android:orientation="vertical"
   ```

3. We will need to populate the new `ViewGroup` (`LinearLayout`) later in our Java code, so give it an ID: `answers`:

   ```
   android:id="@+id/answers"
   ```

4. Like our `TextView` and root `LinearLayout`, make the width `fill_parent`:

   ```
   android:layout_width="fill_parent"
   ```

5. Make the height `wrap_content` so that it doesn't take up more space than all the buttons it will be populated with:

   ```
   android:layout_height="wrap_content"
   ```

The resulting code should look like this:

```
<LinearLayout android:id="@+id/answers"
              android:orientation="vertical"
              android:layout_width="fill_parent"
              android:layout_height="wrap_content"/>
```

What just happened?

You may have noticed that for this example, we have no content in our new LinearLayout. This may seem a little unusual, but in this case, we want to populate it with a variable number of buttons—one for each possible answer to our multiple-choice questions. However, for the next part of the example we need some simple content Button widgets in this LinearLayout so that we can see the entire screen layout in action. Use the following code in your layout resource file to add **Yes!**, **No!**, and **Maybe?** Button widgets to the LinearLayout:

```
<LinearLayout android:id="@+id/answers"
          android:orientation="vertical"
          android:layout_width="fill_parent"
          android:layout_height="wrap_content">
    <Button android:id="@+id/yes"
          android:text="Yes!"
          android:layout_width="fill_parent"
          android:layout_height="wrap_content" />
    <Button android:id="@+id/no"
          android:text="No!"
          android:layout_width="fill_parent"
          android:layout_height="wrap_content" />
    <Button android:id="@+id/maybe"
          android:text="Maybe?"
          android:layout_width="fill_parent"
          android:layout_height="wrap_content" />
</LinearLayout>
```

In Android XML layout resources, any View classes extending from the ViewGroup class are considered containers. Adding widgets to them is as simple as nesting those View elements inside the element of your ViewGroup (as opposed to closing it with no child XML elements).

The following is a screenshot of the preceding **Yes!**, **No!**, **Maybe?** options:

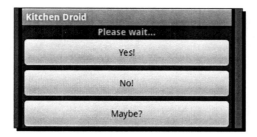

Time for action – adding more buttons

We have two additional buttons to add to the screen layout. One will allow the user to skip the current question; the other will allow them to look at the short list of meals that we have filtered through so far (based on the questions they have already answered).

1. Start by creating an empty `<Button />` element below our answers `ViewGroup` `<LinearLayout />` (but still within the root `LinearLayout` element). Assign it the ID `skip`, so that we can reference it in Java:

   ```
   android:id="@+id/skip"
   ```

2. Create some padding between the answers and the new button by using a margin:

   ```
   android:layout_marginTop="12sp"
   ```

3. Give it the display label **Skip Question**:

   ```
   android:text="Skip Question"
   ```

4. Like all of the previous widgets, the width should be `fill_parent` and the height should be `wrap_content`:

   ```
   android:layout_width="fill_parent"
   android:layout_height="wrap_content"
   ```

5. Now create another empty `<Button />` element below the **Skip Question** button

6. The ID for the new button should be `view`:

   ```
   android:id="@+id/view"
   ```

7. We want this button to display the text: **Feed Me!**:

   ```
   android:text="Feed Me!"
   ```

8. Again, put a little space between the **Skip Question** button, and the new **Feed Me!** button:

```
android:layout_marginTop="12sp"
```

9. Finally, set the width and height of the **Feed Me!** button as with the other elements we've created so far:

```
android:layout_width="fill_parent"
android:layout_height="wrap_content"
```

When you've completed these two buttons, your layout XML file should now end with:

```
<Button android:id="@+id/skip"
        android:text="Skip Question"
        android:layout_marginTop="12sp"
        android:layout_width="fill_parent"
        android:layout_height="wrap_content"/>
<Button android:id="@+id/view"
        android:text="Feed Me!"
        android:layout_marginTop="12sp"
        android:layout_width="fill_parent"
        android:layout_height="wrap_content"/>
</LinearLayout>
```

What just happened

Separation of unrelated user interface objects is a very important part of user interface design. Groups of items can be separated by whitespace, a border, or a box. In our case, we chose to use whitespace, as space also helps make the user interface feel cleaner.

We created our whitespace by using a margin above each of the buttons. Margins and padding work exactly the same way as they (should) do in CSS. A margin is spacing outside of the widget, while padding is spacing inside the widget. In Android, a margin is the concern of the `ViewGroup`, and so its attribute name is prefixed with `layout_`. Because padding is the responsibility of a `View` object, the padding attribute has no such prefix:

```
<Button android:id="@+id/view"
        android:text="Feed Me!"
        android:padding="25sp"
        android:layout_marginTop="12sp"
        android:layout_width="fill_parent"
        android:layout_height="wrap_content"/>
```

The previous code would create extra space between the edge of the `Button` and the text in the middle of it, as well as retaining the margin above the button.

All of the measurements in the preceding example are specified in the sp unit, which is short for "scale independent pixels". Much like CSS, you suffix your measurement numbers with the unit of size that you are specifying the measurement in. Android recognizes the following measurements:

Unit suffix	Full name	Description and uses
px	Pixel	Exactly one pixel of the device screen. This unit is the most common when writing desktop applications, but with the wide variety of phone screen sizes, it becomes much harder to use.
in	Inch	One inch (or the closest approximation). This is based on the physical size of the screen. This is great if you need to work with real world measurements, but again, because of the variations in the size of a device screen, it is not always very useful.
mm	Millimeters	Another real world measurement, made to the closest approximation. This is just a metric version of inches: 25.4 millimeters in 1 inch.
pt	Points	Points are 1/72 of an inch in size. Much like millimeters and inches, they are very useful for sizing things against real-world sizes. They are also commonly used for sizing fonts, and so work well relative to font sizes.
dp or dip	Density-independent-pixels	A single DP is the same size as a single pixel is for a 160 dpi screen. This size is not always a direct ratio, not always precise, but is a best approximation for the current screen.
sp	Scale-independent pixels	Much like the dp unit, it is a pixel scaled according to the user selected font size. This is possibly the best unit to use, as it's based on a user-selected parameter. The user may have increased the font size because they find the screen hard to read. Using an sp unit ensures that your user interface scales with it.

Defining common dimensions

Android also allows you to define your own dimension values as resource constants (note: dimensions, not measurements). This can be useful when you want several view widgets to be the same size, or to define a common font size. Files containing dimension declarations are placed in the /res/values directory in your project. While the actual file name isn't significant, a common name is dimens.xml. Dimensions can technically be included with other value types (that is, strings), but this is not recommended since it makes it harder to trace the dimension that are being applied at runtime.

One advantage of having your dimensions in their own file as opposed to being declared inline) is that you can then localize them based on the size of the screen. This makes screen-resolution-significant scales (such as pixels) much more useful. For example, you can place a `dimens.xml` file with different values into `/res/values-320x240` and another version of the same dimensions into `/res/values-640x480`.

A dimensions resource file is a simple values file (much like `strings.xml`), but dimensions are defined with the `<dimen>` tag:

```
<resources>
    <dimen name="half_width">160px</dimen>
</resources>
```

To access this as a size in a layout XML file, you use a resource reference (much the same way as you access a resource string):

```
<TextView layout_width="@dimen/half_width" />
```

Building a list of common dimensions comes in handy when you want to build complex layouts that will look good on many different screens since it avoids the need to build several different layout XML files.

Have a go hero – improve the styling

Now we have the most basic structure for this user interface, but it doesn't really look too great. Other than the margins between the answer buttons, and the **Skip Question** and **Feed Me!** buttons, you can't really tell them apart. We need to let the user know that these buttons all do different things. We also need to draw more attention to the question, especially if they don't have a lot of time to squint at their screen. You may need the Android documentation, which can be found online at `http://developer.android.com/reference/`.

We have a question at the top of our screen, but as you can see in the previous screenshots, it doesn't stand out much. Therefore, it's not really very clear to the user what they need to do (especially the first time they use the application).

Try making the following styling changes to the question `TextView` at the top of our screen. These will only require you to add some attributes to its XML element:

1. Center the text.
2. Make the text bold.
3. Change the text size to `24sp`.
4. Add `12sp` spacing between the bottom of the question and the answer buttons

The **Feed Me!** button is also very important. This is the button that gives the user access to the list of suggested recipes that the application has filtered based on their answers, so it should look good.

The following styling should help the **Feed Me!** button to stand out nicely (hint: `Button` extends `TextView`):

1. Make the text size `18sp`.
2. Change the text color to a nice red `#9d1111`.
3. Style the text as bold.
4. Add a text shadow: `x=0`, `y=-3`, `radius=1.5`, and `color=white` (`"#fff"`).

When you've finished styling the screen, it should look like the following screenshot:

Limitations of the layout XML format

One of the most obvious limitations of the layout XML format is that you can't dynamically populate part of the `Activity` based on external variables—there are no loops or methods in the XML file.

In our example, this limitation shows itself in the form of our empty `LinearLayout`. Because each question has any number of possible answers, we need a varying number of buttons in the group. For our purposes, we will create the `Button` objects and put them into the `LinearLayout` as part of the Java code.

The other place the XML layout format falls down is dynamically referencing external resources. This can be seen in our example, where we put placeholder text in the `android:text` attribute on the `TextView` element—`question`. We could have referenced an external string using the following syntax:

```
<TextView android:id="@+id/question"
          android:text="@string/question"
          android:gravity="center"
          android:textStyle="bold"
          android:layout_width="fill_parent"
          android:layout_height="wrap_content"/>
```

This will effectively reference a static variable from the `strings.xml` file. It's not suitable for a dynamically selected question, which will change each time we initialize the `Activity`.

Pop quiz

1. What reason do you have for writing your layouts in XML instead of in pure Java code?

    a. Android can read the layout file externally for optimization.

    b. The layout becomes part of the resource selection process.

    c. Your users could download new layouts from the App Store.

    d. The layout can have custom themes applied to it.

2. How would we make the text of the **Next Question** button bold?

    a. Use the `android:typeface` attribute.

    b. Create a custom `Button` implementation.

    c. Add a CSS attribute: `style="font-weight: bold"`.

    d. Use the `android:textStyle` attribute.

3. What would happen if we changed the `LinearLayout` from `vertical` orientation, to `horizontal`?

    a. The layout would turn on its side.

    b. All of the widgets would be squashed together on the screen.

    c. Only the question `TextView` would be visible on the screen.

    d. The question, and possibly some other `View` objects may be visible on the screen depending on the number of pixels available.

    e. The layout would overflow, causing the widgets to appear next to each other, over several lines.

Populating the QuestionActivity

We have a basic user interface, but right now, it's static. We may want to ask our user many different questions, each of which have different answers. We may also want to vary which questions we ask in some way or another. In short, we need some Java code to populate the layout with a question and some possible answers. Our questions are made up of two parts:

- The question
- A list of possible answers

In this example, we will make use of string array resources to store all of the question and answer data. We will use one string array to list the question identifiers, and then one string array for each question and its answers. The advantages of this approach are very similar to the advantages of using a layout XML file instead of hard-coding it. The `res/values` directory of your project will have an auto-generated `strings.xml` file. This file contains string and string-array resources that you want your application to use. Here is the start of our `strings.xml` file, with two questions to ask the user:

```xml
<?xml version="1.0" encoding="UTF-8"?>
<resources>
    <string name="app_name">Kitchen Droid</string>
    <string-array name="questions">
        <item>vegetarian</item>
        <item>size</item>
    </string-array>
    <string-array name="vegetarian">
        <item>Are you a Vegetarian?</item>
        <item>Yes</item>
        <item>No</item>
        <item>I\'m a vegan</item>
    </string-array>
    <string-array name="size">
        <item>How much do you feel like eating?</item>
        <item>A large meal</item>
        <item>Just a nice single serving of food</item>
        <item>Some finger foods</item>
        <item>Just a snack</item>
    </string-array>
</resources>
```

The first item of each `question` array (`vegetarian` and `size`) is the question itself, while each following item is an answer.

Time for action – writing more Java code

1. Open the `QuestionActivity.java` file in an editor or IDE.

2. Import the Android `Resources` class below the package declaration:

```
import android.content.res.Resources;
```

3. In order to start asking the questions from your `strings.xml` file, you'll need a method to look in the `questions <string-array>` and find the name of the array that contains the current question. This is not normally something you need to do with application resources—their identifiers are generally known to you through the `R` class. In this case however, we want to work in the order defined in the `questions <string-array>`, making things a little bit more difficult:

```
private int getQuestionID(Resources res, int index) {
```

4. We can now look at the `questions` string-array, which contains the identifying name of each question (our index string-array):

```
String[] questions = res.getStringArray(R.array.questions);
```

5. We have the array of questions, and we need to find the identifier value. This is much like using `R.array.vegetarian` for the `vegetarian` question, except that it's a dynamic lookup, and therefore much slower than normal. In general, the following line is not recommended, but in our case it's very useful:

```
return res.getIdentifier(
        questions[index],
        "array",
        "com.packtpub.kitchendroid");
```

6. The `QuestionActivity` class will display several questions to the user. We want the application to "play nice" with the phone and its environment. For that reason, each question will be posed in a new instance of `QuestionActivity` (allowing the device to control the display of our `Activity`). However, this method raises an important question: How do we know the index of the question to pose to the user? The answer: Our `Intent`. An `Activity` is started with an `Intent` object, and each `Intent` object may carry any amount of "extra" information (similar to request attributes in the `HttpServletRequest` interface) for the `Activity` to use, sort of like arguments to a `main` method. So, an `Intent` is also like a `HashMap`, containing special data for the `Activity` to use. In our case we use an integer property named `KitchenDroid.Question`:

```
private int getQuestionIndex() {
    return getIntent().getIntExtra("KitchenDroid.Question", 0);
}
```

These two methods form the basis for populating our question screen and navigating our way through a defined list of questions. When complete, they should look like this:

```
private static int getQuestionID(
        final Resources res,
        final int index) {
    final String[] questions = res.getStringArray(R.array.questions);
    return res.getIdentifier(
            questions[index],
            "array",
            "com.packtpub.kitchendroid");
}
private int getQuestionIndex() {
    return getIntent().getIntExtra("KitchenDroid.Question", 0);
}
```

What just happened

The `getQuestionID` method is pretty straight forward. In our code we use `R.array.questions` to access the `<string-array>` which identifies all of the questions we are going to ask the user. Each question has a name in the form of a `String`, and a corresponding resource identification number in the form of an `int`.

In the `getQuestionID` method, we make use of the `Resources.getIdentifier` method, which looks for the resource identifier (the integer value) for a given resource name. The second parameter of the method is the type of resource to look up. This parameter is normally an inner class to the generated `R` class. Finally, we pass the base package that the resource is found in. Instead of all three of these parameters, you could also look up the resource by its full resource name:

```
return res.getIdentifier(
        "com.packtpub.kitchendroid:array/" + questions[index],
        null,
        null);
```

The `getQuestionIndex` method tells us where in the questions `<string-array>` we currently are, and thus, which question to ask the user. This is based on the "extra" information in the `Intent` that triggered the `Activity`. The `getIntent()` method provides you with access to the `Intent` that triggered your `Activity`. Each `Intent` may have any amount of "extra" data, and that data may be any "primitive" or "serializable" type. Here we fetch the `KitchenDroid.Question` extra integer value from our `Intent`, substituting a value of 0 if it has not been set (that is, the default value). If the user taps our icon in the menu, Android won't have specified that value, so we start from the first question.

Dynamically creating widgets

Up to this point we've only used the layout XML file to populate our screen. In some cases, this is just not enough. In this simple example, we want the user to have a list of buttons that they can touch to answer the questions posed to them. We could pre-create some buttons and name them `button1`, `button2`, and so on, but that means limiting the number of possible answers.

In order to create buttons from our `<string-array>` resources, we need to do it in Java. We created a `ViewGroup` earlier (in the form of the `LinearLayout` that we named `answers`). This is where we will add our dynamically created buttons.

Time for action – putting the questions on the screen

Your application now knows where to find the questions to ask, and knows which question it should be asking. Now it needs to put the question on the screen, and allow the user to select an answer.

1. Open the `main.xml` file in your editor or IDE.

2. Remove the **Yes!**, **No!**, and **Maybe?** `Button` elements from the layout resource.

3. Open the `QuestionActivity.java` file in an editor or IDE.

4. We will need a new class field to hold the dynamically-created `Button` objects (for reference):

   ```
   private Button[] buttons;
   ```

5. In order to keep things neat, create a new `private` method to put the questions on the screen: `initQuestionScreen`:

   ```
   private void initQuestionScreen() {
   ```

6. In this method, we assume that the layout XML file has already been loaded into the `Activity` screen (that is, it will be invoked after we `setContentView` in `onCreate`). This means that we can look up parts of the layout as Java objects. We'll need both the `TextView` named `question` and the `LinearLayout` named `answers`:

   ```
   TextView question = (TextView)findViewById(R.id.question);
   ViewGroup answers = (ViewGroup)findViewById(R.id.answers);
   ```

7. These two variables need to be populated with the question and its possible answers. For that we need the `<string-array>` (from our `strings.xml` file) which contains that data, so we need to know the resource identifier for the current question. Then we can fetch the actual array of data:

```
int questionID = getQuestionID(resources, getQuestionIndex());
String[] quesionData = resources.getStringArray(questionID);
```

8. The first element of a `question` string array is the question to pose to the user. The following `setText` call is exactly the same as specifying an `android:text` attribute in your layout XML file:

```
question.setText(quesionData[0]);
```

9. We then need to create an empty array to store references to our `Button` objects:

```
int answerCount = quesionData.length - 1;
buttons = new Button[answerCount];
```

10. Now we're ready to populate the screen. A `for` loop over each of the answer values indexed according to our arrays:

```
for(int i = 0; i < answerCount; i++) {
```

11. Get each answer from the array, skipping the question string at index zero:

```
String answer = quesionData[i + 1];
```

12. Create a `Button` object for the answer and set its label:

```
Button button = new Button(this);
button.setText(answer);
```

13. Finally, we add the new `Button` to our answers object (`ViewGroup`), and reference it in our `buttons` array (where we'll need it later):

```
answers.addView(button);
buttons[i] = button;
```

14. Having done that, just after the `setContentView` calls in `onCreate`, we need to invoke our new `initQuestionScreen` method.

What just happened?

The `findViewById` method traverses the tree of `View` objects looking for a specific identifying integer value. By default, any resource declared with an `android:id` attribute in its resource file will have an associated ID. You could also assign an ID by hand using the `View.setId` method.

Unlike many other user interface APIs, the Android user interface API is geared towards XML development than pure Java development. A perfect example of this fact is that the `View` subclasses have three different constructors, two of which are designed for use with the XML parsing API. Instead of being able to populate the `Button` label in a constructor (as with most other UI APIs), we are forced to first construct the object, and then use `setText` to define its label.

What you do pass into the constructor of every `View` object is a `Context` object. In the preceding example you pass the `Activity` object into the constructor of the answer `Button` objects as `this`. The `Activity` class inherits from the `Context` class. The `Context` object is used by the `View` and `ViewGroup` objects to load the application resources and services that they require in order to function correctly.

You can now try running the application, in which case you'll be greeted with the following screen. You may have noticed that there is additional styling in this screenshot. If you don't have this, you may want to backtrack a little to the previous *Have a go hero* section.

Handling events in Android

Android user interface events work in much the same way as a Swing event-listener or a GWT event-handler. Depending on the type of event you wish to receive, you implement an interface and pass an instance to the widget you wish to receive events from. In our case we have `Button` widgets that fire click-events when they are touched by the user.

The event-listener interfaces are declared in many of the Android classes, so there isn't a single place you can go look for them. Also, unlike most event-listener systems, many widgets may only have one of any given event-listeners. You can identify an event-listener interface by the fact that their class names are prefixed with `On` (much like HTML event attributes). In order to listen for click-events on a widget, you would set its `OnClickListener` using the `View.setOnClickListener` method.

The following code snippet shows how a click-listener might be added to a `Button` object to show a `Toast`. A `Toast` is a small pop-up box which is displayed briefly to give the user some information:

```
button.setOnClickListener(new View.OnClickListener() {
    public void onClick(View clicked) {
        Toast.makeText(this, "Button Clicked!", Toast.LENGTH_SHORT).
            show();
    }
});
```

The preceding event-listener is declared as an anonymous inner class, which is okay when you are passing similar event-listeners to many different widgets. However, most of the time you'll want to be listening for events on widgets you've declared in an XML layout resource. In these cases it's better to either have your `Activity` class implement the required interfaces, or create specialized classes for different event-driven actions. While Android devices are very powerful, they are still limited when compared to a desktop computer or laptop. Therefore, you should avoid creating unnecessary objects in order to conserve memory. By placing as many event-listener methods in objects that will already be created, you lower the overhead required.

Pop quiz

1. When you declare an object in a layout XML file, how do you retrieve its Java object?

    a. The object will be declared in the `R` class.

    b. Using the `Activity.findViewById` method.

    c. By using the `Resources.getLayout` method.

    d. The object will be injected into a field in the `Activity` class.

2. What is the "best" way of listening for events in an Android application?

    a. Declaring the listeners as anonymous inner classes.

    b. Create a separate event listener class for each `Activity`.

    c. Implement the event-listening interfaces in the `Activity` class.

3. Why do you pass `this Activity` into the constructors of `View` objects (that is, `new Button(this)`).

    a. It defines the `Activity` screen they will be displayed on.

    b. It's where event messages will be sent to.

    c. It's how the `View` will reference its operating environment.

Summary

Android comes with some great tools to create and test applications, even if you don't have an Android device handy. That said, there's no replacement for actually touching your application. It's part of what makes Android such a compelling platform, the way it feels and responds (and the emulator just doesn't convey that).

One of the most important tools in an Android developer's arsenal is the resource selection system. With it you can build highly dynamic applications that respond to changes in the devices, and thus, the user environment. Changing the screen layout based on the orientation of the device, or when the user slides out the phone's QWERTY keyboard, lets them know that you've taken their preferences into account when building your application.

When building user interfaces in Android, it's strongly recommended to build at least the layout structure in an XML file. The XML layout files are not only considered as application resources, but Android also strongly favors building XML user interfaces over writing Java code. Sometimes, however, a layout XML file isn't enough, and you need to build parts of the user interface in Java. In this case it's a good idea to define at least a skeleton layout as XML (if possible), and then place the dynamically created `View` objects into the layout by using marker IDs and containers (much like dynamically adding to an HTML document in JavaScript).

When building a user interface, think carefully about the look and feel of the outcome. In our example, we use `Button` objects for the answers to questions. We could have used `RadioButton` objects instead, but then the user would have needed to select an option, and then touch a **Next Question** button, requiring two touches. We could also have used a `List` (which interacts nicely with the fact that it needs to be dynamically populated), however, a `List` doesn't indicate an "action" to the user quite the way a `Button` does.

When coding layouts, be careful with the measurement units that you use. It's strongly recommend that you stick to using `sp` for most purposes—if you can't use one of the special `fill_parent` or `wrap_content` values. Other values are highly dependent on the size of screen, and won't respond to the user preferences. You can make use of the resource selection process to build different screen designs for small, medium, or large screens. You could also define your own measurement unit and base it on the screen size.

Always think about how your user will interact with your application, and how much (or little) time they are likely to have with it. Keeping each screen simple and responsive keeps your users happy.

Now that we've learned how to create a skeleton Android project, and a simple `Activiy`, we can focus on the more subtle problems and solutions of Android user interface design. In the next chapter, we will focus on working with data-driven widgets. Android has several widgets designed specifically for displaying and selecting from more complex data structures. These widgets form the basis of data-driven applications such as an address book or a calendar application.

2
Presenting Data for Views

In the first chapter we covered the basic creation of a project, and how to put together a simple user interface. We backed our first `Activity` with enough code to dynamically generate some buttons that the user can use to answer our multiple-choice questions.

So now we can capture some data, but what about displaying data? One large advantage of software is its ability to present and filter very large volumes of data quickly and in an easy-to-read format. In this chapter we will look at a series of Android widgets that are designed exclusively for presenting data.

Most Android data-centric classes are built on top of `Adapter` objects, and thus extend the `AdapterView` class. An `Adapter` can be thought of as a cross between a Swing Model, and a renderer (or presenter). An `Adapter` object is used to create `View` objects for data objects that your software needs to display to the user. This pattern allows the software to maintain and work with a data-model and only create a graphical `View` for each of the data objects when one is actually needed. This doesn't just help conserve memory, but it is also more logical from a development point of view. As a developer you work with your own data objects instead of trying to keep your data in graphical widgets (which are often not the most robust of structures).

The most common `AdapterView` classes you'll encounter are: `ListView`, `Spinner`, and `GridView`. In this chapter we'll introduce the `ListView` class and `GridView`, and explore the various ways they can be used and how they can be styled.

Listing and selecting data

The ListView class is probably the most common way to display lists of data. It's backed by a ListAdapter object, which is responsible for both holding the data and rendering the data objects in a View. A ListView includes built-in scrolling, so there's no need to wrap it in a ScrollView.

ListView choice modes

The ListView class allows for three basic modes of item selection, as defined by its constants: CHOICE_MODE_NONE, CHOICE_MODE_SINGLE, and CHOICE_MODE_MULTIPLE. The mode for a ListView can be set by using the android:choiceMode attribute in your layout XML file, or by using the ListView.setChoiceMode method in Java.

Choice modes and items

The choice mode of a ListView changes the way the ListView structure behaves, but not the way it looks. The look of a ListView is defined mostly by the ListAdapter, which provides View objects for each of the items that should appear in the ListView.

No selection mode – CHOICE_MODE_NONE

On a desktop system, this would make no sense—a list that doesn't allow the user to choose anything? However, it's the default mode of an Android ListView. The reason is it makes sense when your user is navigating by touch. The default mode of a ListView allows the user to tap on one of the elements, and trigger an action. As a result of this behavior, there's no need for a "Next" button, or anything similar. So the default mode for a ListView is to act like a menu. The following screenshot is a default ListView object displaying a list of different strings from a String array Java object, taken from one of the default ApiDemos examples in Android SDK.

Single selection mode – CHOICE_MODE_SINGLE

In this mode, the `ListView` acts more like a desktop `List` widget. It has the notion of the current selection, and tapping on a list item does nothing more than selecting it. This behavior is nice for things like configuration or settings, where the user expects the application to remember his or her current selection. Another place a single selection list becomes useful is when there are other interactive widgets on the screen. However, be careful not to put too much information in a single `Activity`. It's quite common for a `ListView` to occupy almost an entire screen.

 Single-choice selection: It doesn't directly change the way your list items appear. The look and feel of your list items is defined entirely by the `ListAdapter` object.

Android does, however, provide a collection of sensible defaults in the system resources. In the `android` package you will find an `R` class. It's a programmatic way to access the system's default resources. If you wanted to create a single-choice `ListView` with a `<string-array>` of colors in it, you could use the following code:

```
list.setAdapter(new ArrayAdapter(
        this,
        android.R.layout.simple_list_item_single_choice,
        getResources().getStringArray(R.array.colors)));
```

In this case we use the provided `ArrayAdapter` class from the `android.widget` package. In the second parameter we referenced the Android layout resource named `simple_list_item_single_choice`. This resource is defined by the Android system as a default way to display items in a `ListView` with `CHOICE_MODE_SINGLE`. Most typically this is a label with a `RadioButton` for each object in the `ListAdapter`.

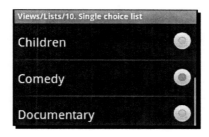

Multiple selection mode – CHOICE_MODE_MULTIPLE

In multi-selection mode, the `ListView` replaces the radio buttons of single-selection mode with normal checkboxes. This design structure is often used on desktops and web-based systems as well. Checkboxes are easily recognized by users, and make it easy to go back and turn options off again. If you wish to use a standard `ListAdapter`, Android provides you with the `android.R.layout.simple_list_item_multiple_choice` resource as a useful default: A label with a `CheckBox` for each object in the `ListAdapter`.

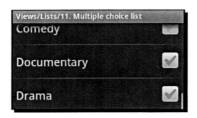

Adding header and footer widgets

Headers and footers in a `ListView` allow you to put additional widgets at the top and bottom of the `List`. The header and footer widgets are by default treated as though they are items in a list (as though they come from your `ListAdapter`). This means that you will be able to select them as though they are data elements in the `List` structure. A very simple example of a header item could be:

```
TextView header = new TextView(this);
header.setText("Header View");
list.addHeaderView(header);
```

Often you don't want your headers and footers to be items in the `ListView`, but instead a label or group of labels identifying parts of the `ListView`, or providing other information. In this case you need to tell the `ListView` that your header or footer views are not selectable list items. This can be done by using the extended implementation of `addHeaderView` or `addFooterView`:

```
TextView footer = new TextView(this);
footer.setText("Footer View");
list.addFooterView(footer, null, false);
```

The `ListView` class integrates headers and footers so tightly into the list structure that you can also provide an `Object` that it will return from the `AdapterView`. `getItemAtPosition(index)` method. In our previous example we have provided `null`. Each header item will offset the index of subsequent views by one (as though you are adding new items to the `ListView`). The third parameter tells the `ListView` whether the header or footer should be counted as a selectable list item (in our previous example it shouldn't).

If you are used to desktop widgets, the header and footer widgets on an Android `ListView` will have a bit of a surprise for you. They will scroll with the rest of the list items, and won't stay attached to the top and bottom of the `ListView` object.

Creating a simple ListView

To introduce the `ListView` class, we'll start a new example which will be enhanced by various subsequent sections of this chapter. The first `Activity` we will create will use a simple `ListView` populated from a `<string-array>` resource.

Time for action – creating a fast food menu

To continue with the food and eating theme, let's build a simple application that allows us to order various types of fast food, and get it delivered! The user will first select where they want to order from, and then select the various foodstuffs that they want to eat.

1. Create a new `android` project using the Android command-line tool:

```
android create project -n DeliveryDroid -p DeliveryDroid -k com.
packtpub.deliverydroid -a SelectRestaurantActivity -t 3
```

2. Open the `/res/values/strings.xml` file in your favorite editor or IDE.

3. Create a string-array structure listing the various fast-food restaurants our users can order from:

```
<string-array name="restaurants">
    <item>The Burger Place</item>
    <item>Mick's Pizza</item>
    <item>Four Buckets \'o Fruit</item>
    <item>Sam\'s Sushi</item>
</string-array>
```

4. Open the `/res/layout/main.xml` file in your favorite editor or IDE.

5. Remove any widget that is inside the default `LinearLayout`.

6. Add a new `<ListView>` element.

7. Assign the `<ListView>` element an ID of `restaurant`:

```
<ListView android:id="@+id/restaurant"/>
```

8. Assign the width and height of the `ListView` to `fill_parent`:

```
android:layout_width="fill_parent"
android:layout_height="fill_parent"
```

9. Since we have a string-array resource of the content we want to populate the `ListView` with, we can reference it directly in our layout XML file:

```
android:entries="@array/restaurants"
```

10. When you've completed the specified steps, you should have a `main.xml` layout file that looks like the following:

```
<?xml version="1.0" encoding="UTF-8"?>
<LinearLayout
    xmlns:android="http://schemas.android.com/apk/res/android"
    android:orientation="vertical"
    android:layout_width="fill_parent"
    android:layout_height="fill_parent">

    <ListView android:id="@+id/restaurant"
            android:layout_width="fill_parent"
            android:layout_height="fill_parent"
            android:entries="@array/restaurants"/>
</LinearLayout>
```

What just happened

If you install your application into the emulator, and run it, you'll be presented with a screen where you can select from the list of restaurants specified in your string-array resource. Notice that the `choiceMode` on the `ListView` is left as `CHOICE_MODE_NONE`, making this into a more direct menu where the user selects their restaurant and is instantly transported to its menu.

In this example, we used the `android:entries` attribute in the layout XML file to specify a reference to a string-array resource with our desired list items in it. Normally, using an `AdapterView` requires you to create an `Adapter` object to create `View` objects for each of the data objects.

Using the `android:entries` attribute allows you to specify the data contents of the `ListView` from your layout resource, instead of requiring you to write the normal Java code associated with an `AdapterView`. It, however, does have two disadvantages to be aware of:

- The `View` objects created by the generated `ListAdapter` will always be the system-specified defaults, and so cannot be easily themed.
- You cannot define data objects that will be represented in the `ListView`. Since string-arrays are easily localized, your application will rely on the index locations of items to determine what they indicate.

You may notice that at the top of the screenshot, the label `Where should we order from?` is not the application default. The label for an `Activity` is defined in the `AndroidManifest.xml` file as follows:

```
<activity
    android:name=".SelectRestaurantActivity"
    android:label="Where should we order from?">
```

Styling the standard ListAdapters

The standard `ListAdapter` implementations require each item be represented in a `TextView` item. The default single-choice and multiple-choice items are built using a `CheckedTextView`, and while there are plenty of other `TextView` implementations in Android, it does limit our options a bit. However, the standard `ListAdapter` implementations are very convenient and provide solid implementations for the most common listing requirements.

Since a `ListView` with `CHOICE_MODE_NONE` is a lot like a menu, wouldn't it be nice to change the items into `Button` objects instead of normal `TextView` items? Technically, a `ListView` can contain any widget that extends `TextView`. However, some implementations are more suitable than others (for example, a `ToggleButtonView` won't maintain the specified text-value when the user touches it).

Defining standard dimensions

In this example we'll be creating various menus for the application. In order to maintain a consistent look and feel, we should define a set of standard dimensions which will be used in each of our layout files. This way we can redefine the sizes for different types of screens. There's nothing more frustrating for a user than only being able to see a partial item because it's been sized bigger than their screen.

Create a new resource file to contain the dimensions. The file should be named `res/values/dimens.xml`. Copy the following code into the new XML file:

```xml
<?xml version="1.0" encoding="UTF-8"?>

<resources>
    <dimen name="item_outer_height">48sp</dimen>
    <dimen name="menu_item_height">52sp</dimen>
    <dimen name="item_inner_height">45sp</dimen>
    <dimen name="item_text_size">24sp</dimen>
    <dimen name="padding">15dp</dimen>
</resources>
```

We declare two height dimensions for the list items: item_outer_height and item_inner_height. The item_outer_height will be the height of the list items, while the item_inner_height is the height of any View object contained inside the list item.

The padding dimension at the end of the file is used to define a standard amount of whitespace between two visual elements. This is defined as dp so it will remain constant based on the DPI of the screen (instead of scaling according to the font size preferences of the user).

Sizing of interactive items

In this styling, you'll notice that the item_outer_height and menu_item_height are 48sp and 52sp, which makes the items in the ListView rather large. The standard size of a list view item in Android is 48sp. The height of a list item is critical. If your users have large fingers, they will struggle to tap on their target list item if you make them too small.

This is a general "good practice" for Android user interface design. If the user needs to touch it, make it big.

Time for action – improving the restaurant list

The list of restaurants we put together earlier is nice, but it's a menu. In order to further emphasize the menu, the text should stand out more. In order to style a ListView with a standard ListAdapter implementation, you will need to specify the ListAdapter object in your Java code.

1. Create a new file in the res/layout directory named menu_item.xml.

2. Create the root XML element as a TextView:

   ```xml
   <?xml version="1.0" encoding="UTF-8"?>
   <TextView />
   ```

3. Import the Android resource XML namespace:

   ```
   xmlns:android="http://schemas.android.com/apk/res/android"
   ```

4. Center the text in the `TextView` widget by setting its gravity:

```
android:gravity="center|center_vertical"
```

5. We assign the `textSize` of the `TextView` to our standard `item_text_size`:

```
android:textSize="@dimen/item_text_size"
```

6. The default color of the text of `TextView` is a bit gray, we want it to be white:

```
android:textColor="#ffffff"
```

7. We want the width of the `TextView` to be the same as the `ListView` that contains it. Since this is for our main menu, its height is `menu_item_height`:

```
android:layout_width="fill_parent"
android:layout_height="@dimen/menu_item_height"
```

8. Now that we have a styled `TextView` resource, we can incorporate it into our menu. Open the `SelectRestaurantActivity.java` file.

9. In the `onCreate` method, after you use `setContentView`, we need a reference to the `ListView` we created earlier in `main.xml`:

```
ListView restaurants = (ListView)findViewById(R.id.restaurant);
```

10. Set the restaurants `ListAdapter` to a new `ArrayAdapter` containing the string-array of restaurants we created in our `values.xml` file:

```
restaurants.setAdapter(new ArrayAdapter<String>(
    this,
    R.layout.menu_item,
    getResources().getStringArray(R.array.restaurants)));
```

What just happened

We first created a new layout XML resource containing the styled `TextView` that we wanted to be used for each list item in our restaurant's `ListView`. The `menu_item.xml` file you wrote should contain the following code:

```xml
<?xml version="1.0" encoding="UTF-8"?>

<TextView xmlns:android="http://schemas.android.com/apk/res/android"
            android:gravity="center|center_vertical"
            android:textSize="@dimen/item_text_size"
            android:textColor="#ffffff"
            android:layout_width="fill_parent"
            android:layout_height="@dimen/menu_item_height" />
```

Unlike our previous layout resources, `menu_item.xml` contained no `ViewGroup` (such as `LinearLayout`). This is due to the fact that the `ArrayAdapter` will attempt to cast the root `View` of the `menu_item.xml` file to a `TextView`. So, if we nested the `TextView` in a `ViewGroup` of some sort, we'd get a `ClassCastException`.

We also created an `ArrayAdapter` instance to reference both our `menu_item` XML resource, and the string-array of restaurants we created earlier. This action eliminates the use of the `android:entries` attribute on the `ListView` in the `main.xml` layout XML resource. If you want, you can remove that attribute. Your `onCreate` method in `SelectRestaurantActivity` should now look as follows:

```
public void onCreate(final Bundle icicle) {
        super.onCreate(icicle);
        setContentView(R.layout.main);
        final ListView restaurants = (ListView)
                findViewById(R.id.restaurant);
        restaurants.setAdapter(new ArrayAdapter<String>(
                this,
                R.layout.menu_item,
                getResources().getStringArray(R.array.restaurants)));
}
```

Try re-installing the application into the emulator with Apache Ant, and you'll now be greeted by a screen that looks a lot more like a menu:

Have a go hero – developing a multiple-choice question application

Try going back to the multiple-choice question application we wrote in *Chapter 1, Developing a Simple Activity*. It uses `LinearLayout` and `Button` objects to display the possible answers to the questions, but it also uses string-arrays for the answers. Try modifying the application to:

- Use a `ListView` instead of a `LinearLayout`
- Style the `ListView` with `Button` objects, as we styled our restaurant menu with `TextView` objects

◆ Make sure you have some margin between the `Button` list items so that they're not too close to each other

Creating custom adapters

When we want to order food, we often want to order more than one of the same item. The `ListView` implementation, and the standard `ListAdapter` implementations allow for us to select a **Cheese Burger** item, but not for us to request **3 Cheese Burgers**. In order to display a menu of different foods that the user can order in multiple quantities, we need a customized `ListAdapter` implementation.

Creating a menu for The Burger Place

For each restaurant in our main menu, we are going to build a separate `Activity` class. In reality, this is not a great idea, but it allows us to investigate different ways of organizing and displaying the menu data. Our first stop is **The Burger Place**, for which we present the user with a list of burgers, and let them tap the ones they want on the screen. Each time they tap a list item, they order another burger. We will display the number of burgers they are ordering in bold to the left of the burger's name. Next to burgers that they aren't ordering, there should be no number (this allows the user to see what they are ordering at a quick glance).

The Burger class

In order to display the menu, we need a simple `Burger` data object. The `Burger` class will hold a name to be displayed in the menu, and the number of `Burger` the user is ordering. Create a `Burger.java` file in the root package of your project with the following code:

```
class Burger {
    final String name;
    int count = 0;
    public Burger(String name) {
        this.name = name;
    }
}
```

You'll notice that there are no getters and setters in the preceding code, and that both the name and count fields are declared as package-protected. In versions of Android prior to 2.2, methods incurred a heavy expense when compared to a straight field lookup. Since this class will be a small part of the rendering procedure (we will be extracting data from it for display), we should make sure we incur as little expense as possible.

Time for action – creating a Burger item layout

The first thing to do in order to create a nice looking menu for **The Burger Place** is to design the menu items. This is done in much the same way as the styling of the restaurant list with a layout XML resource. However, since we will be building the `ListAdapter` ourselves this time, we are not forced to use a single `TextView`, but can instead build a more complex layout.

1. Create a new XML file in the `res/layout` directory named `burger_item.xml`. This file will be used for each burger in the `ListView`.

2. Declare the root of the layout as a `horizontal LinearLayout` (note the height, which will be the height of each item in the `ListView`):

    ```
    <LinearLayout
        xmlns:android="http://schemas.android.com/apk/res/android"
        android:orientation="horizontal"
        android:layout_width="fill_parent"
        android:layout_height="@dimen/item_outer_height">
    ```

3. Next, declare a `TextView`, which we will use as a `counter` for the number of burgers being ordered. We will later access this through its ID:

    ```
    <TextView android:id="@+id/counter" />
    ```

4. The `counter` text size is exactly the same as all of the other list items in the application. However, it should be `bold`, so it can be easily identified and read:

    ```
    android:textSize="@dimen/item_text_size"
    android:textStyle="bold"
    ```

5. We also want the `counter` to be square, so set the width and height exactly the same:

    ```
    android:layout_width="@dimen/item_inner_height"
    android:layout_height="@dimen/item_inner_height"
    ```

6. We also want to center the text inside the `counter`:

    ```
    android:gravity="center|center_vertical"
    ```

7. We'll also need a text space to display the name of the burger:

    ```
    <TextView android:id="@+id/text" />
    ```

8. The text size is standard:

    ```
    android:textSize="@dimen/item_text_size"
    ```

9. We want a little bit of space between the `counter` and the `text` label:

```
android:layout_marginLeft="@dimen/padding"
```

10. The label's width should fill the `ListView`, but we want the size of both `TextView` objects to be the same:

```
android:layout_width="fill_parent"
android:layout_height="@dimen/item_inner_height"
```

11. The text of the label should be centered vertically, to match the location of the `counter`. However, the label should be left-aligned:

```
android:gravity="left|center_vertical"
```

What just happened?

You've just built a very nice `LinearLayout ViewGroup` which will be rendered for each of the burgers we sell from **The Burger Place**. Since the `counter TextView` is a separate object from the label, it can be independently styled and managed. This makes things much more flexible going forward if we want to apply additional styles to them independently. Your complete `burger_item.xml` file should now appear as follows:

```xml
<?xml version="1.0" encoding="UTF-8"?>

<LinearLayout
    xmlns:android="http://schemas.android.com/apk/res/android"
    android:orientation="horizontal"
    android:layout_width="fill_parent"
    android:layout_height="@dimen/item_outer_height">

    <TextView android:id="@+id/counter"
            android:textSize="@dimen/item_text_size"
            android:textStyle="bold"
            android:layout_width="@dimen/item_inner_height"
            android:layout_height="@dimen/item_inner_height"
            android:gravity="center|center_vertical" />

    <TextView android:id="@+id/text"
            android:textSize="@dimen/item_text_size"
            android:layout_marginLeft="@dimen/padding"
            android:layout_width="fill_parent"
            android:layout_height="@dimen/item_inner_height"
            android:gravity="left|center_vertical" />
</LinearLayout>
```

Time for action – presenting Burger objects

The standard `ListAdapter` classes work well if your data objects are either strings or easily represented as strings. In order to display our `Burger` objects nicely on the screen, we need to write a custom `ListAdapter` class. Fortunately, Android provides us with a nice skeleton class for `ListAdapter` implementations named `BaseAdapter`.

1. Create a new class named `BurgerAdapter`, and have it extend from the `android.widget.BaseAdapter` class:

   ```
   class BurgerAdapter extends BaseAdapter {
   ```

2. An `Adapter` is part of the presentation layer, but is also the underlying model of the `ListView`. In the `BurgerAdapter` we store an array of `Burger` objects which we assign in the constructor:

   ```
   private final Burger[] burgers;
   BurgerAdapter(Burger... burgers) {
       this.burgers = burders;
   }
   ```

3. Implement the `Adapter.getCount()` and `Adapter.getItem(int)` methods directly on top of the array of `Burger` objects:

   ```
   public int getCount() {
       return burgers.length;
   }

   public Object getItem(int index) {
       return burgers[index];
   }
   ```

4. An `Adapter` is also expected to provide identifiers for the various items, we will just return their index:

   ```
   public long getItemId(int index) {
       return index;
   }
   ```

5. When an `Adapter` is asked for a `View` of a list item, it may be given an existing `View` object that could be reused. We will implement a simple method to handle this case, and if required, inflate the `burger_item.xml` file we wrote earlier using the `LayoutInflator` class from the `android.view` package:

   ```
   private ViewGroup getViewGroup(View reuse, ViewGroup parent) {
       if(reuse instanceof ViewGroup) {
           return (ViewGroup)reuse;
       }
   ```

```
        Context context = parent.getContext();
        LayoutInflater inflater = LayoutInflater.from(context);
        ViewGroup item = (ViewGroup)inflater.inflate(
                R.layout.burger_item, null);

        return item;
    }
```

6. The most important method for us in the `BurgerAdapter` is the `getView` method. This is where the `ListView` will ask us for a `View` object to represent each list item it needs to display:

```
public View getView(int index, View reuse, ViewGroup parent) {
```

7. In order to fetch the correct `View` for a given item, you'll first need to use the `getViewGroup` method to ensure you have the `burger_item.xml` `ViewGroup` to display the `Burger` item in:

```
ViewGroup item = getViewGroup(reuse, parent);

TextView counter = (TextView)item.findViewById(R.id.counter);
TextView label = (TextView)item.findViewById(R.id.text);
```

8. We'll be populating these two `TextView` objects with the data from the `Burger` object at the requested `index`. The `counter` widget needs to be hidden from the user if the current `count` is zero:

```
Burger burger = burgers[index];

counter.setVisibility(
        burger.count == 0
        ? View.INVISIBLE
        : View.VISIBLE);

counter.setText(Integer.toString(burger.count));
label.setText(burger.name);

return item;
```

What just happened?

We just wrote a custom `Adapter` class to present an array of `Burger` objects to the user in a `ListView`. When a `ListView` invokes the `Adapter.getView` method, it will attempt to pass in the `View` object that was returned from a previous call to `Adapter.getView`. A `View` object will be created for each item in the `ListView`. However, when the data displayed by the `ListView` changes, the `ListView` will ask the `ListAdapter` to reuse each of the `View` objects it generated the first time around. It's important to try and honor this behavior, since it has a direct impact on the responsiveness of your application. In our preceding example, we implemented the `getViewGroup` method so that it would take this requirement into account.

The `getViewGroup` method is also used to inflate the `burger_item.xml` file we wrote. We do this using a `LayoutInflator` object, which is exactly how the `Activity.setContentView(int)` method loads XML layout resources. The `Context` object which we fetch from our `parent ViewGroup` (which will generally be the `ListView`) defines where we will load the layout resource from. If the user hasn't selected a `Burger`, we hide the counter `TextView` using the `View.setVisibility` method. In AWT and Swing, the `setVisible` method takes a `Boolean` parameter, whereas in Android, `setVisibility` takes an `int` value. The reason for this is that Android treats visibility as part of the layout process. In our case we want the `counter` to disappear, but still take up its space in the layout, which will keep the `text` labels left-aligned with each other. If we wanted the counter to vanish and take up no space, we could use:

```
counter.setVisibility(burger.count == 0
        ? View.GONE
        : View.VISIBLE);
```

`ListView` objects will automatically handle the highlighting of a selected item. This includes when the user holds their finger on the item, and when they use a track-pad or directional buttons to navigate the `ListView`. When an item is highlighted, its background generally changes color, according to standard UI conventions.

However, using widgets in a `ListView` that in some way directly captures user input (that is, a `Button` or `EditText`) will cause the `ListView` to stop showing the selection highlighting for that widget. In fact, it will stop the `ListView` from registering `OnItemClick` events completely.

Custom separators in a ListView

If you override the `isEnabled(int index)` method of `ListAdapter`, you can strategically disable specified items in the `ListView`. A common use of this is to turn certain items into logical separators. For example, a section separator in an alphabetically sorted list, containing the first letter of all items in the next "section".

Creating TheBurgerPlaceActivity class

In order to put the `Burger` menu on the screen, and to allow the user to order items, we need a new `Activity` class. We need to know when the user touches the items in the list, for which we will need to implement the `OnItemClickListener` interface. When a specific event occurs (in this case the user touches a specific item in the `ListView`), objects registered as listeners will have a related method invoked with the details of the event that occurred. Android provides a simple `ListActivity` class to provide some default layout and utility methods for this scenario.

Time for action – implementing TheBurgerPlaceActivity

In order to present a `ListView` of `Burger` objects with the `BurgerAdapter` class, we will need to create an `Activity` implementation for **The Burger Place**. The new `Activity` will also be responsible for listening to "touch" or "click" events on the items in the `ListView`. When the user touches one of the items, we need to update the model and `ListView` to reflect that the user has ordered another `Burger`.

1. Create a new class in the root package of your project named `TheBurgerPlaceActivity`, and make sure it extends `ListActivity`:

```
public class TheBurgerPlaceActivity extends ListActivity {
```

2. Override the `Activity.onCreate` method.

3. Invoke the `super.onCreate` to allow normal Android startup.

4. Create an instance of `BurgerAdapter` with some `Burger` objects, and set it as the `ListAdapter` for the `ListActivity` code to use:

```
setListAdapter(new BurgerAdapter(
        new Burger("Plain old Burger"),
        new Burger("Cheese Burger"),
        new Burger("Chicken Burger"),
        new Burger("Breakfast Burger"),
        new Burger("Hawaiian Burger"),
        new Burger("Fish Burger"),
        new Burger("Vegatarian Burger"),
        new Burger("Lamb Burger"),
        new Burger("Rare Tuna Steak Burger")));
```

5. Finally, implement the `onListItemClicked` method with the following code:

```
protected void onListItemClick(
        ListView parent,
        View item,
        int index,
        long id) {

    BurgerAdapter burgers = (BurgerAdapter)
            parent.getAdapter();

    Burger burger = (Burger)burgers.getItem(index);
    burger.count++;
    burgers.notifyDataSetInvalidated();
}
```

What just happened?

This implementation of `TheBurgerPlaceActivity` has a simple hard-coded list of `Burger` objects to display to the user and creates a `BurgerAdapter` to turn these objects into the `burger_item` View objects which we created earlier.

When the user taps a list item, we increment the `count` of the related `Burger` object in the `onItemClick` method. We then call `notifyDataSetInvalidated()` on the `BurgerAdapter`. This method will inform the `ListView` that the underlying data has changed. When the data changes, the `ListView` will re-invoke the `Adapter.getView` method for each item in the `ListView`.

The items in a `ListView` are represented by effectively static `View` objects. This means that the `Adapter` must be allowed to update or recreate that `View` when the data model is updated. A common alternative is to fetch the `View` representing your updated data, and update it directly.

Registering and starting TheBurgerPlaceActivity

In order to start the new `Activity` class from our restaurant menu, you will need to register it in the `AndroidManifest.xml` file. First, open the `AndroidManifest.xml` file in an editor or IDE, and copy the following `<activity>` code into the `<application>...</application>` block:

```
<activity android:name=".TheBurgerPlaceActivity"
        android:label="The Burger Place\'s Menu">

    <intent-filter>
        <action android:name=
                "com.packtpub.deliverydroid.TheBurgerPlaceActivity"/>
    </intent-filter>
</activity>
```

To start the `Activity`, you'll need to go back to `SelectRestaurantActivity` and implement the `OnItemClickListener` interface. After setting the `Adapter` on the `restaurants` `ListView`, set `SelectRestaurantActivity` as the `OnItemClickListener` of the `restaurants` `ListView`. You can start `TheBurgerPlaceActivity` using an `Intent` object in the `onItemClick` method. Your `SelectRestaurantActivity` class should now look like the following code snippet:

```
public class SelectRestaurantActivity extends Activity
        implements OnItemClickListener {

    @Override
    public void onCreate(Bundle icicle) {
        super.onCreate(icicle);
        setContentView(R.layout.main);
```

```
ListView restaurants = (ListView)
        findViewById(R.id.restaurant);
restaurants.setAdapter(new ArrayAdapter<String>(
        this,
        R.layout.menu_item,
        getResources().getStringArray(R.array.restaurants)));
restaurants.setOnItemClickListener(this);
}
public void onItemClick(
        AdapterView<?> parent,
        View item,
        int index,
        long id) {
    switch(index) {
        case 0:
            startActivity(new Intent(
                    this,
                    TheBurgerPlaceActivity.class));
            break;
    }
}
}
```

When you reinstall the application and start it up in the emulator, you'll be able to navigate to **The Burger Place** and place an order for burgers. Pressing the hardware "Back" button in **The Burger Place** menu will take you back to the restaurant menu.

Pop quiz

1. Setting the choice mode on a `ListView` object to `CHOICE_MODE_SINGLE` will:

    a. Add a `RadioButton` to each item.

    b. Do nothing (this is the default).

    c. Make the `ListView` track a "selected" item.

2. A `ListAdapter` defines how a `ListView` displays its items. When will it be asked to reuse a `View` for an item object?

    a. When the data model is invalidated or changed.

    b. On every item, for rubber-stamping.

    c. When the `ListView` redraws itself.

3. When a `ListView` is scrollable, header and footer objects will be positioned:

    a. Above and below the scrolling items.

    b. Horizontally alongside each other, above and below the scrolling items.

    c. Scrolling with the other items.

Using the ExpandableListView class

The `ListView` class is great for displaying small to medium amounts of data, but there are times when it will flood your user with far too much information. Think about an email application. If your user is a heavy email user, or subscribes to a few mailing lists, they may well have several hundred emails in a folder. Even though they may not need to scroll beyond the first few, seeing the scrollbar shrink to a few pixels in size doesn't have a good psychological effect on your user.

In desktop mail clients, you will often group the email list by time: Today, yesterday, this week, this month, and forever (or something similar). Android includes the `ExpandableListView` for this type of grouping. Each item is nested inside a group, and a group can be displayed or hidden by the user. It's a bit like a tree view, but always nested to exactly one level (you can't display an item outside a group).

Massive ExpandableListView groups

There are times where even an `ExpandableListView` will not be enough to keep the amount of data to a reasonable length. In these cases, consider giving your user the first few items in the group and adding a special **View More** item at the end. Alternatively, use a `ListView` for the groups, and a separate `Activity` for the nested items.

Creating ExpandableListAdapter implementations

Since the `ExpandableList` class includes two levels of detail, it can't work against a normal `ListAdapter` which only handles a single level. Instead, it includes the `ExpandableListAdapter` which uses two sets of methods: one set for the group level and another set for the item level. When implementing a custom `ExpandableListAdapter`, it's generally easiest to have your `ExpandableListAdapter` implementation inherit from the `BaseExpandableListAdapter`, as it provides implementations for event registration and triggering.

The `ExpandableListAdapter` will place an arrow pointer on the left side of each group item to indicate whether the group is open or closed (much like a drop-down/combobox). The arrow is rendered on top of the group's `View` object as returned by the `ExpandableListAdapter`. To stop your group label from being partly obscured by this arrow, you'll need to add padding to your list item `View` structures. The default padding for a list item is available as the theme parameter `expandableListPreferredItemPaddingLeft`, which you can make use of:

```
android:paddingLeft=
    "?android:attr/expandableListPreferredItemPaddingLeft"
```

In order to keep your `ExpandableListView` looking consistent, it's a good idea to add the same amount of padding to the normal (child) items of the `ExpandableListView` (to keep their text aligned with that of their parent group), unless you are putting an item on the left-hand side, such as an icon or checkbox.

Have a go hero - ordering customized pizzas

For the `Mick's Pizza` example, we're going to create a menu of categorized pizza toppings. Each topping consists of a name, whether it's 'on' or 'off' the pizza, or 'extra' (for example, extra cheese). Use two `TextView` objects arranged horizontally for each item. The right `TextView` can hold the name of the topping. The left `TextView` can be empty when toppings are not included, `On` when toppings are included, and `Extra` for toppings that the user wants more than the usual amount.

Create an object model with `ToppingCatagory` objects, containing a name and an array of `PizzaTopping` objects. You'll want to store some state whether each topping is ordered, and in what quantity.

You'll also want to implement a `PizzaToppingAdapter` class, extending the `BaseExpandableListAdapter` class. Make use of the default Android `simple_expandable_list_item_1` layout resource for the group label, and a new customized layout resource for the item labels.

When the user taps on a pizza topping, it changes its status between the three values: **Off**, **On**, and **Extra**.

> Using the `ListView.getAdapter()` method will not return your `ExpandableListAdapter` implementation, but a wrapper instead. To fetch the original `ExpandableListAdapter`, you will need to use the `getExpandableListAdapter()` method. You will also want to make use of the `ExpandableListView.OnChildClickListener` interface to receive click events.

When your new `Activity` is complete, you should have a screen which looks something like the following:

Using the GridView class

A `GridView` is a `ListView` with a fixed number of columns, arranged left-to-right, top-to-bottom. The standard (un-themed) Android application menu is arranged like a `GridView`. The `GridView` class makes use of a `ListAdapter` in the exact same format as `ListView`. However, because of its fixed column count, a `GridView` is very well suited for lists of icons.

Using GridViews effectively

A `GridView` can display significantly more information on a single screen than a `ListView`, at the expense of not being able to show as much text information. From a usability point of view, icons are often easier to work with than text. Icons can be recognized more quickly than text, thanks to their colors. When you have information that can be represented using icons, it's a good idea to display it as such. However, remember that icons need to be unique within a single screen preferably within the entire application.

For our next example, we're going to build the **Four Buckets 'o Fruit** menu, using `GridView`. The `GridView` will have an icon for each item on the menu, and the name of the item below the icon. So, when complete, it will look much like the standard Android application menu. This next example will focus less on the implementation of the `ListAdapter`, since it's largely the same as the `ListAdapter` we built for **The Burger Place**.

Icons on touchscreen devices

It's important to think about icons on a touchscreen device. They need to be even more self-explanatory than usual, or be accompanied by some text. With a touchscreen, it's very hard to provide any sort of contextual help, such as a tool-tip. If the user is touching the object, it's often obscured by their finger and/or hand, making the icon and tool-tip invisible.

Time for action – creating the fruit icon

In order to display the various types of fruits as icons, we will need to create a layout XML file. Each icon in the `GridView` will be represented as an instance of this layout, in exactly the same way as list items are represented in a `ListView`. We create each item as an `ImageView` for the icon, with a `TextView` below it for the label.

1. Create a file in the `res/layout` directory named `fruit_item.xml`.

2. Declare the root element of the icon as a vertical `LinearLayout`:

    ```
    <LinearLayout
        xmlns:android="http://schemas.android.com/apk/res/android"
        android:orientation="vertical"
        android:layout_width="fill_parent"
        android:layout_height="fill_parent">
    ```

3. Create the `ImageView` element that will serve as our icon:

    ```
    <ImageView android:id="@+id/icon"
        android:layout_width="fill_parent"
        android:layout_height="wrap_content"/>
    ```

4. Next, create the `TextView` element that will serve as the label:

    ```
    <TextView android:id="@+id/text"
        android:textSize="@dimen/item_description_size"
        android:layout_width="fill_parent"
        android:layout_height="wrap_content"
        android:gravity="center|center_vertical" />
    ```

What just happened?

The `fruit_item.xml` file is a very simple layout for our menu icons, and could be used for many other types of icons represented as a grid. `ImageView` objects will, by default, attempt to scale their content to their size. In our previous example, the root `LinearLayout` has the width and height defined as `fill_parent`. When placed in a `GridView` as a single item, using `fill_parent` as a size will cause the `LinearLayout` to fill the space provided for that grid item (not the entire `GridView`).

Displaying icons in a GridView

We need an object model and `ListAdapter` in order to display the fruits to the user in a `GridView`. The adapter is fairly straightforward at this point. It's a normal `ListAdapter` implementation built on top of an item class and the layout XML we defined for the icons.

For each item of fruit, we will need an object holding both the fruit's name and icon. Create a `FruitItem` class in the root package with the following code:

```
class FruitItem {
    final String name;
    final int image;

    FruitItem(String name, int image) {
        this.name = name;
        this.image = image;
    }
}
```

In the preceding code, we referenced the icon image for the fruit as an integer. When we reference application resources and IDs in Android, it's always with an integer. For this example we're assuming that all of the different types of fruit each have an icon as an application resource. Another option would be to hold a reference to a `Bitmap` object in each `FruitItem`. However, this would have meant holding the full image in memory when the `FruitItem` is potentially not on the screen.

In order for the Android Asset Packaging Tool to recognize and store the icons, you will need to put them in the `res/drawable` directory.

Android Image Resources

Generally, it's considered a good practice in Android to store bitmap images as PNG files. Since you will be accessing these files from your code, make sure they have Java-friendly filenames. The PNG format (unlike JPG) is lossless, can have various different color depths, and correctly handles transparency. This generally makes it a great image format on the whole.

Time for action – building the fruit menu

For the **Four Buckets 'o Fruit** menu, we're going to need a `ListAdapter` implementation to render the `FruitItem` objects into the `fruit_item.xml` layout resources. We'll also need a layout resource for the `GridView` which we will load in our new `Activity` class.

1. Create a new class named `FruitAdapter` extending `BaseAdapter` in the root package of the project.

2. `FruitAdapter` needs to hold and represent an array of `FruitItem` objects. Implement the class using the same structure as the `BurgerAdapter`.

3. In the `ListAdapter.getView` method, set the label and icon as defined in the `fruit_item.xml` layout resource:

```
FruitItem item = items[index];
TextView text = ((TextView)view.findViewById(R.id.text));
ImageView image = ((ImageView)view.findViewById(R.id.icon));
text.setText(item.name);
image.setImageResource(item.image);
```

4. Create a new layout resource to hold the `GridView` that we will use for the **Four Buckets 'o Fruit** menu, and name it `res/layout/four_buckets.xml`.

5. Populate the new layout resource with a three column `GridView`:

```
<GridView
    xmlns:android="http://schemas.android.com/apk/res/android"
    android:numColumns="3"
    android:horizontalSpacing="5dip"
    android:verticalSpacing="5dip"
    android:layout_width="fill_parent"
    android:layout_height="fill_parent"/>
```

What just happened?

The new `four_buckets.xml` layout resource has nothing but a `GridView`. This is unlike the other layout resources we've written so far, especially since the `GridView` has no ID. For this example, the fruit menu `Activity` will contain nothing but the `GridView`, so there's no need for an ID reference or layout structure. We also specified horizontal and vertical spacing of `5dip`. A `GridView` object's default is to have no spacing between its cells, which makes for fairly squashed content. In order to space things out a bit, we ask for some whitespace between each of the cells.

Time for action – creating the FourBucketsActivity

Since we are working with a layout resource with only a `GridView`, and no ID reference, we're going to walk through the creation of the `Activity` step-by-step. Unlike previous `Activity` implementations, we will need a direct reference to the `GridView` defined in `four_buckets.xml`, and this means loading it manually.

1. Start by creating a new class in your project's root package:

   ```
   public class FourBucketsActivity extends Activity {
   ```

2. Override the `onCreate` method, and invoke the super implementation:

   ```
   protected void onCreate(final Bundle istate) {
       super.onCreate(istate);
   ```

3. Get the `LayoutInflator` instance for your `Activity` object:

   ```
   LayoutInflater inflater = getLayoutInflater();
   ```

4. Inflate the `four_buckets.xml` resource and cast its contents directly to a `GridView` object:

   ```
   GridView view = (GridView)inflater.inflate(
           R.layout.four_buckets,
           null);
   ```

5. Set the `ListAdapter` of the `view` object to a new instance of the `FruitAdapter` class, and populate the new `FruitAdapter` with some `FruitItem` objects:

   ```
   view.setAdapter(new FruitAdapter(
           new FruitItem("Apple", R.drawable.apple),
           new FruitItem("Banana", R.drawable.banana),
           new FruitItem("Black Berries", R.drawable.blackberry),
           // and so on
   ```

6. Use `setContentView` to make the `GridView` your root `View` object:

   ```
   setContentView(view);
   ```

7. Register your `FourBucketsActivity` class in your `AndroidManifest.xml`.

8. Add a case to the `SelectRestaurantActivity` to start the new `FourBucketsActivity` when the user selects it.

What just happened?

You just completed the **Four Buckets 'o Fruit** menu. If you re-install the application into your emulator, you'll now be able to go and order fruits (just be careful to have the 16 ton weight ready in case the delivery guy attacks you).

If you look through the `Activity` documentation, you'll notice that while there's a `setContentView` method, there's no corresponding `getContentView` method. Take a closer look and you will notice the `addContentView` method. An `Activity` object may have any number of `View` objects attached to it as "content". This precludes any useful implementation of a `getContentView` method.

In order to get around this limitation, we inflated the layout ourselves. The `getLayoutInflator()` method used is simply a shortcut for `LayoutInflator.from(this)`. Instead of using an ID and `findViewById`, we simply cast the `View` returned directly to a `GridView`, since that's all that our `four_buckets.xml` file contains (much the same way the `ArrayAdapter` class works with `TextView` objects). If we wanted to make things a little more abstract, we could have cast it to an `AdapterView<ListAdapter>`, in which case we could have swapped in implementation in the file with a `ListView`. However, this wouldn't have been very useful for this example.

If you now re-install and run the application, your new `FourBucketsActivity` will present you with a screen similar to the following one:

Have a go hero – Sam's Sushi

The last restaurant on the menu is `Sam's Sushi`. Try using the `Spinner` class along with a `GridView` to create a composite sushi menu. Place the spinner at the top of the screen, with options for different types of sushi:

- Sashimi
- Maki Roll
- Nigiri
- Oshi

- California Roll
- Fashion Sandwich
- Hand Roll

Below the `Spinner`, use a `GridView` to display icons for each different type of fish that the user can order. Here are some suggestions:

- Tuna
- Yellowtail
- Snapper
- Salmon
- Eel
- Sea Urchin
- Squid
- Shrimp

The `Spinner` class makes use of the `SpinnerAdapter` instead of a `ListAdapter`. The `SpinnerAdapter` includes an additional `View` object which represents the drop-down menu. This is most typically a reference to the `android.R.layout.simple_dropdown_item_1line` resource. However, for this example, however, you can probably make use of the `android:entries` attribute on the `Spinner` XML element.

Summary

Data display is one of the most common requirements of a mobile application, and Android has many different options available. The `ListView` is probably one of the most commonly used widgets in the standard Android suite, and styling it allows it to be used to display varying amounts of data, from one line menu items to multi-line to-do notes.

The `GridView` is effectively a tabular version of `ListView`, and is well suited for presenting the user with icon views. Icons have enormous advantages over text, since they can be recognized much more quickly by the user. Icons can also take up significantly less space, and in a `GridView`, you could easily fit four to six icons in a portrait screen without making the user interface cluttered or more difficult to work it. This also frees up precious screen space for other items to be displayed.

Building custom `Adapter` classes not only allows you to take complete control over the styling of the `ListView`, but also determine where the data comes from, and how it's loaded. You could, for example, load the data directly from a web service by using an `Adapter` which generates dummy `View` objects until the web service responds with actual data. Take a good look at the default `Adapter` implementations, they will generally serve your requirements, especially when coupled with a custom layout resource.

In the next chapter, we will take a look at some less generic, more specialized `View` classes that Android provides. As with almost everything in Android, the defaults may be specific, but they can be customized in any number of ways to fit some very unusual purposes.

3
Developing with Specialized Android Widgets

Along with the many generic widgets such as buttons, text fields, and checkboxes, Android also includes a variety of more specialized widgets. While a button is fairly generic, and has use in many situations, a gallery-widget for example, is far more targeted. In this chapter we will start looking at the more specialized Android widgets, where they appear, and how best they can be used.

Although these are very specialized `View` classes, they are very important. As mentioned earlier (and it really can't be stressed enough) one of the cornerstones of good user interface design is **consistency**. An example is the `DatePicker` widget. It's certainly not the prettiest date-selector in the world. It's not a calendar widget, so it's sometimes quite difficult for the user to select exactly which date they want (most people think in terms of "next week Tuesday", and not "Tuesday the 17th"). However, the `DatePicker` is standard! So the user knows exactly how to use it, they don't have to work with a broken calendar implementation. This chapter will work with Android's more specialized `View` and layout classes:

- `Tab` **layouts**
- `TextSwitcher`
- `Gallery`
- `DatePicker`
- `TimePicker`
- `RatingBar`

These classes have very specialized purposes, and some have slight quirks in the way they are implemented. This chapter will explore how and where to use these widgets, and where you need to be careful of their implementation details. We'll also discuss how best to incorporate these elements into an application, and into a layout.

Creating a restaurant review application

In the previous chapter, we built an ordering-in application. In this chapter, we're going to take a look at reviewing restaurants. The application will allow the user to view other people's opinions on the restaurant, a gallery of photos of the restaurant, and finally a section for making an online reservation. We will divide the application into three sections:

◆ **Review**: Review and ratings information for this restaurant

◆ **Photos**: A photo gallery of the restaurant

◆ **Reservation**: Request a reservation with the restaurant

When building an application where all three of these sections need to be quickly available to the user, the most sensible option available is to place each of the sections in a tab on the screen. This allows the user to switch between the three sections without having all of them on the screen at the same time. This also saves screen real estate giving us more space for each section.

The **Review** tab will include a cycling list of comments that people have made about the restaurant being viewed, and an average "star" rating for the restaurant.

Displaying photographs of the restaurant is the job of the **Photos** tab. We'll provide the user with a thumbnail "track" at the top of the screen, and a view of the selected image consuming the remaining screen space.

For the **Reservation** tab, we will want to capture the user's name and when they would like the reservation to be (date and time). Finally we also need to know for how many people the reservation will be made.

Time for action – creating the robotic review project structure

To start this example we'll need a new project with a new `Activity`. The new layout and `Activity` will be a little different from the structures in the previous two chapters. We will need to use the `FrameLayout` class in order to build a tabbed layout. So to begin, we'll create a new project structure and start off with a skeleton that will later become our tab layout structure. This can be filled with the three content areas.

1. Create a new Android project using the Android command-line tool:

   ```
   android create project -n RoboticReview -p RoboticReview -k com.
   packtpub.roboticreview -a ReviewActivity -t 3
   ```

2. Open the `res/layout/main.xml` file in an editor or IDE.

3. Clear out the default code (leaving in the XML header).

4. Create a root `FrameLayout` element:

   ```
   <FrameLayout
       xmlns:android="http://schemas.android.com/apk/res/android"
       android:layout_width="fill_parent"
       android:layout_height="fill_parent">
   ```

5. Inside the new `FrameLayout` element, add a vertical `LinearLayout`:

   ```
   <LinearLayout android:id="@+id/review"
                 android:orientation="vertical"
                 android:layout_width="fill_parent"
                 android:layout_height="wrap_content">
   </LinearLayout>
   ```

6. After the `LinearLayout`, add another empty `LinearLayout` element:

   ```
   <LinearLayout android:id="@+id/photos"
                 android:orientation="vertical"
                 android:layout_width="fill_parent"
                 android:layout_height="wrap_content">
   </LinearLayout>
   ```

7. Then, after the second `LinearLayout` element, add an empty `ScrollView`:

   ```
   <ScrollView android:id="@+id/reservation"
               android:layout_width="fill_parent"
               android:layout_height="fill_parent">
   </ScrollView>
   ```

The `FrameLayout` will be used by the Android tab structures as a content area, each of the child elements will become the contents of a tab. In the preceding layout, we've added in two `LinearLayout` elements for the **Review** and **Photos** sections, and a `ScrollView` for the **Reservation** tab.

What just happened?

We've just started the "restaurant review" application, building a skeleton for the user interface. There are several key parts of this `main.xml` file which we should walk through before continuing the example.

First, our root element is a `FrameLayout`. The `FrameLayout` anchors all of its children to its own top-left corner. In effect, the two occurrences of `LinearLayout` and the `ScrollView` will overlap each other. This structure can be used to form something like a Java AWT `CardLayout`, which will be used by the `TabHost` object to display these objects when their relative tab is active.

Second, each of the `LinearLayout` and the `ScrollView` have an ID. In order to identify them as tab roots, we need to be able to easily access them from our Java code. Tab structures may be designed in XML, but they need to be put together in Java.

Building a TabActivity

In order to continue, we need our `Activity` class to set up the three tab content elements we declared in our `main.xml` file as tabs. By preference, all tabs in Android should have an icon.

The following is a screenshot of the tabs without their icons:

The following is a screenshot of the tabs with the icons:

Creating tab icons

Android applications have a specific look and feel defined by the default widgets provided by the system. In order to keep all applications consistent for users, there are a set of user interface guidelines that application developers should follow. While it's important to have your application stand out, users will often get frustrated with applications that are not familiar or look out of place (this is one of the reasons why automatically ported applications are often very unpopular).

Android tabs and icons

When selecting tab icons for your application, it's considered a good practice to include several different versions of the icon for different screen sizes and densities. The anti-aliased corners that look so good on a high-density screen, look terrible on low-density screens. You can also provide entirely different icons for very small screens, instead of loosing all of your icons details. Android tabs appear raised when they are selected, and lowered in the background when they are not selected. The Android tab icons should appear in the "opposite" etching effect to the tab that they are placed in, that is, lowered when they are selected and raised when they are not selected. The icons therefore have two primary states: selected and unselected. In order to switch between these two states, a tab-icon will generally consist of three resource files:

- The selected icon image
- The unselected icon image
- An XML file describing the icon in terms of its two states

Tab icons are generally simple shapes while the image size is squared (generally at a maximum of 32 x 32 pixels). Different variations of the image should be used for screens of different pixel densities (see *Chapter 1*, *Developing a Simple Activity* for "Resource Selection" details). Generally you will use a dark outset image for the selected state, since when a tab is selected, the tab background is light. For the unselected icon, the opposite is true and a light inset image should be used instead.

The bitmap images in an Android application should always be in the PNG format. Let's call the selected icon for the **Review** tab `res/drawable/ic_tab_selstar.png`, and name the unselected icon file `res/drawable/ic_tab_unselstar.png`. In order to switch states between these two images automatically, we define a special `StateListDrawable` as an XML file. Hence the **Review** icon is actually in a file named `res/drawable/review.xml`, and it looks like this:

```xml
<selector xmlns:android="http://schemas.android.com/apk/res/android"
        android:constantSize="true">

    <item
        android:drawable="@drawable/ic_tab_selstar"
        android:state_selected="false"/>
    <item
        android:drawable="@drawable/ic_tab_unselstar"
        android:state_selected="true"/>
</selector>
```

Note the `android:constantSize="true"` of the `<selector>` element. By default, Android will assume that each state in the resulting `StateListDrawable` object will cause the image to be of a different size, which in turn may cause the user interface to re-run its layout calculations. This can be fairly expensive, so it's a good idea to declare that each of your states is exactly of the same size.

For this example, we'll be using three tab icons, each with two states. The icons are named `review`, `photos`, and `book`. Each one is composed of three files: A PNG for the selected icon, a PNG for the unselected icon, and an XML file defining the state-selector. From our application, we will only make direct use of the state-selector XML files, leaving the Android APIs to pickup the actual PNG files.

Implementing the ReviewActivity

As usual, we will want to have localized text in our `strings.xml` file. Open the `res/values/strings.xml` file and copy the following code into it:

```
<resources>
    <string name="app_name">Robotic Review</string>
    <string name="review">Review</string>
    <string name="gallery">Photos</string>
    <string name="reservation">Reservations</string>
</resources>
```

Time for action – writing the ReviewActivity class

As already said, we will need to set up our tabbed-layout structure in our Java code. Fortunately, Android provides a very useful `TabActivity` class that does much of the heavy lifting for us, providing us with a ready-made `TabHost` object with which we can construct the `Activity` tab structure.

1. Open the `ReviewActivity.java` file generated earlier in an editor or IDE.

2. Instead of extending `Activity`, change the class to inherit `TabActivity`:

   ```
   public class ReviewActivity extends TabActivity
   ```

3. In the `onCreate` method, remove the `setContentView(R.layout.main)` line (generated by the `android create project` utility) completely.

4. Now start by fetching the `TabHost` object from your parent class:

   ```
   TabHost tabs = getTabHost();
   ```

5. Next, we inflate our layout XML into the content view of the `TabHost`:

```
getLayoutInflater().inflate(
        R.layout.main,
        tabs.getTabContentView(),
        true);
```

6. We'll need access to our other application resources:

```
Resources resources = getResources();
```

7. Now we define a `TabSpec` for the **Review** tab:

```
TabHost.TabSpec details =
        tabs.newTabSpec("review").
        setContent(R.id.review).
        setIndicator(getString(R.string.review),
        resources.getDrawable(R.drawable.review));
```

8. Define two more `TabSpec` variables for the **Photos** and **Reservation** tabs using the preceding pattern.

9. Add each of the `TabSpec` objects to our `TabHost`:

```
tabs.addTab(details);
tabs.addTab(gallery);
tabs.addTab(reservation);
```

This concludes the creation of the tab structure for the `ReviewActivity` class.

What just happened?

We built a very basic tabbed-layout for our new `ReviewActivity`. When working with tabs, we didn't simply use the `Activity.setContentView` method, instead we inflated the layout XML file ourselves. Then we made use of the `TabHost` object provided by the `TabActivity` class to create three `TabSpec` objects. A `TabSpec` is a builder object that enables you to build up the content of your tab, similar to the way you build up text with a `StringBuilder`.

The content of a `TabSpec` is the content-view that will be attached to the tab on the screen (assigned using the `setContent` method). In this example, we opted for the simplest option and defined the tab content in our `main.xml` file. It's also possible to lazy-create the tab content using the `TabHost.TabContentFactory` interface, or even to put an external `Activity` (such as the dialer or browser) in the tab by using `setContent(Intent)`. However, for the purposes of this example we used the simplest option.

You'll notice that the `TabSpec` (much like the `StringBuilder` class) supports chaining of method calls, making it easy and flexible to either set up a tab in a "single shot" approach (as done previously), or build up the `TabSpec` in stages (that is, while loading from an external service).

The `indicator` we assigned to the `TabSpec` is what will appear on the tab. In the previous case, a string of text and our icon. As of API level 4 (Android version 1.6) it's possible to use a `View` object as an `indicator`, allowing complete customization of the tab's look and feel. To keep the example simple (and compatible with earlier versions) we've supplied a `String` resource as the `indicator`.

Time for action – creating the Review layout

We've got a skeleton tab structure, but there's nothing in it yet. The first tab is titled **Review**, and this is where we are going to start. We've just finished enough Java code to load up the tabs and put them on the screen. Now we go back to the `main.xml` layout file and populate this tab with some widgets that supply the user with review information.

1. Open `res/layout/main.xml` in an editor or IDE.

2. Inside the `<LayoutElement>` that we named `review`, add a new `TextView` that will contain the name of the restaurant:

```
<TextView android:id="@+id/name"
          android:textStyle="bold"
          android:textSize="25sp"
          android:textColor="#ffffffff"
          android:gravity="center|center_vertical"
          android:layout_width="fill_parent"
          android:layout_height="wrap_content"/>
```

3. Below the new `TextView`, add a new `RatingBar`, where we will display how other people have rated the restaurant:

```
<RatingBar android:id="@+id/stars"
           android:numStars="5"
           android:layout_width="wrap_content"
           android:layout_height="wrap_content"/>
```

4. Keeping this first tab simple, we add a `TextSwitcher` where we can display other people's comments about the restaurant:

```
<TextSwitcher android:id="@+id/reviews"
              android:inAnimation="@android:anim/fade_in"
              android:outAnimation="@android:anim/fade_out"
              android:layout_width="fill_parent"
              android:layout_height="fill_parent"/>
```

The **Review** tab only has three widgets in this example, but more could easily be added to allow the user to input their own reviews.

What just happened

We just put together the layout for our first tab. The `RatingBar` that we created has a width of `wrap_content`, which is really important. If you use `fill_parent`, then the number of stars visible in the `RatingBar` will simply be as many as can fit on the screen. If you want control over how many stars appear on your `RatingBar`, stick to `wrap_content`, but also make sure that (at least on portrait layouts) the `RatingBar` has its own horizontal line. If you install the `Activity` in the emulator now, you won't see anything in either the `TextView` or the `TextSwitcher`.

The `TextSwitcher` has no default animations, so we specify the "in" animation as the default `fade_in` as provided by the `android` package, while the "out" animation will be `fade_out`. This syntax is used to access resources that can be found in the `android.R` class.

Working with switcher classes

The `TextSwitcher` we've put in place is used to animate between different `TextView` objects. It's really useful for displaying things like changing stock-prices, news headlines, or in our case, reviews. It inherits from `ViewSwitcher` which can be used to animate between any two generic `View` objects. `ViewSwitcher` extends `ViewAnimator` which can be used as a sort of animated `CardLayout`.

We want to display a series of comments from past customers, fading between each of them with a short animation. `TextSwitcher` needs two `TextView` objects (which it will ask us to create dynamically), for our example. We want these to be in a resource file.

For the next part of the example, we'll need some comments. Instead of using a web service or something similar to fetch real comments, this example will load some comments from its application resources. Open the `res/values/strings.xml` file and add `<string-array name="comments">` with a few likely comments in it:

```xml
<string-array name="comments">
    <item>Just Fantastic</item>
    <item>Amazing Food</item>
    <item>What rubbish, the food was too hairy</item>
    <item>Messy kitchen; call the health inspector.</item>
</string-array>
```

Time for action – turning on the TextSwitcher

We want the `TextSwitcher` to display the next listed comment every five seconds. For this we'll need to employ new resources, and a `Handler` object. A `Handler` is a way for Android applications and services to post messages between threads, and can also be used to schedule messages at a point in the future. It's a preferred structure to use over a `java.util.Timer` since a `Handler` object will not allocate a new `Thread`. In our case, a `Timer` is overkill, as there is only one task we want to schedule.

1. Create a new XML file in your `res/layout` directory named `review_comment.xml`.

2. Copy the following code into the new `review_comment.xml` file:

```
<TextView
    xmlns:android="http://schemas.android.com/apk/res/android"
    android:gravity="left|top"
    android:textStyle="italic"
    android:textSize="16sp"
    android:padding="5dip"
    android:layout_width="fill_parent"
    android:layout_height="wrap_content"/>
```

3. Open the `ReviewActivity.java` file in your editor or IDE.

4. We'll need to be able to load the `review_comment` resources for the `TextSwitcher`, so `ReviewActivity` needs to implement the `ViewSwitcher.ViewFactory` interface.

5. In order to be update the `TextSwitcher`, we need to interact with a `Handler`, and the easiest way to do that here is to also implement `Runnable`.

6. At the top of the `ReviewActivity` class, declare a `Handler` object:

```
private final Handler switchCommentHandler = new Handler();
```

7. We'll also want to hold a reference to the `TextSwitcher` for our `run()` method when we switch comments:

```
private TextSwitcher switcher;
```

8. In order to display the comments, we'll need an array of them, and an index to keep track of which comment the `TextSwitcher` is displaying:

```
private String[] comments;
private int commentIndex = 0;
```

9. Now, in the `onCreate` method, after you add the `TabSpec` objects to the `TabHost`, read the `comments` string-array from the `Resources`:

```
comments = resources.getStringArray(R.array.comments);
```

10. Next, find the `TextSwitcher` and assign it to the `switcher` field:

```
switcher = (TextSwitcher)findViewById(R.id.reviews);
```

11. Tell the `TextSwitcher` that the `ReviewActivity` object will be its `ViewFactory`:

```
switcher.setFactory(this);
```

12. In order to comply with the `ViewFactory` specification, we need to write a `makeView` method. In our case it's really simple—inflate the `review_comment` resource:

```
public View makeView() {
    return getLayoutInflater().inflate(
            R.layout.review_comment, null);
}
```

13. Override the `onStart` method so that we can post the first timed event on the `Handler` object declared earlier:

```
protected void onStart() {
    super.onStart();
    switchCommentHandler.postDelayed(this, 5 * 1000l);
}
```

14. Similarly, override the `onStop` method to cancel any future callback:

```
protected void onStop() {
    super.onStop();
    switchCommentHandler.removeCallbacks(this);
}
```

15. Finally, the `run()` method alternates the comments in the `TextSwitcher`, and in the `finally` block, posts itself back onto the `Handler` queue in five seconds:

```
public void run() {
    try {
        switcher.setText(comments[commentIndex++]);
        if(commentIndex >= comments.length) {
            commentIndex = 0;
        }
    } finally {
        switchCommentHandler.postDelayed(this, 5 * 1000l);
    }
}
```

Using `Handler` objects instead of creating `Thread` objects means all of the timed tasks can share the main user interface thread instead of each allocating a separate thread. This reduces the amount of memory and CPU load your application places on the device, and has a direct impact on the application performance and battery life.

What just happened?

We just built a simple timer structure to update the `TextSwitcher` with a rotating array of comments. The `Handler` class is a convenient way to post messages and actions between two application threads. In Android, as with Swing, the user interface is not thread-safe, so inter-thread communication becomes very important. A `Handler` object attempts to bind itself to the thread it's created in (in the preceding case, the `main` thread).

It's a prerequisite that a thread which creates a `Handler` object must have an associated `Looper` object. You can set this up in your own thread by either inheriting the `HandlerThread` class, or using the `Looper.prepare()` method. Messages sent to a `Handler` object will be executed by the `Looper` associated with the same thread. By sending our `ReviewActivity` (which implements `Runnable`) to the `Handler` object that we had created in the `main` thread, we know that the `ReviewActivity.run()` method will be executed on the `main` thread, regardless of which thread posted it there.

In the case of long-running tasks (such as fetching a web page or a long-running calculation), Android provides a class that bares a striking resemblance to the `SwingWorker` class, named `AsyncTask`. `AsyncTask` (like `Handler`) can be found in the `android.os` package, and you make use of it by inheritance. `AsyncTask` is used to allow interaction between a background task and the user interface (in order to update a progress bar or similar requirements).

Creating a simple photo gallery

The use of the word `Gallery` is a little misleading, it's really a horizontal row of items with a "single item" selection model. For this example we'll be using the `Gallery` class for what it does best, displaying thumbnails. However, as you'll see, it's capable of displaying scrolling lists of almost anything. Since a `Gallery` is a spinner, you work with it in much the same way as a `Spinner` object or a `ListView`, that is, with an `Adapter`.

Time for action – building the Photos tab

Before we can add images to a `Gallery`, we need the `Gallery` object on the screen. To start this exercise, we'll add a `Gallery` object and an `ImageView` to `FrameLayout` of our tabs. This will appear under the **Photos** tab that we created at the beginning of the chapter. We'll stick to a fairly traditional photo gallery model of the sliding thumbnails at the top of the screen, with the full view of the selected image below it.

1. Open `res/layout/main.xml` in your editor or IDE.

2. Inside the second `LinearLayout`, with `android:id="@+id/photos"`, add a new `Gallery` element to hold the thumbnails:

   ```
   <Gallery android:id="@+id/gallery"
            android:layout_width="fill_parent"
            android:layout_height="wrap_content"/>
   ```

3. `Gallery` objects, by default, squash their contents together, which really doesn't look great in our case. You can add a little padding between the items by using the `spacing` attribute of `Gallery` class:

   ```
   android:spacing="5dip"
   ```

4. We also have tabs directly above the `Gallery`, and we'll have an `ImageView` directly below it. Again, there won't be any padding, so add some using a margin:

   ```
   android:layout_marginTop="5dip"
   android:layout_marginBottom="5dip"
   ```

5. Now create an `ImageView` which we can use to display the full-sized image:

   ```
   <ImageView android:id="@+id/photo"
              android:layout_width="fill_parent"
              android:layout_height="fill_parent"/>
   ```

6. In order to ensure that the full display is scaled correctly, we need to specify the `scaleType` on the `ImageView`:

   ```
   android:scaleType="centerInside"
   ```

The `Gallery` element provides us with the thumbnail track at the top of the screen. The image selected in the `Gallery` will be displayed at full-size in the `ImageView` widget.

What just happened?

We just populated the second tab with the standard widgets required for a basic photo gallery. This structure is very generic, but is also well known and understood by users. The `Gallery` class will handle the thumbnails, scrolling, and selection. However, you will need to populate the main `ImageView` with the selected image, and provide the `Gallery` object with the thumbnail widgets to display on the screen.

The spacing attribute on the `Gallery` element will add some whitespace, which serves as a simple separator between thumbnails. You could also add a border into each of the thumbnail images, border each `ImageView` widget you return for a thumbnail, or use a custom widget to create a border.

Creating a thumbnail widget

In order to display the thumbnails in the `Gallery` object, we will need to create an `ImageView` object for each thumbnail. We could easily do this in Java code, but as usual, it is preferable to build even the most basic widgets using an XML resource. In this case, create a new XML resource in the `res/layout` directory. Name the new file `gallery_thn.xml` and copy the following code into it:

```
<ImageView xmlns:android="http://schemas.android.com/apk/res/android"
           android:scaleType="fitXY"/>
```

That's right, it has just two lines of XML, but to reiterate, this allows us to customize this widget for many different configurations without editing the Java code. While editing the code might not seem like a problem (the resource needs to be recompiled anyway), you also don't want to end up with a long series of `if` statements to decide on exactly how you should create the `ImageView` objects.

Implementing a GalleryAdapter

For the example, we'll stick to using application resources to keep things simple. We'll have two arrays of resource IDs, thumbnails, and the full-size images. An `Adapter` implementation is expected to provide an identifier for each of the items. In this next example, we're going to provide an identifier as the resource identifier of the full-size image, which gives us easy access to the full-size image in classes outside of the `Adapter` implementation. While this is an unusual contract, it provides a convenient way for us to pass the image resource around within an already defined structure.

In order to display your gallery, you'll need some images to display (mine are sized 480 x 319 pixels). For each of these images, you'll need a thumbnail image to display in the `Gallery` object. Generally, these should simply be a scaled-down version of the actual image (mine are scaled to 128 x 84 pixels).

Time for action – the GalleryAdapter

Creating the `GalleryAdapter` is much like the `ListAdapter` classes we created in *Chapter 2, Presenting Data for Views*. The `GalleryAdapter` however, will use `ImageView` objects instead of `TextView` objects. It also binds two lists of resources together instead of using an object model.

1. Create a new Java class in your project root package named `GalleryAdapter`. It should extend the `BaseAdapter` class.

2. Declare an integer array to hold the thumbnail resource IDs:

```
private final int[] thumbnails = new int[]{
    R.drawable.curry_view_thn,
    R.drawable.jai_thn,
    // your other thumbnails
};
```

3. Declare an integer array to hold the full-size image resource IDs:

```
private final int[] images = new int[]{
    R.drawable.curry_view,
    R.drawable.jai,
    // your other full-size images
};
```

4. The `getCount()` method is simply the length of the `thumbnails` array:

```
public int getCount() {
    return thumbnails.length;
}
```

5. The `getItem(int)` method returns the full-size image resource ID:

```
public Object getItem(int index) {
    return Integer.valueOf(images[index]);
}
```

6. As mentioned earlier, the `getItemId(int)` method returns the full-size image resource ID (almost exactly the way that `getItem(int)` does):

```
public long getItemId(int index) {
    return images[index];
}
```

7. Finally, the getView(int, View, ViewGroup) method uses a LayoutInflater to read and populate the ImageView which we created in the gallery_thn.xml layout resource:

```
public View getView(int index, View reuse, ViewGroup parent) {
    ImageView view = (reuse instanceof ImageView)
            ? (ImageView)reuse
            : (ImageView)LayoutInflater.
                    from(parent.getContext()).
                    inflate(R.layout.gallery_thn, null);
    view.setImageResource(thumbnails[index]);
    return view;
}
```

The Gallery class is a subclass of AdapterView and so functions in the same way as a ListView object. The GalleryAdapter will provide the Gallery object with View objects to display the thumbnails in.

What just happened

Much like the Adapter classes built in the last chapter, the GalleryAdapter will attempt to reuse any View object specified in its getView method. A primary difference however, is that this GalleryAdapter is entirely self-contained, and will always display the same list of images.

This example of a GalleryAdapter is extremely simple. You could also build a GalleryAdapter that held bitmap objects instead of resource ID references. You'd then make use of the ImageView.setImageBitmap method instead of ImageView.setImageResource.

You could also eliminate the thumbnail images by having the ImageView scale the full-size images into thumbnails. This would just require a modification to the gallery_thn.xml resource file in order to specify the required size of each thumbnail.

```
<ImageView xmlns:android="http://schemas.android.com/apk/res/android"
        android:maxWidth="128dip"
        android:adjustViewBounds="true"
        android:scaleType="centerInside"/>
```

The adjustViewBounds attribute tells the ImageView to adjust its own size in a way such that it maintains the aspect ratio of the image it contains. We also change the scaleType attribute to centerInside, which will also retain the aspect ratio of the image when it scales. Finally, we set a maximum width for the ImageView. Using the standard layout_width or layout_height attributes is ignored by the Gallery class, so we instead specify the desired thumbnail size to the ImageView (the layout_width and layout_height attributes are handled by the Gallery, while the maxWidth and maxHeight are handled by the ImageView).

This would be a standard speed/size trade-off. Having the thumbnail images takes up more application space, but having the `ImageView` perform the scaling makes the application slower. The scaling algorithm in `ImageView` will also not be as high-quality as the scaling performed in an image-manipulation application such as Adobe Photoshop. In most cases this won't be a problem, but if you have high detail images, you often get "scaling artifacts" with simpler scaling algorithms.

Time for action – making the gallery work

Now that we've got the `GalleryAdapter` working, we need to connect the `Gallery`, the `GalleryAdapter`, and the `ImageView` together, so that when a thumbnail is selected, the full-view of that image is displayed in the `ImageView` object.

1. Open the `ReviewActivity` source code in your editor or IDE.

2. Add `AdapterView.OnItemSelectedListener` to the interfaces that the `ReviewActivity` implements.

3. Below the declaration of the `TextSwitcher`, declare a reference to the `ImageView` which will hold the full-size image:

   ```
   private TextSwitcher switcher;
   private ImageView photo;
   ```

4. At the end of the `onCreate` method, find the `ImageView` named `photo` and assign it to the reference you just declared:

   ```
   photo = ((ImageView)findViewById(R.id.photo));
   ```

5. Now fetch the `Gallery` object as declared in the `main.xml` layout resource:

   ```
   Gallery photos = ((Gallery)findViewById(R.id.gallery));
   ```

6. Create a new `GalleryAdapter` and set it on the `Gallery` object:

   ```
   photos.setAdapter(new GalleryAdapter());
   ```

7. Set the `OnItemSelectedListener` of the `Gallery` object to `this`:

   ```
   photos.setOnItemSelectedListener(this);
   ```

8. At the end of the `ReviewActivity` class, add the `onItemSelected` method:

   ```
   public void onItemSelected(
           AdapterView<?> av, View view, int idx, long id) {

       photo.setImageResource((int)id);
   }
   ```

9. `OnItemSelectedListener` requires an `onNothingSelected` method as well, but we don't need it to do anything for this example.

The `GalleryAdapter` provides the `ReviewActivity` with the resource to load for the full view of the photo through the `id` parameter. The `id` parameter could also be used as an index or identifier for a URL if the image was located on a remote server.

What just happened?

We've now connected the `Gallery` object to the `ImageView` where we will display the full-size image instead of the thumbnail. We've used the item ID as a way to send the resource ID of the full-size image directly to the event listener. This is a fairly strange concept since you'd normally use an object model. However, an object model in this example wouldn't just introduce a new class, it would also require another method call (in order to fetch the image object from the `Adapter` when the event is triggered).

When you specify an `Adapter` on an `AbsSpinner` class like `Gallery`, it will by default attempt to select the first item returned from its new `Adapter`. This in turn notifies the `OnItemSelectedListener` object if one has been registered. However, because of the single-threading model used by the Android user interface objects, this event doesn't get fired immediately, but rather some time after we return from the `onCreate` method. When we call `setAdapter(new GalleryAdapter())` on the `Gallery` object, it schedules a selection change event, which we then receive. The event causes the `ReviewActivity` class to display the first photo in the `GalleryAdapter` object.

If you now reinstall the application in your emulator, you'll be able to go to the **Photos** tab and browse through a `Gallery` of all the images that you had populated the `GalleryAdapter` with.

Pop quiz

1. What would happen in the previous example if you substituted `OnItemSelectedListener` with `OnItemClickListener` (as done in the `ListView` examples)?

    a. The full size won't appear anymore.

    b. The `Gallery` will not rotate the thumbnails when they are touched.

    c. The full-size photo won't appear until a thumbnail is clicked.

2. What is the primary difference between the `ScaleType` values `fitXY` and `centerInside`?

    a. The `fitXY` type will anchor the picture to the top-left, while `centerInside` will center the picture in the `ImageView`.

    b. `fitXY` will cause the picture to distort to the size of the `ImageView`, while `centerInside` will maintain the picture's aspect ratio.

    c. `centerInside` will cause the larger axis to be cropped in order to fit the picture into the `ImageView`, while `fitXY` will scale the picture so that the larger axis is of the same size as the `ImageView`.

3. What dictates the size of a `Gallery` object containing `ImageView` objects when using the `wrap_content` attribute?

    a. The width and height of the `ImageView` objects, as dictated by the size of their content image, or their `maxWidth` and `maxHeight` parameters.

    b. The `itemWidth` and `itemHeight` parameters on the `Gallery` object.

    c. The `LayoutParams` set on the `ImageView` objects (either with the `setLayoutParams` method, or `layout_width`/`layout_height` attributes).

Have a go hero – animations and external sources

Now that you have the basic example working, try improving the user experience a bit. When you touch the images, they should really animate instead of undergoing an instant change. They should also come from an external source instead of application resources.

1. Change the `ImageView` object of full-size images to an `ImageSwitcher`, use the standard Android fade-in/fade-out animations.

2. Remove the thumbnail images from the project, and use the `ImageView` declared in the `gallery_thn.xml` file to scale the images.

3. Change from a list of application resource IDs to a list of `Uri` objects so that the images are downloaded from an external website.

Building the reservation tab

While the **Review** and **Photos** tabs of this example have been concerned with displaying information, the **Reservation** tab will be concerned with capturing the details of a reservation. We really only need three pieces of information:

◆ The name under which the reservation needs to be made

◆ The date and time of the reservation

◆ How many people the reservation is for

In this part of the example we'll create several widgets which have formatted labels. For example, **How Many People: 2**, which will update the number of people as the user changes the value. In order to do this simply, we specify that the widget's text (as specified in the layout file) will contain the format to use for display. As part of the initialization procedure, we read the text from the `View` object and use it to create a format structure. Once we have a format, we populate the `View` with its initial value.

Time for action – implementing the reservation layout

In our `main.xml` layout resource, we need to add the `View` objects which will form the **Reservation** tab. Currently it consists only of an empty `ScrollView`, which enables vertically-long layouts to be scrolled by the user if the entire user interface doesn't fit on the screen.

1. Open the `main.xml` file in your editor or IDE.

2. Inside the `<ScrollView>` we had created for the `Reservation` tab earlier. Declare a new vertical `LinearLayout` element:

```
<LinearLayout android:orientation="vertical"
              android:layout_width="fill_parent"
              android:layout_height="wrap_content">
```

3. Inside the new `LinearLayout` element, create a `TextView` to ask the user under what name the reservation should be made:

```
<TextView android:text="Under What Name:"
          android:layout_width="fill_parent"
          android:layout_height="wrap_content"/>
```

4. After the `TextView` label, create an `EditText` to allow the user to input the name under which reservation is to be made:

```
<EditText android:id="@+id/name"
          android:layout_width="fill_parent"
          android:layout_height="wrap_content"/>
```

5. Create another `TextView` label to ask the user how many people will be going. This includes a format element where we will place the number:

```
<TextView android:id="@+id/people_label"
        android:text="How Many People: %d"
        android:layout_width="fill_parent"
        android:layout_height="wrap_content"/>
```

6. Add a `SeekBar` with which the user can tell us about how many people are going:

```
<SeekBar android:id="@+id/people"
        android:max="20"
        android:progress="1"
        android:layout_width="fill_parent"
        android:layout_height="wrap_content"/>
```

7. Use another `TextView` to ask the user what date the reservation will be on:

```
<TextView android:text="For What Date:"
        android:layout_width="fill_parent"
        android:layout_height="wrap_content"/>
```

8. Add a `Button` to display the date for which the reservation is made. When the user taps this `Button`, we will ask him to select a new date:

```
<Button android:id="@+id/date"
        android:text="dd - MMMM - yyyy"
        android:layout_width="fill_parent"
        android:layout_height="wrap_content"/>
```

9. Create another `TextView` label to ask the time of reservation:

```
<TextView android:text="For What Time:"
        android:layout_width="fill_parent"
        android:layout_height="wrap_content"/>
```

10. Add another `Button` to display the time, and allow the user to change it:

```
<Button android:id="@+id/time"
        android:text="HH:mm"
        android:layout_width="fill_parent"
        android:layout_height="wrap_content"/>
```

11. Finally add a `Button` to make the reservation, and add some margin to separate it from the rest of the inputs in the form:

```
<Button android:id="@+id/reserve"
        android:text="Make Reservation"
        android:layout_marginTop="15dip"
        android:layout_width="fill_parent"
        android:layout_height="wrap_content"/>
```

Several of the preceding widgets include the format of their labels instead of the label literal, the actual label will be generated and set in the Java code. This is because these labels are subject to change when the user changes date, time, or the number of people expected for the reservation.

What just happened?

In the **Reservation** tab, we ask the user how many people the reservation is for, and in order to capture their answer, we make use of a SeekBar object. The SeekBar works in much the same way as a JSlider in Swing, and provides the user with a way of selecting the number of people for the reservation, as long as that number is within a range that we define. SeekBar in Android is actually built on top of the ProgressBar class, and so inherits all of its XML attributes, which will seem a little strange at times. Unfortunately, unlike a JSlider or JProgressBar, the SeekBar class has no minimum value, and since you can't make a reservation for 0 people, we work around this by always adding 1 to the selected value of the SeekBar before display. This means that the default value is 1 (setting the displayed value to 2 people).

 Most people would make a restaurant reservation for two people, hence the default value of 1.

In the **How Many People:** label, we put in a %d, which is a printf marker for where we will put the number of people the reservation is being made for. When the SeekBar is manipulated by the user, we'll update the label with the number the user selects using String.format. In the "date" and "time" Button labels, we want to display the currently selected date and time for the reservation. We set the label in the XML file to the format that we want to display this data in, and we'll parse it later with a standard java.text. SimpleDateFormat.

What about internationalization in our previous example? Shouldn't we have put the labels in the strings.xml file so that the layout doesn't need to change? The answer is: Yes, if you want to internationalize your user interface. Later, make sure you have all of your display text in an application resource file. However, I strongly recommend fetching the format strings directly from the layout, since it allows you to decouple the format data one additional level.

In the preceding layout, you created Button widgets to display the date and time. Why not use a DatePicker and TimePicker object directly? The answer is: They unfortunately don't fit well into normal layouts. They take up a large amount of vertical space, and don't scale horizontally. If we placed a DatePicker and TimePicker inline in this user interface, it would look like the following screenshot on the left, while the actual user interface is the screenshot on the right.

As you can see, the `Button` objects give a much cleaner user interface. Thankfully, Android provides us with a `DatePickerDialog` and `TimePickerDialog` for just this sort of situation. When the user taps on one of the `Button` widgets, we'll pop up the appropriate dialog and then update the selected `Button` label when he approves.

While the use of a `Button` and `Dialog` adds at least two more touches to the user interface, it dramatically improves the look and feel of the application. User interfaces that are not properly aligned will irritate users, even if they can't tell why it's irritating. Screens that users find annoying or irritating are screens that they will avoid, or worse—simply uninstall.

Time for action – initializing the reservation tab

In the **Reservation** tab we made use of formatted labels. These labels shouldn't be displayed to the user as-is, but need to be populated with data before we let the user see them. For this, we need to go to our Java code again and build some functionality to remember the format, and populate the label.

1. Open the `ReviewActivity` Java source in your editor or IDE.

2. Below of all the fields you've declared so far, we need to add some more for the **Reservations** tab. Declare a `String` to remember the formatting of the **How Many People:** label:

    ```
    private String peopleLabelFormat;
    ```

3. Then declare a reference to the **How Many People:** label:

    ```
    private TextView peopleLabel;
    ```

4. Declare a `SimpleDateFormat` object for the format of the date `Button`:

```
private SimpleDateFormat dateFormat;
```

5. Declare a reference to the date `Button`:

```
private Button date;
```

6. Add another `SimpleDateFormat` for the format of the time `Button`:

```
private SimpleDateFormat timeFormat;
```

7. Next, declare a `Button` reference for the time `Button` object:

```
private Button time;
```

8. At the end of the `onCreate` method, we need to initialize the **Reservations** tab. Start by assigning out the `peopleLabel` and fetching the `peopleLabelFormat` using the `TextView.getText()` method:

```
peopleLabel = (TextView)findViewById(R.id.people_label);
peopleLabelFormat = peopleLabel.getText().toString();
```

9. Then fetch the date `Button` reference and its label format:

```
date = (Button)findViewById(R.id.date);
dateFormat = new SimpleDateFormat(date.getText().toString());
```

10. Do the same for the time `Button` and its label format:

```
time = (Button)findViewById(R.id.time);
timeFormat = new SimpleDateFormat(time.getText().toString());
```

11. Now we need to populate the `Button` objects with a default date and time, and for this we need a `Calendar` object:

```
Calendar calendar = Calendar.getInstance();
```

12. If it's later than 4:00p.m., it's likely that the reservation should be made for the next day, so we add one day to the `Calendar` if this is the case:

```
if(calendar.get(Calendar.HOUR_OF_DAY) >= 16) {
    calendar.add(Calendar.DATE, 1);
}
```

13. Now we set the default time of day for a reservation on the `Calendar` object:

```
calendar.set(Calendar.HOUR_OF_DAY, 18);
calendar.clear(Calendar.MINUTE);
calendar.clear(Calendar.SECOND);
calendar.clear(Calendar.MILLISECOND);
```

14. Set the label for the `date` and `time` button from the `Calendar` object:

```
Date reservationDate = calendar.getTime();
date.setText(dateFormat.format(reservationDate));
time.setText(timeFormat.format(reservationDate));
```

15. Now we need the `SeekBar` so that we can fetch its default value (as declared in the layout application resource):

```
SeekBar people = (SeekBar)findViewById(R.id.people);
```

16. Then we can use the label format, and the `SeekBar` value to populate the **How Many People** label:

```
peopleLabel.setText(String.format(
        peopleLabelFormat,
        people.getProgress() + 1));
```

Now we have the various formats in which the labels need to be displayed on the user interface. This allows us to regenerate the labels when the user changes the reservation parameters.

What just happened?

The **Reservations** tab will now be populated with the default data for a reservation, and all the formatting in the labels has disappeared. You will probably have noticed the many calls to `toString()` in the previous code. Android `View` classes generally accept any `CharSequence` for labels. This allows for much more advanced memory management than the `String` class, as the `CharSequence` may be a `StringBuilder`, or may facade a `SoftReference` to the actual text data.

However, most traditional Java APIs expect a `String`, not a `CharSequence`, so we use the `toString()` method to make sure we have a `String` object. If the underlying `CharSequence` is a `String` object, the `toString()` method is a simple `return this;` (which will act as a type cast).

Again, to work around the fact that the `SeekBar` doesn't have a minimum value, we add 1 to its current value in the last line, when we populate the `peopleLabel`. While the `date` and `time` formats are stored as a `SimpleDateFormat`, we store the `peopleLabelFormat` as a `String` and will run it through `String.format` when we need to update the label.

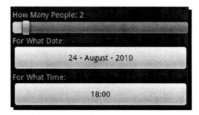

Time for action – listening to the SeekBar

The user interface is now populated with the default data. However, it's not interactive at all. If you drag the `SeekBar` the **How Many People:** label will remain at its default value of **2**. We need an event listener to update the label when the `SeekBar` is used.

1. Open the `ReviewActivity` Java source in your editor or IDE.

2. Add `SeekBar.OnSeekBarChangeListener` to the interfaces that `ReviewActivity` implements.

3. In `onCreate`, after fetching the `SeekBar` with `findViewById`, set its `OnSeekBarChangeListener` to this:

```
SeekBar people = (SeekBar)findViewById(R.id.people);
people.setOnSeekBarChangeListener(this);
```

4. Implement the `onProgressChanged` method to update `peopleLabel`:

```
public void onProgressChanged(
            SeekBar bar, int progress, boolean fromUser) {

    peopleLabel.setText(String.format(
            peopleLabelFormat, progress + 1));
}
```

5. Implement an empty `onStartTrackingTouch` method:

```
public void onStartTrackingTouch(SeekBar bar) {}
```

6. Implement an empty `onStopTrackingTouch` method:

```
public void onStopTrackingTouch(SeekBar bar) {}
```

The `String.format` method is a common method of placing parameters in a localized string in Android. While this is rather different to the normal `java.text.MessageFormat` class, it's the preferred method in Android (although `MessageFormat` is still supported).

What just happened?

When you reinstall the application in the emulator, you'll now be able to use `SeekBar` to select the number of people that the reservation is to be made for. While we didn't implement the `onStartTrackingTouch` or `onStopTrackingTouch` methods, they can be extremely useful if you hide the actual status value by default. For example, you could use a `Dialog` containing icons of people to inform the user how many people the reservation is for. When they touch the `SeekBar`—display the `Dialog`, and then when they release the `SeekBar`—hide the `Dialog` again.

Time for action – selecting date and time

We've made the SeekBar work as expected, but what about the date and time Button widgets? When the users touch them, they expect to be able to select a different date or time for their reservation. For this we'll need a good old OnClickListener, the DatePickerDialog and TimePickerDialog classes.

1. Open the ReviewActivity Java source in your editor or IDE again.

2. Add View.OnClickListener, DatePickerDialog.OnDateSetListener, and TimePickerDialog.OnTimeSetListener to the interfaces that ReviewActivity implements. Your class declaration should now look something like this:

```
public class ReviewActivity extends TabActivity
        implements ViewSwitcher.ViewFactory,
        Runnable,
        AdapterView.OnItemSelectedListener,
        SeekBar.OnSeekBarChangeListener,
        View.OnClickListener,
        DatePickerDialog.OnDateSetListener,
        TimePickerDialog.OnTimeSetListener {
```

3. Implement a utility method to parse a CharSequence into a Calendar object with a specified SimpleDateFormat:

```
private Calendar parseCalendar(
        CharSequence text, SimpleDateFormat format) {
```

4. Open a try block to allow handling of parse errors if the CharSequence is not formatted according to the SimpleDateFormat.

5. Parse the CharSequence into a Date object:

```
Date parsedDate = format.parse(text.toString());
```

6. Then create a new Calendar object:

```
Calendar calendar = Calendar.getInstance();
```

7. Set the time on the Calendar object to the time in the Date object:

```
calendar.setTime(parsedDate);
```

8. Return the parsed Calendar object:

```
return calendar;
```

9. You'll need to `catch(ParseException)` in this method. I recommend wrapping it in a `RuntimeException` and re-throwing it:

```
catch(ParseException pe) {
    throw new RuntimeException(pe);
}
```

10. In the `onCreate` method, after setting the labels of the `date` and `time Button` widgets, set their `OnClickListener` to `this`:

```
date.setText(dateFormat.format(reservationDate));
time.setText(timeFormat.format(reservationDate));
date.setOnClickListener(this);
time.setOnClickListener(this);
```

11. Implement the `onClick` method to listen for when the user taps the `date` or `time Button`:

```
public void onClick(View view) {
```

12. Use the `View` parameter to determine if the clicked `View` is the `date Button`:

```
if(view == date) {
```

13. If so, use the `parseCalendar` method to parse the current value of the `date Button` widget's label:

```
Calendar calendar = parseCalendar(date.getText(), dateFormat);
```

14. Create a `DatePickerDialog` and populate it with the date in the `Calendar`, then `show()` the `DatePickerDialog`:

```
new DatePickerDialog(
        this, // pass ReviewActivity as the current Context
        this, // pass ReviewActivity as an OnDateSetListener
        calendar.get(Calendar.YEAR),
        calendar.get(Calendar.MONTH),
        calendar.get(Calendar.DAY_OF_MONTH)).show();
```

15. Now check if the user has clicked on `View Button` instead of `date`:

```
else if(view == time) {
```

16. If so, parse a `Calendar` using the `time Button` widget's label value:

```
Calendar calendar = parseCalendar(time.getText(), timeFormat);
```

17. Now create a `TimePickerDialog` with the selected time, then `show()` the new `TimePickerDialog` to the user:

```
new TimePickerDialog(
```

```
this, // pass ReviewActivity as the current Context
this, // pass ReviewActivity as an OnTimeSetListener
calendar.get(Calendar.HOUR_OF_DAY),
calendar.get(Calendar.MINUTE),
false) // we want an AM / PM view; true = a 24hour view
.show();
```

18. Now implement the `onDateSet` method to listen for when the user accepts the `DatePickerDialog` with a new date selected:

```
public void onDateSet(
        DatePicker picker, int year, int month, int day)
```

19. Create a new `Calendar` instance to populate the date into:

```
Calendar calendar = Calendar.getInstance();
```

20. Set the year, month, and day on the Calendar:

```
calendar.set(Calendar.YEAR, year);
calendar.set(Calendar.MONTH, month);
calendar.set(Calendar.DAY_OF_MONTH, day);
```

21. Set the label of the `date Button` to the formatted `Calendar`:

```
date.setText(dateFormat.format(calendar.getTime()));
```

22. Implement the `onTimeSet` method to listen for when the user accepts the `TimePickerDialog` after selecting a new time:

```
public void onTimeSet(TimePicker picker, int hour, int minute)
```

23. Create a new `Calendar` instance:

```
Calendar calendar = Calendar.getInstance();
```

24. Set the `Calendar` object's `hour` and `minute` fields according to the parameters given by the `TimePickerDialog`:

```
calendar.set(Calendar.HOUR_OF_DAY, hour);
calendar.set(Calendar.MINUTE, minute);
```

25. Set the label of the `time Button` by formatting the `Calendar` object:

```
time.setText(timeFormat.format(calendar.getTime()));
```

Having stored the format for the `date` and `time` objects, we can now display the values selected by the user in the `Button` widgets. When the user has selected a new date or time we update the `Button` labels to reflect the new selections.

What just happened

If you install and run the application in the emulator, you can now tap on either the `date` or `time Button` widgets, and you will be greeted by a modal `Dialog` allowing you to select a new value. Beware of overusing modal `Dialog` widgets, because they block access to the rest of your application. You should avoid using them for displaying status messages as they effectively render the rest of the application useless during that time. If you do display a modal `Dialog`, ensure that there is some way for the user to dismiss the `Dialog` without any other interaction (that is, a **Cancel** button or something similar).

The first advantage to using a `DatePickerDialog` and `TimePickerDialog` comes from the fact that both include **Set** and **Cancel** buttons. This allows the user to manipulate the `DatePicker` or `TimePicker`, and then cancel the changes. If you used an inline `DatePicker` or `TimePicker` widget, you could provide a **Reset** button, but this would take up additional screen space, and generally would seem out-of-place (until it's actually needed).

Another advantage of the `DatePickerDialog` over the `DatePicker` widget is that the `DatePickerDialog` displays a long-format of the selected date in it's title area. This long-format date generally includes the day of the week that the user has currently selected. The "day of the week" is a field that is noticeably missing from the `DatePicker` widget, which makes it surprisingly difficult to use. Most people think in terms of "next Thursday", instead of "the 2nd of August, 2010." Having the day of the week visible makes the `DatePickerDialog` a much better choice for date selection than an inline `DatePicker`.

Creating complex layouts with Include, Merge, and ViewStubs

In this chapter we've built a single layout resource with three different tabs in it. As a result of this, the `main.xml` file has become quite large and hence, more difficult to manage. Android provides several ways in which you can break up large layout files (such as this one) into smaller chunks.

Using Include tags

The `include` tag is the simplest one to work with. It's a straight import of one layout XML file into another. For our previous example, we could separate each tab out into its own layout resource file, and then `include` each one in the `main.xml`. The `include` tag has only one mandatory attribute: `layout`. This attribute points to the layout resource to be included. This tag is not a static or compile-time tag, and so the included layout file will be selected through the standard resource selection process. This allows you to have a single `main.xml` file, but then add a special `reviews.xml` file (perhaps for Spanish).

The `layout` attribute on the include tag is **not** prefixed with the `android` XML namespace. If you attempt to use the `layout` attribute as `android:layout`, you won't get any compile-time errors, but your application will strangely fail to run.

The `include` element can also be used to assign or override several attributes of the root included element. These include the element `android:id`, and any of the `android:layout` attributes. This allows you to reuse the same layout file in several parts of your application, but with different layout attributes and a different ID. You can even `include` the same layout file several times on the same screen, but with a different ID for each instance. If we were to change our `main.xml` file to include each of the tabs from other layout resources, the file would look something more like this:

```
<?xml version="1.0" encoding="UTF-8"?>
<FrameLayout xmlns:android="http://schemas.android.com/apk/res/
android"
              android:layout_width="fill_parent"
              android:layout_height="fill_parent">
    <include
        android:id="@+id/review"
        layout="@layout/review"/>
    <include
        android:id="@+id/photos"
        layout="@layout/photos"/>
    <include
        android:id="@+id/reservation"
        layout="@layout/reservations"/>
</FrameLayout>
```

Merging layouts

The `include` element is very fine and well when you want to include a single `View` or `ViewGroup` into a larger layout structure. However, what if you want to include multiple elements into a larger layout structure, without implying the need for a root element in the included structure? In our example each tab needs a single root `View` in order that each tab carries a single and unique ID reference.

However, having an additional `ViewGroup` just for the sake of an `include` can adversely affect the performance of large layout trees. In this case, the `merge` tag comes to the rescue. Instead of declaring the root element of a layout as a `ViewGroup`, you can declare it as `<merge>`. In this case, each of `View` objects in the included layout XML will become direct children of the `ViewGroup` that includes them. For example, if you had a layout resource file named `main.xml`, with a `LinearLayout` that included a `user_editor.xml` layout resource, then the code would look something like this:

```
<LinearLayout android:orientation="vertical">
    <include layout="@layout/user_editor"/>
    <Button android:id="@+id/save"
            android:text="Save User"
            android:layout_width="fill_parent"
            android:layout_height="wrap_content"/>
</LinearLayout>
```

The simple implementation of the `user_editor.xml` looks something like this:

```
<LinearLayout
    xmlns:android="http://schemas.android.com/apk/res/android"
    android:orientation="vertical"
    android:layout_width="fill_parent"
    android:layout_height="wrap_content">

    <TextView android:text="User Name:"
            android:layout_width="fill_parent"
            android:layout_height="wrap_content"/>

    <EditText android:id="@+id/user_name"
            android:layout_width="fill_parent"
            android:layout_height="wrap_content"/>

    <!-- the rest of the editor -->
</LinearLayout>
```

However, when this is included into the `main.xml` file, we embed the `user_editor.xml` `LinearLayout` into the `main.xml` `LinearLayout`, resulting in two `LinearLayout` objects with identical layout attributes. Obviously it would be much better to simply put the `TextView` and `EditView` from `user_editor.xml` directly into the `main.xml` `LinearLayout` element. This is exactly what the `<merge>` tag is used for. If we now re-write the `user_editor.xml` file using the `<merge>` tag instead of a `LinearLayout`, it looks like this:

```
<merge xmlns:android="http://schemas.android.com/apk/res/android">
    <TextView android:text="User Name:"
            android:layout_width="fill_parent"
            android:layout_height="wrap_content"/>
```

```
<EditText android:id="@+id/user_name"
        android:layout_width="fill_parent"
        android:layout_height="wrap_content"/>
<!-- the rest of the editor -->
</merge>
```

Note that we no longer have the `LinearLayout` element, instead the `TextView` and `EditView` will be added directly to the `LinearLayout` in the `main.xml` file. Beware of layouts that have too many nested `ViewGroup` objects, as they are almost certain to give trouble (more than about ten levels of nesting is likely to cause your application to crash!). Also be careful with layouts that have too many `View` objects. Again, more than 30 is very likely to cause problems or make your application crash.

Using the ViewStub class

When you load a layout resource that includes another layout, the resource loader will immediately load the included layout into the memory, in order to attach it to the layout you've requested. When `main.xml` is read in by the `LayoutInflator`, so are the `reviews.xml`, `photos.xml`, and `reservations.xml` files. In situations with very large layout structures, this can consume a huge amount of your application memory, and even cause your application to crash. The Android API includes a specialized `View` named `ViewStub` which allows lazy-loading of layout resources.

A `ViewStub` is by default a zero-by-zero sized empty `View`, and when it's specialized, `inflate()` method is invoked. It loads the layout resource and replaces itself with the loaded `View` objects. This process allows the `ViewStub` to be garbage-collected as soon as its `inflate()` method has been called.

If we were to make use of a `ViewStub` in the example, you would need to lazy-initialize the content of a tab when it is selected by the user. This also means that none of the `View` objects in a tab would exist until that tab has been selected. While using a `ViewStub` is a bit more work than a straight `include`, it can allow you to work with much larger and more complex layout structures than would otherwise be possible.

Any layout attributes set on a `ViewStub` will be passed on to its inflated `View` object. You can also assign a separate ID to the inflated layout. If we wanted to include each of our tabs in a `ViewStub`, the `main.xml` file would look something like this:

```
<?xml version="1.0" encoding="UTF-8"?>
<FrameLayout
        xmlns:android="http://schemas.android.com/apk/res/android"
        android:layout_width="fill_parent"
        android:layout_height="fill_parent">

<ViewStub android:id="@+id/review"
```

```
                        android:inflatedId="@+id/inflated_review"
                        android:layout="@layout/review"/>
        <ViewStub  android:id="@+id/photos"
                        android:inflatedId="@+id/inflated_photos"
                        android:layout="@layout/photos"/>
        <ViewStub  android:id="@+id/reservations"
                        android:inflatedId="@+id/inflated_reservations"
                        android:layout="@layout/reservations"/>
    </FrameLayout>
```

Note that unlike the `include` tag, the `ViewStub` requires the `android` XML namespace for its `layout` attribute. After you `inflate()` one of the `ViewStub` objects, it will no longer be available by its original `android:id` reference. Instead, you will be able to access the inflated layout object using the `android:inflatedId` reference.

Have a go hero – separate the tabs

Extract each of the tabs into its own layout resource file, and use the `include` tag to load each of them. This shouldn't require any changes to the Java source code.

For more of a challenge, try using `ViewStub` objects instead of the `include` tag. This will require you to break up the `onCreate` method and listen for when tabs are clicked. For this you'll need to use `TabHost.OnTabChangeListener` to know when to load a specific tab's content.

Summary

Tabs are a great way of breaking an `Activity` into different areas of work. With limited screen real estate, they are a great way to make an `Activity` more accessible to the user. They also have a performance impact since only one tab is rendered on the screen at a time.

The `RatingBar` and `SeekBar` are two different methods of capturing, or displaying numeric data to the user. While they are closely related, and both function in the same way, each class is used to address different types of data. Keep in mind the limitations of both of these, before deciding whether and where to use them.

The `Gallery` class is brilliant for allowing the user to view a large number of different objects. While in this example we used it to simply display thumbnails, it could be used as a replacement for tabs in a web browser by displaying a list of page thumbnails above the actual browser view. All you need to do to customize its function is to change the `View` objects returned from the `Adapter` implementation.

When it comes to date and time capturing, try to stick to using the `DatePickerDialog` and `TimePickerDialog` instead of their inline counterparts (unless you have good reason). The use of these `Dialog` widgets helps you conserve screen space and improve the user experience. When they open a `DatePickerDialog` or `TimePickerDialog`, they have better access to the editor than you can generally provide as part of your user interface (especially on a device with a small screen).

In the next chapter, we'll take a closer look at `Intent` objects, the activity stack, and the lifecycle of an Android application. We'll investigate how `Intent` objects and the activity stack can be used as a way to keep applications more usable. Also, we shall learn about improving the reuse of `Activity` classes.

4
Leveraging Activities and Intents

In many ways Android application management appears to be inspired by JavaScript and the web browser and rightly so! The web browser model has proved itself as a mechanism that users find easy to work with. Android as a system, Android has many things in common with a web browser, some of which are obvious, and others that you will need to look a little deeper for.

The Activity Stack is much like a single-directional web browser history. When you launch an `Activity` *using the* `startActivity` *method, you effectively hand control back to the Android system. When the user pushes the hardware "Back" button on their phone, the default action is to pop the top* `Activity` *off the stack, and display the one underneath (not always the one that started it).*

In this chapter we'll explore a little of how Android runs an application and manages `Activity` instances. While not strictly necessary for user interface design, it's important to know how this works. Properly leveraging these concepts will help you ensure a consistent user interface experience. As you will also see, it will help you improve the performance of your application, and allow you to reuse more of your application components.

It's also important to understand how an `Activity` is created (and when it is created), as well as how Android decides what `Activity` to create. We'll also look at some good practices to follow when building an `Activity` class, and how to behave nicely within the confines of an Android application.

We've already encountered the "Activity Stack" in *Chapter 1, Developing a Simple Activity* and *Chapter 2, Presenting Data for Views* where we constructed `Intent` objects to launch specific `Activity` classes. When you used the hardware "Back" button, you were automatically taken to the previous `Activity` instance, no code needed (much like a web-browser). For this chapter we'll be looking at:

- The life cycle of an `Activity` object
- Using the `Bundle` class to maintain application state
- Exploring the relationship between an `Intent` and an `Activity`
- Passing data into an `Activity` through an `Intent`

Exploring the Activity class

The life cycle of an `Activity` object is much more like a Java `Applet` than a normal application. It may be started, paused, resumed, paused again, killed, and then brought back to life in a seemingly random order. Most Android devices have very good performance specifications. However, most of them appear underpowered when compared to the top-of-the-range devices. For those devices that do have good specifications, users tend to demand a lot more from them than the cheaper devices. On a phone, you're never going to get away from the fact that you have many applications and services sharing a very limited device.

An `Activity` may be garbage-collected any time it is not visible to the user. This means it may be your application that is running, but because the user is looking at a different `Activity`, any non-visible or background `Activity` objects may be shut down or garbage-collected in order to save memory. By default, the Android APIs will handle these shut down/start up cycles elegantly by storing their state before a shut down, and restoring it when they are re-created. A very simple diagram of the life cycle of an application with two `Activity` instances is shown in the following figure. When the "Main Activity" is paused, it becomes eligible for garbage-collection by the system. If this happens, it will first store its state in a temporary location, restoring the state when it is brought back to the foreground.

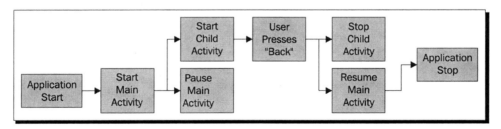

Storage of user interface state

If an `Activity` is stopped, all `View` objects that have an ID assigned will attempt to store their state before they are made available for garbage-collection. However, this state is only stored for the lifetime of the application. When the application is shut-down, this state is lost.

While it's possible to use the `setContentView` method over and over again to change the content on the screen (much the way you might build a wizard interface with an AWT `CardLayout` object), it's considered a very bad idea. You are effectively trying to take the control away from Android, which will always create problems for you. If for example, you developed an application with only one `Activity` class, and used multiple layout resources or your own custom `ViewGroup` objects to represent different screens, you would also have to take control of the hardware "Back" button on the device in order to allow the user to go backwards. Your application is released in the Android market, and a few months later a handset manufacturer decides to put a "Forward" button onto their new phone (in the same style as the "Forward" button on a web-browser). The Android system would be patched to handle this change to the device, but your application would not be. As a result, your users get frustrated with your application because "it doesn't work properly".

Using Bundle objects

In the `onCreate` method of the `Activity` class, we've been accepting a `Bundle` parameter named `saveInstanceState`, as you may have guessed. It's where state information is stored between stops and starts of an `Activity`. Despite what it looks like, a `Bundle` object is not a form of persistent storage. When the configuration of a device context changes (for example when the user selects a new language, or changes from "portrait" to "landscape" mode), the current `Activity` is "restarted". For this to happen, Android requests the `Activity` save its state in a `Bundle` object. It then shuts down and destroys the existing instance, and then creates a new instance of the `Activity` (with the new configuration parameters) with the `Bundle` that the state information was saved in.

The `Bundle` class is effectively a `Map<String, ?>` containing any number of values. Since `Bundle` objects are used to store short term state (that is, the blog post a user was busy typing), they are mostly used to store the state of `View` objects. They have two major advantages over standard Java serialization in this regard:

- You are forced to implement the storage of the object manually. This requires some thought as to how the object will be stored, and what parts of it need to be stored. For example, most of the time in a user interface, you don't need to store the layout information, since that can be recreated from the layout file.
- Being a key-value structure, a `Bundle` is more future-proof and flexible than a serialized object. You can leave out values that are set to their defaults, reducing the size of the `Bundle`.

A `Bundle` object is also a type-safe structure. If you use the `putString` method, only then `getString` or `getCharSequence` will work to retrieve the object. I strongly advise that when using the `get` methods of `Bundle`, you should always provide a default value.

Before an `Activity` is paused by the Android system, the system requests that it save any state information in a `Bundle` object. To do this, the `onSaveInstanceState` method will be invoked on the `Activity`. This happens before the `onPause` method. In order to restore the state of the `Activity`, the system will invoke the `onCreate` method with the saved state `Bundle`.

Handling Activity crashes

If an `Activity` class throws an uncaught exception, the user will get the dreaded **Force Close** dialog box. Android will attempt to recover from these errors by terminating the Virtual Machine, and re-opening the root activity, providing a `Bundle` object with the last known state from `onSaveInstanceState`.

The `View` class also has an `onSaveInstanceState` method, as well as a corresponding `onRestoreInstanceState` method. As mentioned earlier, the `Activity` class' default functionality will attempt to save each `View` object with an ID within a `Bundle`. This is another good reason to stick to XML layouts instead of building your own. Having a reference to a `View` object is not enough for it to be saved and restored, and while you can assign IDs in Java code, it clutters your user interface code even more.

Time for action – building an example game: "guess my number"

We want to build a simple example that will save and restore its state from a `Bundle` object. For this example, we have a very simple "guess my number" game. The `Activity` object picks a number between one and ten and challenges the user to guess it.

The basic user interface layout for this example will need a label telling the user what to do, an input area for them to input their guess, and a button to tell the application they wish to input a guess. The following diagram is a basic idea of how the user interface should be structured:

I am thinking of a number between 1 to 10. Can you guess what it is?

Guess!

If the user were to get an SMS while playing this game, there's a strong chance that we will lose the number he is trying to guess. For this reason we will store the number that he is trying to guess in a `Bundle` object when the system asks us to save our state. We'll also need to look for the stored number when starting up.

1. From a command-prompt, create a new project named `GuessMyNumber`:

```
android create project -n GuessMyNumber -p GuessMyNumber -k com.
packtpub.guessmynumber -a GuessActivity -t 3
```

2. Open the default `res/layout/main.xml` file in an editor or IDE.

3. Remove the default content within the `LinearLayout` element.

4. Add a new `TextView` to serve as a label, to tell the user what to do:

```
<TextView android:text=
    "I'm thinking of a number between 1 and 10. Can you guess what
it is?"
    android:layout_width="fill_parent"
    android:layout_height="wrap_content"/>
```

5. Create a new `EditText` where the users will enter their guess. Use the `android:numeric` attribute of `TextView` to enforce only `integer` input:

```
<EditText
    android:id="@+id/number"
    android:numeric="integer"
    android:layout_width="fill_parent"
    android:layout_height="wrap_content"/>
```

6. Add a `Button` that the users can click on to submit their guess:

```
<Button android:id="@+id/guess"
    android:text="Guess!"
    android:layout_width="fill_parent"
    android:layout_height="wrap_content"/>
```

7. Now open the `GuessActivity.java` file in your editor or IDE.

8. Make the `GuessActivity` class implement `OnClickListener`:

```
public class GuessActivity
    extends Activity implements OnClickListener {
```

9. Create a field variable to store the number the user is supposed to guess:

```
private int number;
```

10. Create a utility method to generate a random number between one and ten:

```
private static int random() {
    return (int)(Math.random() * 9) + 1;
}
```

11. In the `onCreate` method, directly after the call to `super.onCreate`, check to make sure the `Bundle` passed in is not `null`:

```
if(savedInstanceState != null) {
```

12. If the `Bundle` isn't `null`, then attempt to fetch the stored `Number` from it:

```
number = savedInstanceState.getInt("Number", random());
```

13. If the `Bundle` is `null`, the Activity is running as a new instance—generate a random number:

```
else {
    number = random();
}
```

14. Then `setContentView` to the `main.xml` layout resource:

```
setContentView(R.layout.main);
```

15. Find the `Button` object you declared in the `main.xml` layout resource:

```
Button button = (Button)findViewById(R.id.guess);
```

16. Set the `Button` object's `OnClickListener` to the `GuessActivity` object:

```
button.setOnClickListener(this);
```

17. Now override the `onSaveInstanceState` method:

```
protected void onSaveInstanceState(Bundle outState) {
```

18. Be sure to first allow the default `Activity` behavior:

```
super.onSaveInstanceState(outState);
```

19. Then store the `number` variable in the `Bundle`:

```
outState.putInt("Number", number);
```

20. We need to override the `onClick` method to handle the user's guess:

```
public void onClick(View clicked) {
```

21. Find the `EditText` where the user enters the guessed number:

```
EditText input = (EditText)findViewById(R.id.number);
```

22. Parse the current value of the `EditText` as an integer:

```
int value = Integer.parseInt(input.getText().toString());
```

23. If the number they guessed is too low, use a `Toast` to tell them:

```
if(value < number) {
    Toast.makeText(this, "Too low", Toast.LENGTH_SHORT).show();
}
```

24. If the number they guessed is too high, again use a `Toast` to tell them:

```
else if(value > number) {
    Toast.makeText(this, "Too high", Toast.LENGTH_SHORT).show();
}
```

25. If they successfully guessed the correct number, then congratulate them:

```
else {
    Toast.makeText(
            this,
            "You got it! Try guess another one!",
            Toast.LENGTH_SHORT).show();
```

26. Then generate a new number for the user to guess:

```
    number = random();
}
```

The `Toast` class is used in the previous code to display the output messages for **Too high**, **Too low**, and **You got it!** The `Toast` class is the perfect mechanism for displaying short output messages, and they automatically disappear after a few seconds. However they're not suitable for long messages as the user has no control over them, and cannot leave the message open or close it on command as they are entirely non-interactive.

What just happened

In the previous example, we listened for a call to `onSaveInstanceState` in order to record the number that the user is supposed to guess. We also have the current guess which the user most recently made, in the form of an `EditText`. Since we assigned an ID value to `EditText` in the `main.xml` file, the call to `super.onSaveInstanceState` will handle the storage of the `EditText` widget's exact state (potentially including "selection" and "focus" state).

In the `onCreate` method, the example first checks to make sure that the `Bundle` is not null. If Android is attempting to create a new instance of the `GuessActivity` object, it won't pass in any saved state. If however, we have a `Bundle` object, we invoke the `Bundle.getInt` method to attempt to fetch our previously stored `number` value. We also pass in a `random()` number as a second parameter. If the `Bundle` object (for whatever reason) doesn't have a stored `Number`, it will return this random number, eliminating the need for us to check such a condition.

As a quick side-note, the example made use of the `android:numeric` attribute of the `TextView` class to enforce `integer` input on the `EditText` object. Switching to a numeric view stops the user from entering anything except "valid" characters. It also affects the soft-keyboard. Instead of displaying the full keyboard, it will only display the numbers and symbols.

Creating and consuming intents

The `Intent` class is Android's primary method of "late binding". It's a form of very loose coupling which allows you to specify an action (along with some parameter data), while not specifying how the action should be carried out. For example, you may specify `browse to http:// www.packtpub.com/` using an `Intent`, but you don't need to specify how Android should carry out this action. It may use the default "browser" application, or another web browser the user has installed, or it may even ask the user how exactly they want to get to `http:// www.packtpub.com/`. There are two primary types of `Intent`:

- Explicit Intents
- Implicit Intents

So far we've only made use of explicit `Intent` objects, where we specify the exact class we want to run. These are very important when switching from one `Activity` to another, as your application may depend on the exact implementation of an `Activity`. An implicit `Intent` is one where instead of specifying the exact class which we want to work with, we include an abstract name for the action we want carried out. Generally, an implicit `Intent` will have much more information content, due to the following reasons:

♦ To allow the system to make a good selection of which component to interact with

♦ `Intent` may point to a more generic structure than we would have built ourselves and a more generic structure often requires more information about how it is expected to behave

`Intent` objects are what really make Android different from other (more traditional) operating systems. They level the playing field between applications, and allow the user much more choice in how they want to run their phones. It's perfectly plausible for the user to not just install a new web browser, but also a new menu, desktop, or even dialler application.

Each `Activity` instance holds onto the `Intent` object that started it. In *Chapter 1, Developing a Simple Activity,* we made use of the `Activity.getIntent()` method to fetch some parameters from the `Intent` object, which in turn told us which question to ask the user.

Defining Intent actions

The first thing looked at in an implicit `Intent` is its action. The action defines what the `Intent` "does", but not how it does it, or what it does it to. The `Intent` class defines a long series of constants which represent common actions. These common actions always have some form of backing logic, which is generally defined by the phone system. Thus they are always available to be used by an application.

For example, you wanted to present the users with the dialler application, so they could dial a phone number and make a call, you would use an `Intent` with `ACTION_DIAL`:

```
startIntent(new Intent(Intent.ACTION_DIAL));
```

The action value of an `Intent` is matched against one of the actions defined for an `Activity`. An `Activity` may have any number of actions that it may perform, and they're all specified as part of an application's `AndroidManifest.xml` file. For example, you wanted to define an `askQuestion` action and bind it to an `Activity`, your `AndroidManifest.xml` file would contain an `Activity` entry which would look something like this:

```
<activity
    android:name=".AskQuestionActivity"
```

```
        android:label="Ask Question">

    <intent-filter>
        <action android:name="questions.askQuestion"/>
        <category android:name="android.intent.category.DEFAULT"/>
    </intent-filter>
</activity>
```

An `Activity` may have any number of `<intent-filter>` elements, each defining a different type of match to perform on an `Intent`. The `Activity` with the closest match to any given `Intent` is chosen to perform the action requested by the `Intent` object.

Passing data in an Intent

Presenting the user with the dialler application in order to let them dial a phone number is very nice, but what if we actually need them to dial a phone number? The `Intent` class doesn't just work by using the action, it also provides a default space for us to tell it what we want the action to be performed on. It's not brilliantly useful being able to open a web browser without being able to tell the browser what URL to go to, is it?

The default data provided by an `Intent` is provided as a `Uri` object. The `Uri` can be made to technically point to absolutely anything. For our earlier code snippet, we started the dialler to let the user dial a phone number. How would we then tell the dialler: "Dial 555-1234"? Simple, just take a look at the following code:

```
startActivity(new Intent(
        Intent.ACTION_DIAL,
        Uri.parse("tel://5551234")));
```

Adding extra data to an Intent

Sometimes a `Uri` doesn't allow enough data to be specified. For these cases, the `Intent` class provides you with a `Map` space of key-value pairs, called "extra" data. The methods for accessing the extra data correspond to the methods in the `Bundle` class. Back in *Chapter 1, Developing a Simple Activity*, we used the extra data to keep track of which question we were asking the user.

When defining generic `Activity` classes (such as file viewers), it's a good idea to work on a three phase fall-back system when looking for operational data:

   ◆ Any custom (non-standard) parameters can be passed in extra fields (and none of them should be mandatory)

   ◆ Inspect the data `Uri` to see what information you should be working with

   ◆ If no data `Uri` is specified, fall-back gracefully to a logical default, and provide some functionality to the user

Have a go hero – generic questions and answers

Go back to the example question and answer application from *Chapter 1, Developing a Simple Activity*. Rework the QuestionActivity class to use the data Uri to specify the question ID (by name) instead of the extra parameters.

Also, allow for the full question to be passed in using "extra" parameters—a parameter Question for the question text to ask the user, and a parameter Answers, specifying a string array of possible answers to the given question.

Using advanced Intent features

An Intent object is designed to indicate a single action as requested by the user. It's a self-contained request, and in some ways it is quite similar to an HTTP request, containing both, the action to carry out, and the resource upon which the action should be carried out, and any additional information that may be required.

In order to find the Activity (service or broadcast receiver) that will handle an Intent, the system makes use of intent-filters (as we discussed briefly earlier). Each intent-filter indicates a single type of action that could be carried out by the Activity. When two or more Activity implementations match an Intent, the system sends out an ACTION_PICK_ACTIVITY Intent to allow the user (or some automated system) to select which of the Activity implementations should be used to handle the Intent. The default behavior is to ask the users which of the Activity implementations they wish to use.

Getting data back from an Intent

An Intent is not always a one-way structure, some Intent actions will provide feedback. A great example of this is Intent.ACTION_PICK. The Intent.ACTION_PICK action is a way to ask the user to "pick" or select some form of data (a common use would be to ask the user to select a person or phone number from their contacts list).

When you need information back from an Intent, you use the startActivityForResult method instead of the normal startActivity method. The startActivityForResult method accepts two parameters, the Intent object to execute, and a useful int value which will be passed back to you.

As mentioned earlier, when another Activity is visible instead of yours, your Activity is paused, and may even be stopped and garbage-collected. For this reason, the startActivityForResult method returns immediately and you can generally assume your Activity will be paused directly after you return from your current event (passing control back to the system).

In order to get information back out of the Intent you triggered, you will need to override the onActivityResult method. The onActivityResult method is invoked every time an Intent started with startActivityForResult returns some data to you. The first parameter passed back into the onActivityResult method is the same integer value that you passed into the startActivityForResult method (allowing you to pass simple parameters back).

> **Passing information to another Activity**
>
> If you intend for an Activity implementation to pass information back to its caller, you can make use of the Activity.setResult method to pass both, a result-code and an Intent object with your response data.

Pop quiz

1. When does onCreate get passed a valid Bundle object?

    a. Every time the Activity is created

    b. When the application stored information in the Bundle in a previous execution

    c. When the Activity is being restarted due to configuration changes, or a crash

2. When is the onSaveInstanceState method invoked?

    a. After the onStop method

    b. Before the onPause method

    c. When the Activity is being restarted

    d. Before the onDestroy method

3. A Bundle object will be stored until:

    a. The application is closed

    b. The Activity is no longer visible

    c. The application is uninstalled

Time for action – viewing phone book contacts

In this example we will delve a little deeper into the workings of the Android system. We're going to override the default "view contact" option, providing our own Activity to view contacts from the phonebook on the device. When the user tries to open a contact to e-mail or call them, they will be presented with an option to view the contact using our Activity instead of the default one.

1. Start by creating a new project from the command line:

    ```
    android create project -n ContactViewer -p ContactViewer -k com.
    packtpub.contactviewer -a ViewContactActivity -t 3
    ```

2. Open the `res/layout/main.xml` layout resource in an editor or IDE.

3. Remove the default content within the `LinearLayout` element.

4. Add a new `TextView` object to contain the contact's display name:

    ```
    <TextView android:id="@+id/display_name"
            android:textSize="23sp"
            android:textStyle="bold"
            android:gravity="center"
            android:layout_width="fill_parent"
            android:layout_height="wrap_content"/>
    ```

5. Then add a `Button` which will be used to "dial" the default phone number of the displayed contact:

    ```
    <Button android:id="@+id/phone_number"
            android:layout_marginTop="5sp"
            android:layout_width="fill_parent"
            android:layout_height="wrap_content"/>
    ```

6. Open the `ViewContactActivity.java` source file in your editor or IDE.

7. Make `ViewContactActivity` implement `OnClickListener`:

    ```
    public class ViewContactActivity
            extends Activity implements OnClickListener {
    ```

8. After the `setContentView(R.layout.main)` in the `onCreate` method, find the `TextView` object you have created, to show the contact's name in:

    ```
    TextView name = (TextView)findViewById(R.id.display_name);
    ```

9. Then find the `Button` widget to display the phone number in:

    ```
    Button number = (Button)findViewById(R.id.phone_number);
    ```

10. Now use the `Activity.managedQuery` method to query the contact's database for the data `Uri` specified in our `Intent`:

    ```
    Cursor c = managedQuery(
            getIntent().getData(),
            new String[]{
                People.NAME,
                People.NUMBER
            },
            null,
    ```

```
        null,
        null);
```

11. In a `try {} finally{}` block, tell the `Cursor` to `moveToNext()` and make sure it does so (this works in exactly the same way as `ResultSet.next()`):

```
if(c.moveToNext()) {
```

12. Fetch and display the contact display name from the `Cursor`:

```
name.setText(c.getString(0));
```

13. Fetch and display the contact default phone number from the `Cursor`:

```
number.setText(c.getString(1));
```

14. In the `finally{}` block, close the `Cursor`:

```
finally {
    c.close();
}
```

15. Now set the `OnClickListener` of the `number Button` to `this`:

```
number.setOnClickListener(this);
```

16. Override the `onClick` method:

```
public void onClick(View clicked) {
```

17. We know that the `number Button` is what was clicked (it's the only `View` with an event-listener at this point). Cast the `View` parameter to a `Button` so that we can use it:

```
Button btn = (Button)clicked;
```

18. Create an `Intent` object to dial the selected phone number:

```
Intent intent = new Intent(
        Intent.ACTION_DIAL,
        Uri.parse("tel://" + btn.getText()));
```

19. Use `startActivity` to open the dialler application:

```
startActivity(intent);
```

20. Now open the `AndroidManifest.xml` file in your editor or IDE.

21. Before the declaration of the `<application>` element, we need permission to read the contacts list:

```
<uses-permission
    android:name="android.permission.READ_CONTACTS" />
```

22. Change the label of the `ViewContactActivity` to **View Contact**:

```
<activity
    android:name=".ViewContactActivity"
    android:label="View Contact">
```

23. Remove all of the default content inside the `<intent-filter>` element.

24. Declare an `<action>` type of `ACTION_VIEW` for this `<intent-filter>`:

```
<action android:name="android.intent.action.VIEW"/>
```

25. Set the `<catagory>` of this `<intent-filter>` to `CATAGORY_DEFAULT`:

```
<category android:name="android.intent.category.DEFAULT"/>
```

26. Add a `<data>` element to filter `person` entries (this is a MIME type):

```
<data
    android:mimeType="vnd.android.cursor.item/person"
    android:host="contacts" />
```

27. Add another `<data>` element to filter `contact` entries:

```
<data android:mimeType="vnd.android.cursor.item/contact"
    android:host="com.android.contacts" />
```

When installed on a device, the preceding code will become an option for opening "Contacts" in the user's address book. As you can see, replacing part of the standard Android framework is very simple, and allows more seamless integration of applications with the base system than is possible with a more conventional application architecture.

What just happened

If you install this application on the emulator, you'll notice that in the launcher, there's no icon to start it up. That's because this application doesn't have a main entry point like all of the others we've written thus far. Instead, if you open the "Contacts" application, and then click on one of the contacts in the address book, you'll be greeted by the following screen:

If you select the second icon, your new `ViewContactActivity` will be started in order to view the selected contact. The user (as you can see) also has the ability to use your application in preference to the default (for as long as your application remains available on the device).

Overriding a default behavior is a very important decision when developing a new application. Android makes it very easy to do, and as you can see, a third-party application can slot in almost seamlessly between two of the default applications. In a normal operating system environment, you would need to write an entire "contacts manager", while in Android you need only write the bits that interest you.

This is a part of your user interface design since you can use it to extend the functionality of various default parts of the system. For example, if you wrote a chat application, such as a "Jabber" client, you could embed the client in the **View contact** `Activity` for each contact in the user's address book that was linked with a Jabber ID. This would allow users to chat with available contacts directly from their address book, instead of having to go to your application. You application becomes a way for them to check a contact's status, and possibly avoid a phone call entirely.

Summary

Implementing an `Activity` at the correct granularity is an important part of your user interface design process. Although it's not a graphical part directly, it defines how the system will interact with your application, and thus how the user will interact with it.

It's a good idea to keep implicit intents in mind when structuring how your `Activity` will be started. Creating a generic `Activity` allows for other applications to integrate seamlessly with your own, effectively turning your new application into a platform for other developers to work with. An implicitly started `Activity` can be replaced or extended by another application, or it can be re-used in other application. In both cases, the user becomes free to customize your application in much the same way that they can customize the wallpaper image or theme.

Always try and provide a single `Activity` implementation for each action the user might want to take, don't make an `Activity` do too many things in the same screen. A very good example of granularity is the "Contacts" application—there's a contact list, contact viewer, contact editor, and the dialler application.

When working with tabbed interfaces (as we did in the previous chapter), it's possible to specify the tab content as an `Intent`, effectively embedding the `Activity` in your application. I would strongly urge you to consider doing exactly this when building a tabbed user interface, since it allows each tab to be re-used by your application far more easily, while also allowing third-party developers to create extensions to your interface, one tab at a time.

So far we've only really worked with the `LinearLayout` class, and while it's a great base for simple user interfaces, it's almost never enough. In the next chapter, we'll be looking at the many other types of layouts that Android provides by default, exploring the way in which each layout works, and how they can be used.

5
Developing Non-linear Layouts

Non-linear layouts are normally a completely fundamental subject of user interface design. However, on a device with a small screen (as many Android devices are), it doesn't always make sense. That said, Android devices can be turned to landscape mode, where suddenly you have an abundance of horizontal space, and limited vertical space. In these situations (and as we'll see, in many other situations as well), you will want to work with a layout other than the plain old LinearLayout *structure we've worked with so far.*

The real power of Android layouts comes from the same place as the power of the old Java AWT LayoutManagers—*by combining the different layout classes with each other. For example, combining a* FrameLayout *with other* ViewGroup *implementations allows you to layer various parts of the user interface on top of each other.*

It's important to consider how your layout will act on screens of different sizes. While Android does allow you to select different layouts based on the screen size of the device, this means that you will have to maintain multiple layouts for the different screen sizes and densities which your application will encounter in the wild. As far as possible you should make use of the tools that Android provides, and work with layouts that will scale according to the size of the various View objects.

In this chapter, we'll look into the various other layout styles that Android provides us with by default, and investigate various alternative uses for each one of them. We'll also take a closer look at how you specify parameters for different layouts, and how they can help in usability, as opposed to simply putting your widgets in a particular order.

Time for action – creating a layouts example project

Before we walk through each of the layouts, we need a common project inside which we will showcase each of them.

1. From a command prompt, create a new project named **Layouts**:

```
android create project -n Layouts -p Layouts -k com.packtpub.
layouts -a LayoutSelectorActivity -t 3
```

2. Delete the standard `res/layout/main.xml` layout resource file.

3. Open the `res/values/strings.xml` file in an editor or IDE.

4. Add a new `<string-array>` by the name of `layouts` to the file:

```
<string-array name="layouts">
```

5. Add the following items to the new `<string-array>` element:

```
<item>Frame Layout</item>
<item>Table Layout</item>
<item>Custom Layout</item>
<item>Relative Layout</item>
<item>Sliding Drawer</item>
```

6. Open the `LayoutSelectorActivity` source file in your editor or IDE.

7. Have the class inherit from `ListActivity` instead of `Activity`:

```
public class LayoutSelectorActivity extends ListActivity {
```

8. In the `onCreate` method, set the contents of your `ListActivity` you declared in the `strings.xml` resource file to your `layouts` array:

```
setListAdapter(new ArrayAdapter<String>(
        this,
        android.R.layout.simple_list_item_1, Have the class
inherit from"
        getResources().getStringArray(R.array.layouts)));
```

9. Override the `onListItemClick` method:

```
protected void onListItemClick(
        ListView l,
        View v,
        int position,
        long id) {
```

10. Create a `switch` statement on the `position` parameter:

```
switch(position) {
```

11. Add a `default` clause (the only one for now) to let yourself know that you haven't implemented an example for the selected item yet:

```
default:
    Toast.makeText(
            this,
            "Example not yet implemented.",
            Toast.LENGTH_SHORT).show();
```

What just happened?

The new project will serve as a basis for each of the examples in this chapter. For each layout we work through, we'll build a new `Activity` that will become part of this application. Currently, the application consists of only a menu for accessing each of the layout examples. The idea as of now is to fill each one with something interesting.

In this chapter, we will explore not just the basic layouts, but also how they can be made to interact with each other.

FrameLayout

The `FrameLayout` class anchors each of its widgets at the top-left corner of itself. This means each child widget is drawn on top of the previous one. This can be used to simulate a `CardLayout` from AWT by using `View.setVisible` to show one of the children while hiding all the others (this is effectively how `TabHost` works).

As `FrameLayout` actually paints all of its visible children, it can be used to layer the child widgets on top of each other. It produces very strange effects in some cases, while in other cases it can be amazingly useful. For example, darkening out all of the widgets except one can be achieved by using a semi-transparent `View` object and a `FrameLayout`. The inactive widgets are the first layer in the `FrameLayout`, a semi-transparent `View` object is the second, and the active widgets are the third.

Common uses

The most common use of `FrameLayout` is probably in combination with `TabHost`—to hold the content `View` objects for each tab. You can also use it to simulate a more desktop feel, by layering widgets on top of each other. It can also be used very effectively in games, to display the in-game menu, or draw an animated background behind the game's main menu.

By combining a `FrameLayout` object with widgets that also take up the entire screen, you can make use of the `gravity` attribute to place objects more precisely on top of other widgets. For this, you'll generally want each of the `FrameLayout` children to be a `ViewGroup` of some sort, since they generally don't paint in a background unless told to (leaving the lower layers visible).

A `FrameLayout` is also capable of displaying a `foreground`. While all `View` objects have a `background` attribute, `FrameLayout` includes a `foreground` (which is also an optional `Drawable`). The `foreground` will be painted on top of all of the child widgets, allowing a "frame" to be displayed.

Time for action – developing a FrameLayout example

To really understand what a `FrameLayout` does, and how it can be used, it's best to kick it around a bit with an example. In this example, we'll use a `FrameLayout` to layer some `Button` widgets on top of an `ImageView`, and show-and-hide a `TextView` message when one of the buttons is clicked.

For this example to work, you're going to need an image to serve as a background image. I'm going to use a photo of one of my friends. As always, place your image in the `res/drawable` directory, and try to use a PNG file.

1. Create a new layout resource file named `res/layout/frame_layout.xml`.

2. Declare the root element as a `FrameLayout` consuming all available space:

```
<FrameLayout
    xmlns:android="http://schemas.android.com/apk/res/android"
    android:layout_width="fill_parent"
    android:layout_height="fill_parent">
```

3. Inside the `FrameLayout`, create an `ImageView` to serve as the background image. It should scale to fill all the available space:

```
<ImageView android:src="@drawable/jaipal"
           android:scaleType="centerCrop"
           android:layout_width="fill_parent"
           android:layout_height="fill_parent"/>
```

4. Now create a vertical `LinearLayout` where we will place two `Button` objects at the bottom of the screen:

```
<LinearLayout android:orientation="vertical"
              android:gravity="bottom"
              android:layout_width="fill_parent"
              android:layout_height="fill_parent">
```

5. Create a `Button` that we will use to toggle one of the child layers of our `FrameLayout` (creating a dialog-like effect):

```
<Button android:text="Display Overlay"
        android:id="@+id/overlay_button"
        android:layout_width="fill_parent"
        android:layout_height="wrap_content"/>
```

6. Create another `Button` to quit the demo and go back to the menu:

```
<Button android:text="Quit"
        android:id="@+id/quit"
        android:layout_marginTop="10sp"
        android:layout_width="fill_parent"
        android:layout_height="wrap_content"/>
```

7. After the `</LinearLayout>`, create a final `TextView` element that we will show and hide when the first button is clicked. By default it's hidden:

```
<TextView android:visibility="gone"
        android:id="@+id/overlay"
        android:textSize="18sp"
        android:textStyle="bold"
        android:textColor="#ffff843c"
        android:text="This is a text overlay."
        android:gravity="center|center_vertical"
        android:layout_width="fill_parent"
        android:layout_height="fill_parent"/>
```

8. Create a new `FrameLayoutActivity` Java class in the root package of your project, and open the source file in your editor or IDE. The new class needs to extend from `Activity` and implement the `OnClickListener` class (for events from those two `Button` widgets):

```
public class FrameLayoutActivity
        extends Activity implements OnClickListener {
```

9. Override the `onCreate` method:

```
protected void onCreate(Bundle savedInstanceState) {
```

10. Invoke the `super.onCreate` method to get the `Activity` code working:

```
super.onCreate(savedInstanceState);
```

11. Set the content layout to the `frame_layout` resource you just created:

```
setContentView(R.layout.frame_layout);
```

12. Find the `overlay` `Button` widget you declared in the `frame_layout` resource file and create a reference to it:

```
Button overlay = (Button)findViewById(R.id.overlay_button);
```

13. Set its `OnClickListener` to the new `FrameLayoutActivity` object:

```
overlay.setOnClickListener(this);
```

14. Find the `quit` `Button` widget:

```
Button quit = (Button)findViewById(R.id.quit);
```

15. Then set it's `OnClickListener` to the `FrameLayoutActivity` object:

```
quit.setOnClickListener(this);
```

16. The `OnClickListener` interface requires us to implement an `onClick` method with the following signature:

```
public void onClick(View view) {
```

17. Create a `switch` statement on the ID of the `View` parameter:

```
switch(view.getId()) {
```

18. If the `View` clicked by the user widget is the `overlay_button` `Button`, then use the following:

```
case R.id.overlay_button:
```

19. Fetch the `overlay` `View` object from the layout:

```
View display = findViewById(R.id.overlay);
```

20. Toggle its visibility according to its current state, then `break` from the switch:

```
display.setVisibility(
        display.getVisibility() != View.VISIBLE
        ? View.VISIBLE
        : View.GONE);
break;
```

21. If the `View` clicked by the user widget is the `quit` `Button`, then use the following:

```
case R.id.quit:
```

22. Invoke the `finish()` method, and `break` from the `switch` statement:

```
finish();
break;
```

23. Open the `LayoutSelectorActivity` Java source in your editor or IDE.

24. In the `onListItemClick` method, create a new `case` in the `switch` statement, for `position` value `0`:

```
case 0:
```

25. Start the `FrameLayoutActivity` using an explicit `Intent`:

```
startActivity(new Intent(this, FrameLayoutActivity.class));
break;
```

26. Open the `AndroidManifest.xml` file in an editor or IDE.

27. Add the new `FrameLayoutActivity` to the manifest file:

```
<activity android:name=".FrameLayoutActivity"
        android:label="Frame Layout Example"/>
```

What just happened?

The new `FrameLayoutActivity` makes use of a simple three layer `FrameLayout`. We use an `ImageView` object to draw a nice background image, on top of which we placed our two buttons. While the third layer (the `TextView` widget) is invisible until the top button is clicked, it's important to note that not only is the background of the top `TextView` transparent, it also delegates click events to widgets that are technically underneath it (the `TextView` has a widget and height that consumes the entire `FrameLayout`). This will continue to work, even if the background of the `TextView` is opaque. It has more to do with the fact that the `TextView` is not "clickable". If you would have added an `OnClickListener` to the `overlay TextView` object, the button underneath it would have stopped working. This means you need to be careful how you layer widgets in a `FrameLayout` (although so long as one widget doesn't take up the same space as another, this won't become a problem for you).

In this example, we added a **Quit** button to the layout, and used the `finish()` method to close the `Activity` when the `Button` was clicked. You'll find that you generally don't use the `finish()` method directly since the user will mostly be moving forward through your application. If a user wants to go back, they will most often use the hardware "Back" button, or press the hardware "Home" button to exit your application entirely.

A final note on the above example—in the `frame_layout.xml` file, we declare the `overlay` as a `TextView` widget. However, in the Java code we access it using the `View` class instead of `TextView`. This is a simple case of decoupling. Unless you're working in a performance-centric piece of code, it's a good idea to reference your layout widgets as high up the class-tree as possible. This will allow you to modify your user interface much more quickly later on. In this case, you could change the simple `TextView` to an entire `LinearLayout` without the need to change the Java code at all.

Following are two screenshots of the `FrameLayout` example, with and without the `overlay TextView` enabled. This sort of layout is perfect for use in a game menu or a similar structure where you need to layer different widgets on top of each other.

Table Layout

The `Table Layout` arranges its children in a HTML-style grid. It's a bit like the AWT `Grid Layout` class, but with much more flexibility. Unlike most other layout classes in Android, `Table Layout` uses its own specialized direct-child `View` class, named `Table Row`. The `Table Layout` class also doesn't allow you to define the number of rows or columns (making it far more like an HTML `<table>` element). Instead, the number of rows and columns is calculated by the number of widgets in the `Table Layout` and its `Table Row` children.

A cell in a `Table Layout` may consume any number of rows and columns, although the default for a `View` placed inside a `Table Row` is to take up exactly a single table cell. However, if you place a `View` as a direct child of a `Table Layout`, it will consume an entire row.

`Table Layout` is also a relative layout structure, which is vitally important when working with Android devices. Being able to align everything based on grid lines allows your user interface to scale from the lowest resolution on a tiny phone, to a high-density screen on a 7-inch tablet.

The `android:gravity` attribute comes into play far more in a `Table Layout` than in many of the other layout classes. What looks great on a small screen may look completely different on a large screen, not due to the size of the screen, but instead due to the scaling of the fonts used. Be careful, especially with the vertical alignment of labels and widgets. The easiest way to start with this is to vertically center all of your table widgets, and work from there. Be sure to test any table based layout on a variety of screen resolutions and sizes.

Common uses

Most commonly you'll find yourself using a `Table Layout` to arrange input form. It's also useful for laying out complex information, especially when making some `View` objects span several rows and columns. The most important trait of `Table Layout` comes from the fact that it aligns its cells in a very strict manner, and the fact that its a relative-size layout.

A `Table Layout` can also be used to achieve an effect similar to the AWT `Border Layout` class. Generally, when sizing a `Table Layout` to fit the entire screen, it becomes a very different tool to a simple grid, allowing you to fit a `Scroll View` in the middle of the control widgets.

By using a `Table Layout` inside a `FrameLayout`, you can arrange a control `View` on top of a content `View` (think of the controls in Google Maps). Also, try to bear in mind that unlike an AWT `GridLayout`, the size of a `View` inside a `TabelLayout` is not attached to size of the table-cell in which it is placed. By making use of the `gravity` attribute (and possibly a layout margin), you can place a `View` object within the table-cell, leading to layouts that are far more user-friendly.

Using TableLayout for a memory game

To demonstrate the `TableLayout`, I thought it would be fun to write a simple memory-card game. You're presented with a grid (in the form of a `TableLayout`) of "cards" which you can touch to effectively turn over. You can then attempt to match all these cards, with the contents that are displayed on the cards (you're only allowed to turn over two at a time). For this example, you'll need some images to place on the cards (I've re-used the fruit icons from the delivery example). In this application, we'll also be creating a simple placeholder image, in the form of an XML file.

To create the placeholder image, create a new XML resource in the `res/drawable` directory, named `line.xml`. This will be a "shape" resource. Shape resources are very useful for creating simple, scalable shapes. Also, shape resource files can make use of any color, texture, or gradient which you can provide from your code.

Copy the following code into the `line.xml` file in order to create the simple placeholder image for our example:

```xml
<?xml version="1.0" encoding="UTF-8"?>
<shape xmlns:android="http://schemas.android.com/apk/res/android"
        android:shape="line">
    <stroke android:width="3dp"
            android:color="#ff000000"/>
    <padding android:left="1dp"
             android:top="1dp"
             android:right="1dp"
             android:bottom="1dp"/>
</shape>
```

Time for action – developing a simple memory game

Unlike almost all previous example, we'll generate the layout entirely in Java code in this game. The main reason for this is that the content is highly repetitive, each cell containing almost exactly the same widget. We use a `TableLayout` to create the grid, and display the "cards" in `ImageButton` widgets. To encapsulate the individual card behavior, we create a `MemoryCard` inner-class which holds a reference to the `ImageButton` it controls.

1. Create a new Java class in the root package of your project, and name it `TableLayoutActivity`.

2. Make the new class extend `Activity`:

   ```java
   public class TableLayoutActivity extends Activity {
   Declare and array of all the icon resources to use as card
   images, there must be eight images resources declared in this
   array:private static final int[] CARD_RESOURCES = new int[]{
       R.drawable.apple,
       R.drawable.banana,
       R.drawable.blackberry,
       // …
   };
   ```

3. You'll need a timer in order to flip cards back over, so declare a `Handler`:

   ```java
   private final Handler handler = new Handler();
   ```

4. Declare an array of `MemoryCard` objects:

   ```java
   private MemoryCard[] cards;
   ```

5. We either have one or two cards turned over (that we want to keep track of). Declare a placeholder for the first:

```
private MemoryCard visible = null;
```

6. If there are two cards turned over, but they don't match, we disable touch with a simple `boolean` switch (our event listeners will check this):

```
private boolean touchEnabled = true;
```

7. Now declare an inner class named `MemoryCard` which implements the `OnClickListener` interface:

```
private class MemoryCard implements OnClickListener {
```

8. The `MemoryCard` class holds a reference to an `ImageButton`:

```
private ImageButton button;
```

9. The `MemoryCard` class also has a value, which is a reference to the image resource on its face:

```
private int faceImage;
```

10. Finally, a `MemoryCard` uses a `boolean` value to remember its state (whether the face image, or the placeholder image is visible):

```
private boolean faceVisible = false;
```

11. Declare a constructor for the `MemoryCard` class, it only needs to take the resource identifier for the face image:

```
MemoryCard(int faceImage) {
```

12. Store the `faceImage` resource identifier for later use:

```
this.faceImage = faceImage;
```

13. Create a new `ImageButton` object, using the `TableLayoutActivity` object as its `Context` (which the `ImageButton` will use to load the images):

```
this.button = new ImageButton(TableLayoutActivity.this);
```

14. Set the size of the `ImageButton` to a fixed 64 x 64 pixels:

```
this.button.setLayoutParams(new TableRow.LayoutParams(64, 64));
```

15. Set the scale-type so that icons are made to fit into the `ImageButton`, then set the image to the placeholder resource:

```
this.button.setScaleType(ScaleType.FIT_XY);
this.button.setImageResource(R.drawable.line);
```

16. Assign the `MemoryCard` object as the `OnClickListener` of the `ImageButton` object:

```
this.button.setOnClickListener(this);
```

17. For convenience later on, the `MemoryCard` needs a `setFaceVisible` method, which will toggle between showing the placeholder and the `faceImage` resource:

```
void setFaceVisible(boolean faceVisible) {
    this.faceVisible = faceVisible;
    button.setImageResource(faceVisible
            ? faceImage
            : R.drawable.line);
}
```

18. Implement the `onClick` method in the `MemoryCard` class:

```
public void onClick(View view) {
```

19. First, make sure that the face isn't currently visible (so we're turned down), and that touch is enabled (and some other cards aren't about to be turned face-down again):

```
if(!faceVisible && touchEnabled) {
```

20. If these conditions are met, we tell the `TableLayoutActivity` that we've been touched and want to be turned face-up:

```
onMemoryCardUncovered(this);
```

21. After the `MemoryCell` inner class, create a simple utility method in the `TableLayoutActivity` to create an ordered array of `MemoryCell` objects with a specific size:

```
private MemoryCard[] createMemoryCells(int count) {
```

22. When we create each of the `MemoryCell` objects, we create them in pairs, and in the same sequence as was specified in our array of icon resources:

```
MemoryCard[] array = new MemoryCard[count];
for(int i = 0; i < count; i++) {
    array[i] = new MemoryCard(CARD_RESOURCES[i / 2]);
}
```

23. When complete, return the new array of `MemoryCell` objects:

```
return array;
```

24. Now override the `onCreate` method:

```
protected void onCreate(Bundle savedInstanceState) {
```

25. Invoke the `Activity.onCreate` method:

```
super.onCreate(savedInstanceState);
```

26. Now create a new `TableLayout` object, passing it the `TableLayoutActivity` as a `Context` for loading styles and resources:

```
TableLayout table = new TableLayout(this);
```

27. By default, we create a four-by-four grid:

```
int size = 4;
cards = createMemoryCells(size * size);
```

28. Then we shuffle it to randomize the order:

```
Collections.shuffle(Arrays.asList(cards));
```

29. Create each of the required `TableRow` objects, and populate it with the `ImageButtons`, created by the `MemoryCard` objects in the grid:

```
for(int y = 0; y < size; y++) {
    TableRow row = new TableRow(this);
    for(int x = 0; x < size; x++) {
        row.addView(cards[(y * size) + x].button);
    }
    table.addView(row);
}
```

30. Set the `Activity` content view to the `TableLayout` object:

```
setContentView(table);
```

31. Now we write the `onMemoryCardUncovered` method, which is called by the `MemoryCard.onClick` implementation:

```
private void onMemoryCardUncovered(final MemoryCard cell) {
```

32. First, check to see if there is a currently `visible` MemoryCard, if not, the card touched by the user is turned face-up and we remember it:

```
if(visible == null) {
    visible = cell;
    visible.setFaceVisible(true);
}
```

33. If there is already a face-up card, check to see if they have the same image. If the images are the same, disable the `ImageButton` widgets so we ignore the events:

```
else if(visible.faceImage == cell.faceImage) {
    cell.setFaceVisible(true);
    cell.button.setEnabled(false);
```

```
            visible.button.setEnabled(false);
            visible = null;
    }
```

34. Finally, if the face images don't match, we turn the card touched by the user face-up and flip our `touchEnabled` switch so that the `MemoryCard` objects will ignore all other touch events for a second:

```
else {
    cell.setFaceVisible(true);
    touchEnabled = false;
```

35. Then we post a delayed message on our `Handler`, which will turn both cards face-up again and re-enable touch events:

```
handler.postDelayed(new Runnable() {
    public void run() {
        cell.setFaceVisible(false);
        visible.setFaceVisible(false);
        visible = null;
        touchEnabled = true;
    }
}, 1000); // one second before we flip back over again
```

What just happened

In the previous example, it should be obvious to see why we wrote the layout code manually, building it in an XML file would have been terribly repetitive. You'll notice that the code creates a `TableRow` object as the direct children of the `TableLayout`, just as we would have in an XML file.

The `onClick` method of `MemoryCard` uses the `touchEnabled` switch to determine whether or not to call `onMemoryCardUncovered`. However, neither does this stop the user from pressing the `ImageButton` objects, nor does it stop the objects from responding to the user (although they won't turn over). For a more user-friendly experience, it would be better to use the `setClickable` method on each of the enabled `ImageButton` objects, to stop them completely from reacting to the user's touch.

When we create the `ImageButton` objects, we pre-size them at 64 x 64 pixels. While this is fine for the big emulator screen, there are plenty of devices that wouldn't fit the 4 x 4 grid of buttons on the screen. I would recommend you use an XML resource to create the `ImageButton` objects.

The previous code uses `setLayoutParams(new TableRow.LayoutParams(64, 64));` to set the size of the `ImageButton` objects. It's important to note that because we are placing the `ImageButton` objects into a `TableRow`, their `LayoutParams` must be of the type `TableRow.LayoutParams`. If you try changing to a generic `ViewGroup.LayoutParams`, then the user interface won't layout (it'll just be blank). Following are two screenshots of the working application:

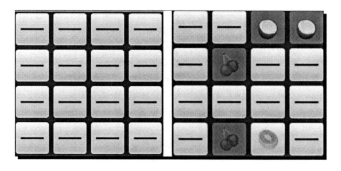

Have a go hero

The `TableLayout` example works great, but the location of the grid isn't great (on the top left of the screen), and having it against a black background is quite dull. Time to make it look great!

Start by using a `FrameLayout` to add a background image to the game. This will enhance the overall appeal of the game by adding more color. You should also take this opportunity to center the grid on the screen. Having it in the top left makes it look lopsided somehow.

You should also try removing the `touchEnabled` switch, instead using `setClickable` on each of the `ImageButton` objects. This will stop them from providing a visual "press and release" feedback when you're about to turn cards face-down.

AbsoluteLayout/Custom Layouts

Do not use AbsoluteLayout! AbsoluteLayout is Deprecated! That said, there are times when using the `AbsoluteLayout` class makes sense. So why shouldn't you use the `AbsoluteLayout` class, and where should you use it? The answer to the first question is very simple—all of the child widgets of an `AbsoluteLayout` have their locations specified exactly, they don't change size or location on different screens. It also makes your layout almost impossible to re-use (for example, importing it into another layout, or embedding it into another application).

If you're going to work with an `AbsoluteLayout`, you should approach it in either one of the following two ways:

1. Carefully build a separate layout XML for each different screen size.

2. Write your layout data in Java code instead of XML.

The first is impractical unless you specify that the application only runs on specific devices, and the layout cannot be used outside of your application. The second option however, opens up the "right" way—write a custom layout manager. Since `AbsoluteLayout` requires strict locations, and doesn't allow easy interaction with the measuring of child `View` objects, the best way to define layouts that don't fit well into any of the over layout classes is to define a custom layout in your own `ViewGroup` class.

Developing your own Layouts

Since `AbsoluteLayout` is deprecated, and yet many people seem to insist on using it, this example will be to demonstrate not just how easy it is to write your own `ViewGroup` class defining a new layout, but also how easy it is to then integrate that layout into a layout XML resource. This will thus prove that there is no compelling reason to use an `AbsoluteLayout` (unless it really makes sense).

Time for action – creating a custom layout

To really demonstrate the use of a custom layout, you need to try building something unusual. In the following example, you'll put together a `ViewGroup` that arranges its children in a nice circle. It's not a very brilliant layout, nor is it particularly useful, but circles are nice to look at, and it would provide useful negative space in the screen center (which could be filled using a `FrameLayout`).

1. Create a new Java source file in the root package of the project named `CircleLayout.java`, and open it in your editor or IDE.

2. Declare the `CircleLayout` as extending the `ViewGroup` class:

    ```
    public class CircleLayout extends ViewGroup
    ```

3. Declare the three `ViewGroup` constructors and have them delegate directly to the `ViewGroup` default constructors:

    ```
    public CircleLayout(Context context) {
        super(context);
    }
    // ...
    ```

4. We'll need to know the largest number of pixels taken up by a child `View` object's width, and the largest number of pixels taken up by a child `View` object's height. To avoid unnecessary overhead, we take this opportunity to `measure` the child `View` objects as well. Declare a utility method named `measureChildrenSizes` to perform these two operations:

```
private int[] measureChildrenSizes(int sw, int sh) {
```

5. Declare an `int` to hold the maximum width and height we find:

```
int maxWidth = 0;
int maxHeight = 0;
```

6. Create a `for` loop to iterate over each of the child `View` objects in this `CircleLayout` object:

```
for(int i = 0; i < getChildCount(); i++) {
```

7. Declare a reference to `View` at the current index:

```
View child = getChildAt(i);
```

8. As a layout widget, your class will be responsible for setting the display size for all of it's child widgets. In order to know a child widget's desired width and height, you need to use the `measureChild` method in the `ViewGroup` class:

```
measureChild(child, sw, sh);
```

9. Test the width and height of the child `View` object against the maximum width and height variables you created earlier:

```
maxWidth = Math.max(maxWidth, child.getMeasuredWidth());
maxHeight = Math.max(maxHeight, child.getMeasuredHeight());
```

10. At the end of the method, return an array containing the maximum width and height found during the procedure:

```
return new int[]{maxWidth, maxHeight};
```

11. Implement the `onLayout` method of `ViewGroup`:

```
protected void onLayout(boolean changed,
        int l, int t, int r, int b) {
```

12. Calculate the width and height of our available space:

```
int w = r - l;
int h = b - t;
```

13. Declare a variable to hold the number of child `View` objects:

```
int count = getChildCount();
```

14. Perform the measurement of all child `View` objects against the amount of available space:

```
int[] max = measureChildrenSizes(w, h);
```

15. Subtract the maximum width and height from the available space so that all the child `View` objects will fit on the screen:

```
w -= max[0];
h -= max[1];
```

16. Calculate the center point in the `CircleLayout`:

```
int cx = w / 2;
int cy = h / 2;
```

17. Create a `for` loop to iterate over each of the child `View` objects again:

```
for(int i = 0; i < count; i++) {
```

18. Declare a variable to hold the current child `View` object:

```
View child = getChildAt(i);
```

19. Calculate the x and y locations of the child `View` object:

```
double v = 2 * Math.PI * i / count;
int x = l + (cx + (int)(Math.cos(v) * cx));
int y = t + (cy + (int)(Math.sin(v) * cy));
```

20. Invoke the layout method of the child `View` object with the calculated coordinates in the circle:

```
child.layout(
        x, y,
        x + child.getMeasuredWidth(),
        y + child.getMeasuredHeight());
```

What just happened?

The `CircleLayout` class is a very simple implementation of a `ViewGroup`. Except for the requested width and height of its children, it has no special attributes that can be used in an XML resource. However, it will take notice of the sizing that you declare for its children, and so the `layout_width` and `layout_height` attributes will work normally.

It's important to note that in order to make use of a custom `View` or `ViewGroup` from a layout XML resource, you need to have all three default constructors overridden.

The Layout Inflater will make use of one of these constructors to create instances of your class. If the one it wants to use isn't in place, you will get the dreaded **Force Close** dialog when you try and inflate the layout XML file.

The CircleLayout has its own utility method to handle the measuring of its child View objects. Generally, a ViewGroup would use the ViewGroup.measureChildren utility method to see that all of its child View objects are measured before performing the actual layout. However, we need to iterate over the list of child View objects in order to find the largest used width and height, so instead of performing the iteration three times, we perform the measurements ourselves.

Using the CircleLayout

To make use of your custom ViewGroup implementation, it's good to know that Android has you covered as far as the XML layout resources are concerned. When you need to reference a custom View or ViewGroup class from an XML layout resource, you simply use the full class name instead of the simple class name. The following is a simple example of an XML layout that uses the CircleLayout:

```
<com.packtpub.layouts.CircleLayout
    xmlns:android="http://schemas.android.com/apk/res/android"
    android:layout_width="fill_parent"
    android:layout_height="fill_parent">

    <Button android:text="Button1"
            android:layout_width="wrap_content"
            android:layout_height="wrap_content"/>

    <Button android:text="Button2"
            android:layout_width="wrap_content"
            android:layout_height="wrap_content"/>

    <!-- 10 Buttons in total works nicely

</com.packtpub.layouts.CircleLayout>
```

Time for action – finishing the CircleLayout example

We've got the CicleLayout implementation, but we should really include it in our "layouts" example now. To do that we'll need a layout resource XML file, a new CircleLayoutActivity class. We also need to register the new Activity with both, Android (in the manifest file), and with our LayoutSelectorActivity class (in its event listener).

1. Copy the preceding XML layout into a new file named `res/layout/circle_layout.xml`. It works best with around ten widgets added as children of the `CircleLayout` ViewGroup.

2. Create a new Java source file in the root package of your project named `CircleLayoutActivity.java`. Open this in your editor or IDE.

3. `CircleLayoutActivity` must extend the `Activity` class:

```
public class CircleLayoutActivity extends Activity {
```

4. Override the `onCreate` method of `Activity`:

```
protected void onCreate(Bundle savedInstanceState) {
```

5. Invoke the super class:

```
super.onCreate(savedInstanceState);
```

6. Set the content view to the `circle_layout` layout resource:

```
setContentView(R.layout.circle_layout);
```

7. Open the `AndroidManifest.xml` file in your editor or IDE.

8. After the `TableLayoutActivity` declaration, declare the new `CircleLayoutActivity`:

```
<activity android:name=".CircleLayoutActivity"
        android:label="Circle Layout Example"/>
```

9. Open the `LayoutSelectorActivity` source file in your editor or IDE.

10. In the `onListItemClick` method, before the `default` case, add a new `case` statement to start the `CircleLayoutActivity`:

```
case 2:
    startActivity(new Intent(
        this, CircleLayoutActivity.class));
    break;
```

What just happened?

You now have a new `Activity` implementation that uses your own customized `ViewGroup` implementation. Custom `ViewGroup` classes are not just useful when you have a hard-to-express layout that the standard `ViewGroup` implementations don't handle very well. A custom `ViewGroup` is also an option when the default `ViewGroup` implementations are too slow for a particular structure that you want to implement.

The "layouts" example that you've been building in this chapter will now have a working **Custom Layout** menu item. Click it and you'll be presented with the following screenshot. Try adding widgets other than `Button` objects, and maybe even try throwing in a child `ViewGroup` and see what happens.

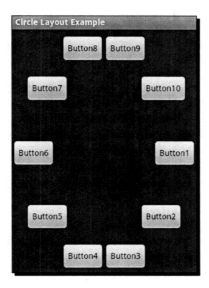

Pop quiz

1. Layout generally happens in two phases, what's the first phase called?

    a. Pre-layout

    b. Calculation

    c. Parent layout

    d. Measurement

2. What do the four parameters of the layout method signify?

    a. x, y, width, and height.

    b. Left, top, right, and bottom.

    c. The size of the parent `ViewGroup`.

3. How can a custom `ViewGroup` implementation read layout XML attributes?

    a. They are injected into setters by the `LayoutInflator`.

    b. They are loaded with the `View.getAttribute` method.

    c. They read it from the `AttributeSet` object passed into the `ViewGroup` constructor.

RelativeLayout

The RelativeLayout class is arguably the most powerful layout that Android provides. It's a relative layout, managing widgets of varying sizes, and aligning widgets against each other instead of against their parent or grid-lines. In some ways, RelativeLayout has a striking resemblance to the Swing GroupLayout class, although it is nowhere near as complex. Each widget in a RelativeLayout is positioned against either another widget, or against its parent (the RelativeLayout itself).

RelativeLayout calculates the location of each child in a single loop, so it relies strongly on the order in which you specify the children. However, this doesn't mean that you must specify the widgets in the order they are displayed on the screen. Due to the nature of a RelativeLayout, the child widgets are often declared and displayed in a different order. This also requires that any user interface element used for aligning other widgets must have an ID assigned to it. This includes even non-interactive user interface elements which would normally not need an ID, must now be assigned one, even though they will never be used outside of the layout.

Using a RelativeLayout is extremely flexible, but may also require some careful planning. As with any user interface, it helps enormously to draw the layout on paper first. Once you have a paper diagram, you can start to plan how you will build the layout according to the rules specified by the RelativeLayout class.

Common uses

The uses of RelativeLayout are very similar to those of TableLayout. It's great for drawing up forms and content views. However, RelativeLayout is not confined to the grid pattern of TableLayout, and can therefore create relationships between widgets that are physically far away from each other on the screen (that is, by aligning them with each other).

RelativeLayout positions and sizes a widget either according to other widgets in the same RelativeLayout, and/or according to the boundaries of the RelativeLayout itself. This means some widgets may be placed at the top of the screen, and you can align another group of widgets at the bottom of the screen, as shown in the following diagram.

Integrating the RelativeLayout

When faced with a contact editor, a `RelativeLayout` is the perfect tool to produce an easy-to-use user interface. For the next example, we build a very simple contact editing user interface including an image of the user.

Time for action – creating a contact editor

This example requires that some of the user interface elements are declared out-of-order (as discussed earlier). We'll also include **Save** and **Cancel** `Button` widgets at the bottom of the screen. This example goes back to declaring the user interface in a resource XML file rather than writing it in Java code. For this example, you'll need a placeholder image for the user's contact photo. A 64 x 64 pixel PNG file is about the right size to work with (I used a big smiley image).

1. Start by creating a new XML layout file named `res/layout/relative_layout.xml`. Open this file in your editor or IDE.

2. Declare the root element as a full-screen `RelativeLayout`:

```
<RelativeLayout
    xmlns:android="http://schemas.android.com/apk/res/android"
    android:layout_width="fill_parent"
    android:layout_height="fill_parent">
```

3. Create an `ImageButton` that will have an icon of the user on it. The `ImageButton` should be aligned to the top-left of the screen, and have a place-holder image in it:

```
<ImageButton android:src="@drawable/face"
             android:id="@+id/photo"
             android:layout_alignParentTop="true"
             android:layout_alignParentLeft="true"
             android:layout_width="wrap_content"
             android:layout_height="wrap_content"/>
```

4. Add an `EditText` where the user can type a contact's name. Align this to the right bottom of the `ImageButton`:

```
<EditText android:text="Unknown"
          android:id="@+id/contact_name"
          android:layout_alignBottom="@id/photo"
          android:layout_toRightOf="@id/photo"
          android:layout_width="fill_parent"
          android:layout_height="wrap_content"/>
```

5. Now add a `TextView` to act as a label for the `EditText` widget. We align this to the right of the `ImageButton`, but above the `EditText`:

```
<TextView android:text="Contact Name:"
        android:id="@+id/contact_label"
        android:layout_above="@id/contact_name"
        android:layout_toRightOf="@id/photo"
        android:layout_width="wrap_content"
        android:layout_height="wrap_content"/>
```

6. We'll need an **Edit** `Button` to allow the user to edit the list of phone numbers for the contact. Position this on the right side of the screen, and below the `EditText`. We add a margin at the top of this `Button` to give a logical separation in the user interface:

```
<Button android:id="@+id/edit_numbers"
        android:text="Edit"
        android:paddingLeft="20dp"
        android:paddingRight="20dp"
        android:layout_below="@id/contact_name"
        android:layout_alignParentRight="true"
        android:layout_marginTop="10dp"
        android:layout_width="wrap_content"
        android:layout_height="wrap_content"/>
```

7. Create a nice big `TextView` as a label to the phone numbers, which we will list below the new `TextView` and **Edit** `Button`:

```
<TextView android:text="Contact Numbers:"
        android:id="@+id/numbers_label"
        android:textSize="20sp"
        android:layout_alignBaseline="@id/edit_numbers"
        android:layout_alignParentLeft="true"
        android:layout_width="wrap_content"
        android:layout_height="wrap_content"/>
```

8. Now create a `TableLayout` to hold a list of the contact person's phone numbers, center-align this `TableLayout` in the `RelativeLayout`, and position it below the **Contact Numbers** label with a slight margin:

```
<TableLayout android:layout_below="@id/edit_numbers"
            android:layout_marginTop="5dp"
            android:layout_centerInParent="true"
            android:layout_width="wrap_content"
            android:layout_height="wrap_content">
```

9. Add two `TableRow` elements with some dummy content to the `TableLayout`:

```
<TableRow>
    <TextView android:text="Home"
              android:layout_marginRight="20dp"/>
    <TextView android:text="555-987-5678"/>
</TableRow>
<TableRow>
    <TextView android:text="Mobile"
              android:layout_marginRight="20dp"/>
    <TextView android:text="555-345-7654"/>
</TableRow>
```

10. Create the **Save** `Button` positioned at the bottom-left of the screen:

```
<Button android:text="Save"
        android:id="@+id/save"
        android:layout_alignParentLeft="true"
        android:layout_alignParentBottom="true"
        android:layout_width="100sp"
        android:layout_height="wrap_content"/>
```

11. Create a **Cancel** `Button` positioned at the bottom-right of the screen:

```
<Button android:text="Cancel"
        android:id="@+id/cancel"
        android:layout_alignParentRight="true"
        android:layout_alignParentBottom="true"
        android:layout_width="100sp"
        android:layout_height="wrap_content"/>
```

What just happened

Many of the user interface elements in the previous example are declared in an order that is contrary to the logical layout order, while others are positioned relative to the `RelativeLayout` itself and can therefore be placed anywhere in the XML file.

The **Contact Name** label and editor are positioned relative to the "contact photo", which in turn is relative to the screen (or `RelativeLayout`). However, because we want the label to appear directly above the editor, we need to declare and position the `EditText` element before the `TextView` element.

The **Contact Name** `EditText` element uses a width of `fill_parent`, which in a `RelativeLayout` simply fills the available horizontal space (or vertical space if it's used on a widget's height). This is a useful feature when you want an element to simply consume the rest of a "line", or span across the entire screen (that is, for a dividing line). In a `RelativeLayout` you cannot use two layout attributes that conflict with the same axis of a widget. For example, you use the `layout_toRightOf` and `layout_alignRight` on the same `View` widget.

Time for action – integration with the layout example

The integration of the `RelativeLayout` example is almost identical to the integration of the custom `CircleLayout` example that you wrote earlier. Integration will require a new `Activity` implementation, and then we need to register it with Android and the `LayoutSelectorActivity`.

1. Create a new Java source file in the root package of the "layouts" example project, named `RelativeLayoutActivity.java`. Open this in your editor or IDE.

2. The new `RelativeLayoutActivity` needs to extend the `Activity` class:

```
public class RelativeLayoutActivity extends Activity {
```

3. Override the `onCreate` method:

```
protected void onCreate(Bundle savedInstanceState) {
```

4. Invoke the `super` class to set up its state:

```
super.onCreate(savedInstanceState);
```

5. Set the content view of the new `Activity` to the `relative_layout` XML layout resource created earlier:

```
setContentView(R.layout.relative_layout);
```

6. Open the `AndroidManifest.xml` file in your editor or IDE.

7. Register `RelativeLayoutActivity` after `CircleLayoutActivity`:

```
<activity android:name=".RelativeLayoutActivity"
          android:label="Relative Layout Example"/>
```

8. Open `LayoutSelectorActivity` Java source code in your editor or IDE.

9. In the `onListItemClick` method, declare a new `case` statement before the `default` statement and start the new `RelativeLayoutActivity`:

```
case 3:
    startActivity(new Intent(
            this, RelativeLayoutActivity.class));
    break;
```

What just happened?

Now that the RelativeLayoutActivity is integrated with the rest of the layout example, you can fire up the emulator and take a look at the screen you just built. As you can see in the following screenshot, this design is much more user-friendly than most of the other designs we've built so far. The main reason for this is the ability to group and align widgets in ways that logically relate to each other, rather than being forced to confine to the requirements of the chosen ViewGroup.

However, this flexibility doesn't come without a price. The RelativeLayout structures are far more easily broken than other ViewGroup implementations, and in many cases won't offer you much additional flexibility. In the preceding example, we embedded a TableLayout to display the list of contact numbers instead of displaying them directly under the RelativeLayout element. Not only is TableLayout better suited to this task, but it also allows us to center-align the numbers as a single group instead of aligning them to the left and right of the RelativeLayout.

RelativeLayout combined with either an embedded ScrollView or a FrameLayout is a brilliant way of providing toolbars for more content-centric user interfaces. When you have a media-centric user interface (with full-screen maps, video, photos, or something similar), using a RelativeLayout to arrange the tool buttons around the outside of the screen and then placing the actual content behind it with a FrameLayout works extremely well as can be seen in many Android applications such as Google Maps or the default browser application. This design also allows you to show or hide the tool buttons based on the user's interaction with the application, giving them a better view of the media content when they are not interacting with the toolset.

SlidingDrawer

If you've used an un-themed Android installation (such as the emulator), or most themed versions of Android, then you've used a SlidingDrawer. It's the widget that drives the opening and closing of the launcher menu. While it is not exactly a layout in its own right, a SlidingDrawer allows you to make a large number of lesser-used widgets very quickly available to the user. This makes it an important widget to consider when developing a new user interface.

Generally, it'll be a decision between using a menu and a SlidingDrawer. While a menu is great for displaying action items, a SlidingDrawer can display any content you want. However, a SlidingDrawer also has some restrictions on its use. For example, it requires that you place it within a FrameLayout or RelativeLayout instance (of which FrameLayout is far more typical) in order to function correctly.

A SlidingDrawer is in some ways a form of disclosure widget. It consists of a handle and content. By default, only the handle is visible on the screen, until the user touches or pulls the handle to open the SlidingDrawer and display the content section.

Common uses

The open/close content nature of the SlidingDrawer class makes it ideal for the application launcher in Android. By default, it is hidden away so the desktop is visible and usable, until you tap the handle in order to view the list of available applications.

This also makes SlidingDrawer a brilliant tool for building applications such as strategy games. Instead of giving your user all the available build options (for example), restrict the default screen view to the key map elements. When they want to build something, or check some status information, they can tap or drag open a SlidingDrawer from the bottom of the screen, revealing all the build/command options.

Generally, when you have actions or information that the user won't need to interact often with, a SlidingDrawer is a great way to present it. It can also be opened and closed from your Java code when key events that require the user's attention occur.

The handle element of the SlidingDrawer is also a full View or ViewGroup, which allows you to put status messages in it. Another common use of the slidingdrawer widget is that the status bar at the top of most Android devices is often implemented as a SlidingDrawer. A summary is displayed on the handle when an event occurs, and the user can drag open the content to view the complete details of the most recent events.

Creating a SlidingDrawer example

To keep the `SlidingDrawer` example nice and simple, we're going to re-use the `CircleLayout` example with one main modification—the background color needs to change. If the background of a `SlidingDrawer` is not specifically set, the background will be transparent. Generally, this is undesirable since the content behind the open `SlidingDrawer` widget is then visible, and interferes with the content of the `SlidingDrawer`.

Time for action – creating a SlidingDrawer

For this example, we'll be placing a `SlidingDrawer` widget on top of an image (I've once again chosen a photo of one of my friends as my background). For the handle of the `SlidingDrawer`, we'll make use of the line drawable XML file that was created for the `TableLayoutActivity`. For the content of the `SlidingDrawer`, we'll make use of the `circle_layout` resource.

1. Open the `res/layout/circle_layout.xml` file in your editor or IDE.

2. On the root element declaration, set the background attribute to black:

```
<com.packtpub.layouts.CircleLayout
    xmlns:android="http://schemas.android.com/apk/res/android"
    android:background="#ff000000"
    android:layout_width="fill_parent"
    android:layout_height="fill_parent">
```

3. Create a new layout resource file named `sliding_drawer.xml`, and open this file in your editor or IDE.

4. Declare the root element of this layout as a `FrameLayout`:

```
<FrameLayout
    xmlns:android="http://schemas.android.com/apk/res/android"
    android:layout_width="fill_parent"
    android:layout_height="fill_parent">
```

5. Inside the `FrameLayout`, create an `ImageView` to contain the background image. Remember to set the scale-type and size so the image fills the screen:

```
<ImageView android:src="@drawable/jaipal"
            android:scaleType="centerCrop"
            android:layout_width="fill_parent"
            android:layout_height="fill_parent"/>
```

6. Declare the `SlidingDrawer` widget. You'll need to forward-reference the handle and content widgets since they don't exist yet:

```
<SlidingDrawer android:handle="@+id/handle"
                android:content="@+id/content"
                android:layout_width="fill_parent"
                android:layout_height="fill_parent">
```

7. Inside the `SlidingDrawer` element, create an `ImageView` with the placeholder `line` drawable resource that you created for the `TableLayoutActivity` earlier:

```
<ImageView android:id="@id/handle"
            android:src="@drawable/line"
            android:layout_width="fill_parent"
            android:layout_height="12dp"/>
```

8. Also inside the `SlidingDrawer` element, include the `circle_layout` layout resource, assigning its ID as "content":

```
<include android:id="@id/content"
          layout="@layout/circle_layout"/>
```

What just happened?

You'll notice that in the previous example, the `SlidingDrawer` adds the ID references to its handle and content widgets, while the widgets themselves appear to access these IDs instead of declaring them:

```
<SlidingDrawer android:handle="@+id/handle"
                android:content="@+id/content"
                android:layout_width="fill_parent"
                android:layout_height="fill_parent">
```

This is a side effect of how the `SlidingDrawer` class works. it needs the ID values before it needs the widgets themselves. This technique is much like a forward-reference, except the object is not technically created. The `@+` syntax tells the resource compiler that we are creating a new id, but not a new object. When we later declare the `ImageView` element using the `@id/handle` value as its `id`, we are in fact referencing the value that was generated when we declared the `SlidingDrawer`.

Time for action – sliding drawer integration

Now it's time to plug the `SlidingDrawer` example into the "layouts" example. This, like all the other integrations, involves a new `Activity`, and registering the new `Activity` with Android and `LayoutSelectorActivity`.

1. Create a new Java source file in the root package of the "layouts" example project named `SlidingDrawerActivity.java`. Open this in your editor or IDE.

2. The new `SlidingDrawerActivity` needs to extend the `Activity` class:

    ```
    public class SlidingDrawerActivity extends Activity {
    ```

3. Override the `onCreate` method:

    ```
    protected void onCreate(Bundle savedInstanceState) {
    ```

4. Invoke the super class to set up its state:

    ```
    super.onCreate(savedInstanceState);
    ```

5. Set the content view of the new `Activity` to the `sliding_drawer` XML layout resource created earlier:

    ```
    setContentView(R.layout.sliding_drawer);
    ```

6. Open the `AndroidManifest.xml` file in your editor or IDE.

7. Register the `SlidingDrawerActivity` after the `RelativeLayoutActivity` is declared:

    ```
    <activity android:name=".SlidingDrawerActivity"
            android:label="Sliding Drawer Example"/>
    ```

8. Open the `LayoutSelectorActivity` Java source code in your editor or IDE.

9. In the `onListItemClick` method, declare a new `case` statement before the `default` statement and start the new `SlidingDrawerActivity`:

    ```
    case 3:
        startActivity(new Intent(
                this, SlidingDrawerActivity.class));
        break;
    ```

What just happened?

You've just completed all of the layout examples in this chapter. The `default` condition in your `switch` statement should never trigger again! The `SlidingDrawer` example is very simple, but demonstrates well how versatile this widget can be. If this example was (for instance) a paint application, the `SlidingDrawer` would be the perfect place to hide a list of the more complex painting functions available.

The handle of this `SlidingDrawer` example is a simple `ImageView`, but it can be any `View` or `ViewGroup` (a `TableLayout`, if you wanted). However, you want to avoid the handle becoming interactive (that is, a `Button` or `EditText` widget). An interactive widget in the handle will cause problems when the user touches it. Although the widget remains fully functional, and can be dragged up and down like a handle, touching it to start an interaction will cause the `SlidingDrawer` to open or close itself. To stop this from happening, you can optionally turn the "touch to toggle" option of the `SlidingDrawer` off with the `allowSingleTap` attribute:

```
<SlidingDrawer android:handle="@+id/handle"
               android:content="@+id/content"
               android:allowSingleTap="false"
               android:layout_width="fill_parent"
               android:layout_height="fill_parent">
```

That said, having an `EditText` (or similar) as a handle for a `SlidingDrawer` makes very little sense, and is likely to make your users rather irritated with you. As far as possible, you should make sure that the handle of your `SlidingDrawer` widgets looks like something the user can drag. The default handle of the launcher application is a great example.

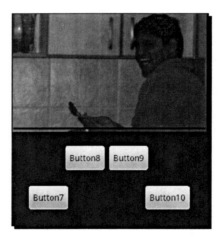

Summary

Working through the examples in this chapter should have given you a good look into the layouts that are available by default in Android, as well as a look at how they are implemented (and how new ones can be implemented when needed). In most cases, these `ViewGroup` implementations will serve any layout needs you have, but it remains important to keep the following principals in mind when building Android layouts:

- ◆ Different devices have different size and resolution screens
- ◆ Use negative space (white space) and lines to separate groups of widgets
- ◆ You will almost certainly need to modify the layout in the future

That last point is particularly important when choosing to use the `RelativeLayout` class. While it offers your far more power than the other implementations, a badly put-together `RelativeLayout` can be very difficult and time consuming to maintain.

In the coming chapter, we'll take a look at how capturing input, and the validation of that input should be taken as a user interface design decision. We'll also work through some examples that can be used as a foundation for future user interface developments.

6
Validating and Handling Input Data

Unfortunately, the validation and handling of input in an application is often an afterthought in the design process. These should be at the forefront of your thoughts during the second round of drafts for the user interface. A touchscreen device offers many more opportunities to streamline the capturing of data from the user, in many cases removing the need for sanitation or validation, while at the same time massively improving the user's experience with the application.

Android provides an excellent toolset to capture many different types of data from the user, while also providing loose coupling between your application components in the form of `Intent` structures. By using several smaller `Activity` classes to capture data, while at the same time abstracting the functionality to capture different types of input, you'll be able to more easily reuse the input capturing `Activity` classes, not just within the application, but in other applications as well. Further, by registering the `Activity` correctly, you'll allow other applications to override, or make use of your `Activity` implementation, allowing the users to select their preferred capturing mechanism.

Dealing with undesirable input

Often applications require specific types of input from their users. An application captures input from its user in order for the user to tell it something about the world. This could be anything, from what the user is looking for (that is, a search term), to something about the users themselves (that is, their age). In most of these cases, the users can be guided in the way they give the input using mechanisms, such as an auto-completion box. However, if a user can give you "undesirable" input, then somewhere along the line one of them will.

Undesirable input can be anything ranging from text where a number is expected, through to a search term that yields no results. In both cases, you need to do three things:

1. Inform the user about the format you expect the data to be in
2. Let them know that they entered undesirable data
3. Let them re-enter the data

Correctly labeling input

Your first defense against undesirable input from your users is to correctly label of an input widget. This doesn't just mean, having a label that reads as follows:

```
Date of Birth (dd/mm/yy):
```

It means using the correct widget to capture the data. Your input widgets are a form of a label, they indicate to the user what sort of data you expect them to enter. In many cases, they can be used to stop the user from entering invalid data, or at least make it less likely.

 Keep in mind the way that users expect things to work, and that they expect to be able to select things quickly. If you need them to give your application the name of a country, don't use a `Spinner` and force them to scroll through a seemingly endless list of names.

Signaling undesirable input

If the user does enter something unwanted or useless, you need to tell them, and fast! The sooner you let the user know that they've given you something useless, the sooner they can correct it and get back to using your application.

A common mistake is to simply `Toast` the user when they press a **Save** or **Submit** button. While this is okay if you can only determine their mistake at that point, but you can almost always figure it out beforehand.

Bear in mind that on a touchscreen device, while you have a "focused" widget, it doesn't play the same role as on a desktop system, and the user isn't going to "tab" off the widget. This means that as far as possible, your user interface should respond live to the user's actions, not wait for them to do something else (that is, select another widget) before giving them some feedback. If they do something that makes another form element invalid to use, disable it. If they do something that makes a group of widgets invalid, hide the entire group from them or put it on a different screen.

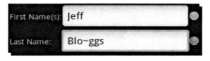

Coloring and icons are both great ways to quickly tell the user they've got something wrong. You can take the additional step of disabling any sort of **Save**, **Next**, or **Submit** button when you realize that some of the user's input is wrong. However, if you do disable such a button, ensure that it is clear which form element has undesirable data on it, and make sure it is on their screen. A great alternative is to `Toast` the user when they select a **Next** button, and scroll to the invalid element.

Make use of background (or asynchronous) messages if you need to check the users' input against some remote service. This will allow you to validate the user's content as they are using the application. It'll also allow you to signal that something is wrong without stopping them from using the rest of the form. They can always come back to the invalid field and correct it.

Recovering from undesirable input

Always ensure that fixing a mistake is as painless as possible for the user. The more work they have to do to correct a misspelled word (or similar), the more likely it is that they will stop using the application. The easiest way to recover from undesirable input (which happens to fit nicely with the above comments) is to tell the user about it before they have a chance to move to another part of the process. However, this isn't always possible.

There are times when you need to pop up a **Please Wait** dialog during a process that will (generally as a side effect) validate the users input. In these cases, it's wise to use a `ProgressDialog` so you don't move the user away from your current `Activity` during this phase. This will have two important side effects:

- You don't add unnecessary layers to the activity stack
- The input the user gave is still available when you close the `ProgressDialog`

Giving users direct feedback

When accepting text or other keyboard input from the users, it's best to signal its validity to the users while they are still entering it. A common method is to use an `ImageView` to the right of the `EditText` widget, and changing the image content to signal whether the user has entered valid or invalid content. The image displayed in the `ImageView` can be set, based on whether the input is currently valid or not. This gives the user a live view of the validation process. This mechanism also works well for signaling variable levels of validation (that is, when the input is not strictly valid or invalid, but rather good quality or undesirable quality), such as in the case of a password input.

You can either make use of image icons, or simply use an Android drawable XML resource to represent the validity (that is, green for valid, red for invalid). This also means that your icon will scale to any size that you prescribe to it in your layout XML file.

Colors and icons

It's often a good idea to use a non-color indicator to differentiate icons. Someone who is color blind may find it difficult or impossible to tell the difference between two icons unless you change the shape as well as the color. Having your "valid" icon as a green circle, and your "invalid" icon as a red hexagon will make your application more usable.

In order to avoid cluttering your screen with icons, you may want to display only the validation icon next to the field the user is currently working with. It's a good idea however, to make use of the `INVISIBLE View` state instead of `GONE` in order to avoid changing the layout when the user changes the focus of the user interface. At the same time, please ensure that validation icons are the same size.

Avoiding invalid input entirely

Remember that with a mobile device, time is often a constraint for the user. For this reason (and for simple usability reasons) you should generally strive to avoid invalid input from your users entirely. Android provides you with several mechanisms with which to do this, and it's wise to make use of them at every opportunity. Generally, you will want to make use of widgets that avoid validation requirements. This is almost always an option in Android, and even when your requirements are more complex than simple type information, you can generally customize the widget to stop the user from breaking your validation rules.

Capturing date and time

As we've already discussed, when inputting date and time you should make use of `DatePicker` and `TimePicker` widgets, or the `DatePickerDialog` and `TimePickerDialog` to avoid the layout issues that the primitive widgets introduce.

Avoid creating your own calendar widget unless it's a hard requirement of your application. You may not like how a `DatePickerDialog` looks, but users have seen them in other Android applications and know how to use them. It's also possible that these standard widgets are improved in future Android releases, giving your application an improvement with no work from your side.

You may find that you need additional validation for date and time inputs, especially when capturing date or time ranges. For example, if you ask a user for a date of birth, the user shouldn't be able to enter a field that indicates any time later than "today" (unless it's an expected date of birth). While the `DatePicker` class has an event listener which allows you to listen for changes to its data (and `DatePickerDialog` implements this event listener), you cannot use this event listener to cancel the change event.

Therefore, in order to **Cancel** the event, you need to change the input back to something valid while the event is executing. This is a surprisingly simple trick in Android. Since the events are executed on the same thread that does the painting, it allows you to change the value before the invalid data is rendered on the screen. The following is a simple example of a `ValidatingDatePickerDialog` which you can use in order to implement a simple level of date validation in your application. Another such class could be easily written for `TimePickerDialog` if you needed one.

```java
public class ValidatingDatePickerDialog extends DatePickerDialog {
    private int lastValidYear;
    private int lastValidMonth;
    private int lastValidDay;
    private ValidationCallback callback = null;

    public ValidatingDatePickerDialog(
            final Context context,
            final OnDateSetListener callBack,
            final int year,
            final int monthOfYear,
            final int dayOfMonth) {
        super(context, callBack, year, monthOfYear, dayOfMonth);
        setValidData(year, monthOfYear, dayOfMonth);
    }

    protected void setValidData(
            final int year,
```

```
                 final int monthOfYear,
                 final int dayOfMonth) {

        lastValidYear = year;
        lastValidMonth = monthOfYear;
        lastValidDay = dayOfMonth;
    }
    @Override
    public void onDateChanged(
                 final DatePicker view,
                 final int year,
                 final int month,
                 final int day) {

        if(callback != null && !callback.isValid(year, month, day)) {
            view.updateDate(
                     lastValidYear,
                     lastValidMonth,
                     lastValidDay);
        } else {
            super.onDateChanged(view, year, month, day);
            setValidData(year, month, day);
        }
    }
    public void setValidationCallback(
                 final ValidationCallback callback) {
        this.callback = callback;
    }
    public ValidationCallback getValidationCallback() {
        return callback;
    }
    public interface ValidationCallback {
        boolean isValid(int year, int monthOfYear, int dayOfMonth);
    }
}
```

This method of handling validation can be used in most Android widgets that don't offer implicit validation of their events, and it offers a much better user experience than giving the user a `Toast` with the text **Please enter a valid date of birth**. It also avoids the need for additional layers of validation in your application.

Using spinners and ListView for selection

There are many times when the user needs to select something from a list of possible values in an application. We've already discussed `Spinner` and `ListView` widgets in *Chapter 2, Presenting Data for Views*. However, they offer several features that can be very useful when it comes to validation. They are implicitly validated widgets, that is, it's impossible for the user to enter incorrect data since the possible values for input are defined by the application. However, what about when the set of valid items changes based on other user input, or some external source of information? In these cases, several options are available to you.

Changing the data set

The simplest method of stopping the user from selecting a value that is no longer valid is to remove it from the data set. We've already done a similar thing in `BurgerAdapter`, in *Chapter 2, Presenting Data for Views,* where we modified the data set when the user touched certain items. Modifying the data set of an `AdapterView` is a good idea because it "takes the option off the menu". However, it doesn't work well with the `Spinner` class, since, if the item is removed off the screen, the user will be left wondering what happened to the item that was there just a second ago (and may be concerned that they are going mad).

In order not to confuse or frustrate your users, you should only remove items from a `Spinner` or `ListView` data set if the item will probably not be added back into the data set. A good example of this requirement is a list of Wi-Fi networks available, or Bluetooth devices within range. In both of these cases, the list of available items is defined by the environment. The user will accept that the displayed options are not always going to be available to them, and new items may appear from time to time.

Disabling selections

An alternative and usually more user-friendly method of stopping certain items from being selected is to disable them. You can make the `ListView` or `Spinner` ignore items by overriding the `isEnabled(int)` method in the `ListAdapter` class. However, this method will only disable the item at the event level, the item will still appear as enabled (it's primary purpose is to define separator views).

In order to visually disable an item, you'll need to disable the `View` that the item is displayed in. This is a very effective way of telling the user, "You've changed something that has made this item unavailable". Graphically disabling an item also lets the user know that it may become available in the future.

Capturing text input

The most difficult inputs to work with are the various forms of text input. I find that working with a soft keyboard may not be as quick as working with a hardware keyboard, but from a development point of view it offers something that a hardware keyboard does not—flexibility. When I want to enter text into a field, a soft keyboard's state will indicate the type of input that is valid for that field. If I'm supposed to enter a phone number, the keyboard can display only numbers, or even change into a dial pad. This not only indicates to me what I'm supposed to do, but also stops me from inputting anything that would cause a validation error.

The Android `TextView` (and thus the `EditText`) widgets provide you with a host of different options and methods by which you can define complex validation rules for text input. Many of these options are also understood by various soft keyboards, allowing them to display subsets of the full keyboard based on how the `TextView` widget has been configured. Even if not fully understood by the soft keyboard (or if a hardware keyboard is in use), the rules of the specified option must be adhered to. The easiest way to tell the `EditText` what type of data you want it to capture is with the `inputType` XML attribute.

As you'll see from the `inputType` documentation, all of its possible values are different combinations of the bit masks available in the `android.view.inputmethod.InputType` interface. The options available as values to the `inputType` attribute will cover most cases where you need to capture a specific type of input. You can also create your own, more complex input types by using the `TextView.setRawInput` or `TextView.setKeyboardListener` methods.

Keyboard listeners

As far as possible, you should either use the input type or a standard `KeyListener` to handle your text validation. Writing a `KeyListener` is a non-trivial task, and in some cases may see you implementing a custom soft keyboard. A `KeyListener` in Android, which defines an input type other than TYPE_NULL, may not have its listener events (onKeyDown, onKeyUp, and onKeyOther) invoked at all if a soft keyboard is present. The key events of a `KeyListener` are only used to accept or reject events from a hardware keyboard. Software keyboards use the input type attribute of a `TextView` to decide what functionality they should provide to the user.

Autocompleting text input

The `Spinner` and `ListView` widgets are great ways to ask your user to select from a predefined list of options. However, both have a major flaw in that they don't scale well to very long lists. While the implementation and performance are both very good, users just don't like looking through massive lists of data. The standard way to solve this problem is to provide an auto completed text input widget.

Autocompleted input widgets are also often used with a history of past options that the user has given, or to suggest possible ways the user may want to "complete" their input. The Android `AutoCompleteTextView` widget is an `EditText` with autocompletion capabilities. It uses a `ListAdapter` (which must also implement the `Filterable` interface) to find and display the list of possible suggestions to the user.

However, an `AutoCompleteTextView` has two major flaws:

◆ It's still a `TextView` and the user is not forced to select one of the suggested items, this means that its content must be validated separately.

◆ The suggestion list is displayed directly below the widget, consuming a fair amount of screen space. Combined with a soft keyboard for input, the user interface may become cluttered or almost unusable on a small screen

Both of these issues can be solved by using the `AutoCompleteTextView` class carefully and sparingly. They are brilliantly useful when you need a search box, URL input, or something similar but they are often not suitable for placing in the middle of the screen (they are best placed at the top where they have plenty of space for the suggestion list).

Pop quiz

1. When does the `onKeyDown` event in `KeyboardListener` get invoked?

   a. When a system-wide key down event is broadcast

   b. Depends on whether the system has a hardware keyboard

   c. When a hardware keyboard key is pressed

   d. When one of the hardware interface control buttons is pressed

2. When would you use a `Toast` to notify the user of a validation error?

   a. When they make a mistake (that is, check a checkbox that shouldn't be checked)

   b. After they tab off the invalid widget

   c. After receiving a validation error from an external service

3. In an IM (Instant Messaging) application, if one of the user's contacts goes offline, how do you update the `ListView` of contacts to reflect this change?

   a. Graphically disable the users icon in the `ListView` and move it to the bottom of the `ListView`

   b. Remove the user from the `ListView`

   c. Disable the users icon in the `ListView`

Building activities for results

There are times when none of the default widgets in Android will fulfill your input requirements on their own, and you need some sort of composite input structure. In these cases, you can either create a `Dialog` widget, or build a new `Activity`. `Dialog` widgets are useful when their content is kept small (two or three lines of widgets at maximum) because they visually remain on top of the current `Activity`. However, this means that they consume additional resources (since their calling `Activity` cannot be swapped out into the background), and because they have their own decorations they don't have as much available screen space to work on as an `Activity`.

In *Chapter 4, Leveraging Activities and Intents,* we discussed the notion of `Activity` classes that hand data back to their callers. This is a great technique to use when you need some additional form of validation or you want to isolate a particular input widget (or group of widgets). You can specify some result data in the `Activity.setResult` methods. Generally, an `Acitivity` would just specify a success or failure result (using the `RESULT_OK` and `RESULT_CANCELLED` constants). It's also possible to hand back data by populating an `Intent` for the purpose:

```
Intent result = new Intent();
result.putExtra("paymentDetails", paymentDetails);
setResult(RESULT_OK, result);
```

The `Intent` data will be passed into the parent `Activity` object's `onActivityResult` method when you invoke the `finish()` method, along with the result code.

Generic filtering search Activity

As discussed earlier in the chapter, there are times where you have a predefined list of objects and you want your user to select one of them. The list is too large for the user to scroll through (for example, a list of all the countries in the world), but it's also a defined list, so you don't want them to be able to select free text.

In this case, a filterable `ListView` is generally the best suited option. While the `ListView` class has filtering capabilities, it doesn't work very well (if at all) on devices without hardware keyboards. For this reason, it's wise to make use of an `EditText` widget to allow the user to filter the contents of the `ListView`.

This sort of requirement is a very common one, and so in this section we'll look at building an `Activity` that is almost entirely generic in its capability to filter and select data. This example will provide two mechanisms for displaying the data to the user. One through a `Cursor`, and another through a simple `Object` array. In both cases, the task of filtering the `ListView` is left up to the `ListAdapter` implementation, keeping the implementation relatively simple.

Time for action – creating the ListItemSelectionActivity

This is a fairly large and somewhat complex example to work through, so I'll break it into bite size chunks, each with a goal. The first thing we want is an `Acitivity` class with a nice looking layout. The layout we'll build is an `EditText` above a `ListView`, each one with an ID that can be used by the `Acitivity`.

1. Create a new project to contain your `ListItemSelectionActivity` class:
    ```
    android create project -n Selector -p Selector -k com.packtpub.
    selector -a ListItemSelectionActivity -t 3
    ```

2. Open the `res/layout/main.xml` file in an editor or IDE.

3. Remove any of the default layout code.

4. Ensure that the root element is a `LinearLayout` consuming the available screen space in the `Activity`:
    ```
    <LinearLayout
        xmlns:android="http://schemas.android.com/apk/res/android"
        android:orientation="vertical"
        android:layout_width="fill_parent"
        android:layout_height="fill_parent">"
    ```

5. Inside the root element, declare an `EditText` with an ID of `input` and an `inputType` of `textFilter` to indicate that it will filter another widget's content:
    ```
    <EditText android:id="@+id/input"
            android:inputType="textFilter"
            android:layout_width="fill_parent"
            android:layout_height="wrap_content"/>
    ```

6. After the `EditText`, we declare a `ListView` which consumes the remaining space:
    ```
    <ListView android:id="@+id/list"
            android:layout_width="fill_parent"
            android:layout_height="fill_parent"/>
    ```

7. Open the `ListItemSelectionActivity` Java source file in an editor or IDE.

8. Declare a `ListAdapter` field at the top of the class:

```
private ListAdapter adapter;
```

9. After the `ListAdapter` field, declare a `Filter` field:

```
private Filter filter;
```

10. In the `onCreate` method, make sure you are loading the `main.xml` as the content view for the `ListItemSelectionActivity`:

```
setContentView(R.layout.main);
```

11. Then fetch the `ListView` declared in the XML file for our later use:

```
ListView list = (ListView)findViewById(R.id.list);
```

12. Finally, fetch the `EditText` declared in the XML file for our later use:

```
EditText input = (EditText)findViewById(R.id.input);
```

What just happened?

You've now got a skeleton of the `ListItemSelectionActivity` class. The application will be able to run at this point, presenting you with an empty `ListView` and an `EditText`. The `ListAdapter` and `Filter` fields declared at the top of the class will be used in later stages to hold the list information, and filter what is visible on the screen.

Time for action – creating an ArrayAdapter

The `ListItemSelectionActivity` class will accept list content from two different sources. You can either specify a database query `Uri` that will be used to select two columns from an external source, or you can specify an `Object` array as extra data in the `Intent` object. For the next task, we'll write a private utility method to create an `ArrayAdapter` from the `Intent` object.

1. Open the `ListItemSelectionActivity` Java source file in your editor or IDE.

2. Declare a new utility method to create a `ListAdapter` for `Intent`:

```
private ListAdapter createArrayAdapter(Intent intent) {
```

3. Fetch an `Object` array from the extra data in `Intent`:

```
Object[] data = (Object[])intent.getSerializableExtra("data");
```

4. If the array is not `null`, and not empty, return a new `ArrayAdapter` object which will display the contents of the array in the standard list item resources defined by Android:

```
if(data != null && data.length > 0) {
return new ArrayAdapter<Object>(
    this,
    android.R.layout.simple_list_item_1,
    data);
```

5. If the array is either null or empty, throw an `IllegalArgumentException`:

```
else {
    throw new IllegalArgumentException(
            "no list data specified in Intent: "
            + intent);
}
```

What just happened?

You just wrote a very basic utility method to extract an `Object` array from an `Intent`, and return it. The method throws an `IllegalArgumentException` if the array doesn't exist, or if it's empty. This is a valid response since we will look for the array *after* looking for a database query. If we aren't given any data from outside, then this `Activity` cannot be executed. It's useless to ask a user to select an item from a blank list.

 Remember that it's intended that this `Activity` be started by another `Activity`, not directly by the user through the applications menu. For that reason, we want to give useful feedback to ourselves or other developers when the `Activity` is not used in the way it's intended.

Time for action – creating the CursorAdapter

The `CursorAdapter` is much more complex to set up than the `ArrayAdapter`. For one thing, we offer more options with the `CursorAdapter` than we did with the `ArrayAdapter`. Our `CursorAdapter` can be made to display either one or two line list items, based on whether there are one or two columns specified. While the `ArrayAdapter` includes some default filtering logic, we need to provide a little more support for the `CursorAdapter`.

1. To start with, we allow for two different column naming conventions to be used, along with some defaults. Declare a utility method to find the expected column names from the `Intent`:

```
private String getColumnName(
        final Intent intent,
        String primary,
        String secondary,
        String def) {
```

2. First, try and use the `primary` attribute name to get a column name:

```
String col = intent.getStringExtra(primary);
```

3. If the column name is `null`, try the `secondary` attribute name:

```
if(col == null) {
    col = intent.getStringExtra(secondary);
}
```

4. If the column name is still `null`, use the default value:

```
if(col == null) {
    col = def;
}
```

5. `return` the column name:

```
return col;
```

6. Now, declare another utility method that will create the actual `CursorAdapter` to be used in the `ListView`:

```
private ListAdapter createCursorAdapter(Intent intent) {
```

7. Find the name of the first column to be displayed:

```
final String line1 = getColumnName(intent, "name", "line1",
"name");
```

8. Find the name of the optional second column to be displayed:

```
String line2 = getColumnName(
        intent, "description", "line2", null);
```

9. We now have two possible paths—a single line list item, or a double line list item. These are very similar in their construction, so we declare some variables to hold those values that are different between the two paths:

```
int listItemResource;
final String[] columns;
String[] displayColumns;
int[] textIds;
```

10. If the `line2` column name has been specified, we use the following code:

```
if(line2 != null) {
```

11. We will be using a two-line list item resource:

```
listItemResource = android.R.layout.two_line_list_item;
```

12. The database query needs to select the _id column, and both columns that were specified in the `Intent`:

```
columns = new String[]{"_id", line1, line2};
```

13. However, the list items will only display the two specified columns:

```
displayColumns = new String[]{line1, line2};
```

14. The `CursorAdapter` needs to know the resource IDs of the `TextView` widgets declared in the `two_line_list_item` resource:

```
textIds = new int[]{android.R.id.text1, android.R.id.text2};
```

15. If the second column name was not specified in the `Intent`, the `ListView` should have single-line items:

```
else {
listItemResource = android.R.layout.simple_list_item_1;
```

16. We only need to request the _id column, and the single column name:

```
columns = new String[]{"_id", line1};
```

17. The items in the list should have the contents of the requested column in them:

```
displayColumns = new String[]{line1};
```

18. We don't need to tell the `CursorAdapter` which widget ID to look for in a single-line list item resource:

```
textIds = null;
```

19. After the `else` clause, we will have the required variables populated. We can run our initial database query and get the full list of data for presenting it to the user:

```
Cursor cursor = managedQuery(
        intent.getData(),
        columns,
        null,
        null,
        line1);
```

20. We can now create the `CursorAdapter` to wrap the database `Cursor` object for the `ListView`. We use the `SimpleCursorAdapter` implementation:

```
CursorAdapter cursorAdapter = new SimpleCursorAdapter(
        this,
        listItemResource,
        cursor,
        displayColumns,
        textIds);
```

21. In order for the user to filter the list, we need to give the `CursorAdapter` a `FilterQueryProvider`. Declare the `FilterQueryProvider` as an anonymous inner class:

```
cursorAdapter.setFilterQueryProvider(
        new FilterQueryProvider() {
```

22. Inside the anonymous `FilterQueryProvider`, declare the `runQuery` method which will be called each time the user types a key:

```
public Cursor runQuery(CharSequence constraint) {
```

23. We can return a `managedQuery` which simply performs an SQL `LIKE` on the first column that we are rendering in the `ListView`:

```
return managedQuery(
        intent.getData(),
        columns,
        line1 + " LIKE ?",
        new String[] {constraint.toString() + '%'},
        line1);
```

24. Finally, the `createCursorAdapter` method can return the `CursorAdapter`:

```
return cursorAdapter;
```

What just happened?

This utility method handles the creation of the `CursorAdapter` for the time when a query `Uri` is specified in our `Intent`. This structure allows filtering of very large data sets, since it's (generally) built on top of the SQL Lite database. Its performance is directly related to the structure of the database table it will query.

As a result of the potentially enormous size of a database query, the `CursorAdapter` classes don't do any filtering of the data set themselves. Instead, you are required to implement the `FilterQueryProvider` interface to create and run a new query for each change to the filter. In the preceding example, we created a `Cursor` which is exactly the same as the default `Cursor`, but we add `selection` and `selectionArgs` to the query. This `LIKE` clause will tell SQL Lite to only return rows starting with the filter that the user has typed.

Time for action – setting up the ListView

We now have implementations to create both types of ListAdapter that this Activity can filter. Now we need a utility method to figure out which one to use, and return it; and then we want to use the new utility method to set the ListAdapter on the ListView widget.

1. Declare a new method to create the desired ListAdapter object:

```
protected ListAdapter createListAdapter() {
```

2. Fetch the Intent object that was used to start the Activity:

```
Intent intent = getIntent();
```

3. If the data Uri in the Intent is not null, return a CursorAdapter for the given Intent. Otherwise, return an ArrayAdapter for the given Intent:

```
if(intent.getData() != null) {
return createCursorAdapter(intent);
else {
    return createArrayAdapter(intent);
}
```

4. In the onCreate method, after finding the two View objects from the layout, create the desired ListAdapter with the new utility method:

```
adapter = createListAdapter();
```

5. Assign the Filter field to the Filter given by the ListAdapter:

```
filter = ((Filterable)adapter).getFilter();
```

6. Set the ListAdapter on the ListView:

```
list.setAdapter(adapter);
```

What just happened?

This code now references both the created ListAdapter object and the Filter that it works with. You'll notice that if you run the application now, you'll get a **Force Close** dialog when you open it. That's because the code now requires some sort of data to populate the ListView with. While not desirable for a normal application, this is really a reusable component which could be used in a variety of situations.

Time for action – filtering the list

Although the code is all set up to display the list, and even to filter it, we haven't yet attached the `EditText` box to the `ListView`, so typing in the `EditText` will have absolutely no effect at the moment. We need to listen for changes to the `EditText` box, and request that the `ListView` be filtered based on what is typed. This will involve the `ListItemSelectionActivity` class listening for events on the `EditText` and then asking the `Filter` object to narrow the available set of items.

1. The `ListItemSelectionActivity` should be made to implement the `TextWatcher` interface:

```
public class ListItemSelectionActivity extends Activity
        implements TextWatcher
```

2. After setting the `ListAdapter` on the `ListView` in the `onCreate` method, add the `ListItemSelectionActivity` as a `TextWatcher` on the `EditText` widget:

```
input.addTextChangedListener(this);
```

3. You'll need to declare empty implementations of the `beforeTextChanged` and `onTextChanged` methods, since we're not really interested in these events:

```
public void beforeTextChanged(
        CharSequence s,
        int start,
        int count,
        int after) {
}

public void onTextChanged(
        CharSequence s,
        int start,
        int count,
        int after) {
}
```

4. Then declare the `afterTextChanged` method, which we are interested in:

```
public void afterTextChanged(Editable s) {
```

5. In the `afterTextChanged` method, we simply ask the `Filter` of the current `ListAdapter` to filter the `ListView`:

```
filter.filter(s);
```

What just happened?

The `TextWatcher` interface is used in order to track changes to a `TextView` widget. Implementations will be able to listen for any changes to the actual content of the `TextView`, regardless of the source of the change. While the `OnKeyListener` and `KeyboardListener` interfaces are mostly there to handle hardware keyboard events, the `TextWatcher` handles changes from hardware keyboards, soft keyboards, and even internal calls to `TextView.setText`.

Time for action – returning the selection

The `ListItemSelectionActivity` can now be used to display a list of possible items, and filter through them by typing in an `EditText` above the `ListView`. However, we have no way of letting the user actually select one of the options from the `ListView` in order to pass it back to our parent `Activity`. This requires nothing more than a simple implementation of the `OnItemClickListener` interface.

1. The `ListItemSelectionActivity` class now needs to implement the `OnItemClickListener` interface:

```
public class ListItemSelectionActivity extends Activity
        implements TextWatcher, OnItemClickListener {
```

2. After registering as a `TextWatcher` in the `onCreate` method, register as an `OnItemClickListener` on the `ListView`:

```
list.setOnItemClickListener(this);
```

3. Override the `onItemClick` method to listen for the user's selection:

```
public void onItemClick(
        AdapterView<?> parent,
        View clicked,
        int position,
        long id) {
```

4. Create an empty `Intent` object to pass back to our parent `Activity`:

```
Intent data = new Intent();
```

5. If the `ListAdapter` is a `CursorAdapter`, the id passed into the `onItemClick` will be the database _id column value for the selection. Add this value to the `Intent`:

```
if(adapter instanceof CursorAdapter) {
data.putExtra("selection", id);
```

6. If the `ListAdapter` is not a `CursorAdapter`, we add the actual selected `Object` to the `Intent`:

```
else {
    data.putExtra(
            "selection",
            (Serializable)parent.getItemAtPosition(position));
}
```

7. Set the result code to `RESULT_OK`, and pass the `Intent` back:

```
setResult(RESULT_OK, data);
```

8. The user has made their selection, so we're now finished with this part:

```
finish();
```

What just happened?

The `ListItemSelectionActivity` is now complete and ready for use. It offers much the same functionality as an `AutoCompleteTextView`, except that being an independent `Activity`, it offers the user a much larger list of suggestions, and the user must select an item from the `ListView` instead of being able to simply type their input data.

Using the ListItemSelectionActivity

You will need to specify what data you want the user to select from, as part of the `Intent` that starts a `ListItemSelectionActivity`. As already discussed, there are effectively two paths:

◆ Pass in an array of some sort (which is perfect for use within your own application)

◆ Give it a database query `Uri` and the column names you want displayed (which is great if you want to use it from another application)

Since the `ListItemSelectionActivity` returns its selection (and it's not much use if it doesn't), you need to start it with the `startActivityForResult` method instead of the normal `startActivity` method. If you want to pass it an array of `String` objects to select from, you could use something similar to the following intent = new Intent(this, ListItemSelectionActivity.class):

```
intent.putExtra("data", new String[] {
    "Blue",
    "Green",
    "Red",
    // more colors
});
startActivityForResult(intent, 101);
```

Given enough colors in the above `data` array, you would be presented with a `ListItemSelectionActivity` screen which could be filtered for the user's desired color. The following is a screenshot of how the resulting screen would look:

In order to receive the results back from the `ListItemSelectionActivity`, you will need to listen for the results in the `onActivityResult` method (as discussed in *Chapter 4, Leveraging Activities and Intents*). If, for example, you simply wanted to `Toast` the result of the confirmed selection, you could use the following code:

```
@Override
protected void onActivityResult(
        int requestCode,
        int resultCode,
        Intent data) {

    super.onActivityResult(requestCode, resultCode, data);

    if(requestCode == 101 && resultCode == RESULT_OK) {
        Object obj = data.getSerializableExtra("selection");
        Toast.makeText(
                this,
                String.valueOf(obj),
                Toast.LENGTH_LONG).show();
    }
}
```

Finally, how would you use a database query with the `ListItemSelectionActivity`? This is amazingly easy to show, and is probably the most exciting feature of the `ListItemSelectionActivity`. The following code snippet will let the user select one of the contacts from their phone book:

```
Intent intent = new Intent(
        this,
        ListItemSelectionActivity.class);

intent.setData(People.CONTENT_URI);
intent.putExtra("line1", People.NAME);
intent.putExtra("line2", People.NUMBER);

startActivityForResult(intent, 202);
```

Have a go hero!

The `ListItemSelectionActivity` can filter and select almost anything. Try building up a list of all the countries in the world (many such lists are available online), and then create an `Activity` which asks you to select one using a `ListItemSelectionActivity`.

Summary

How you accept input from your users, and how you validate that input plays a crucial part in the overall experience your users will have with your application. Software should help the users along and tell them what it expects at each step. This not only makes an application easier to use, but also much faster to work with.

Using the `ListItemSelectionActivity`, will often help your users trawl through large data sets, while protecting them from making a choice that they don't want to, or is invalid. It's a very commonly used type of widget and is seen in many different applications (in various forms). Android, at present, doesn't have a generic class to perform this job quite as easily.

In the next chapter, we'll start taking a look at a fairly modern form of user feedback: animation. Android has excellent support, not just for animating parts of your user interface, but also for composing complex custom animations. Animation can play a vital part in a user's enjoyment of an application. This is not only because it looks great, but also because it gives visual queues of what the application is currently doing, and what effect their actions are having.

7
Animating Widgets and Layouts

Animations are an important element in the user interface design of a modern application. However, it's also easy to overuse animations in your designs. A general guideline for animation use in a non-game application is—only animate user interactions and notifications, and keep the duration short so that it doesn't impact the user's experience negatively. For a game, more animation is generally acceptable (or even expected).

So why animate user interaction and not (for example) the background of your application? For one thing, animating the background of an application is distracting, and if you are trying to capture or present important information to the user, it's unprofessional (no matter how good it looks). Animations are also very important in regards to notifications. Movement on the screen draws attention, thus what would normally be a large pop-up dialog can be replaced by a small animating icon. A perfect example of such an icon is the "downloading" icon which is placed at the top left of the notification area of an Android device when the Android **Market** application is downloading new software or updates.

Layout animations and transitions provide useful status information to the user. When using a screen transition you tell your user what has just happened, or what is about to happen. Different transitions signify different events to your users, knowing what transition to use for each different activity will let your users know what kind of action is about to be taken. Layout animations are an important part of your user feedback, leaving them out or using the wrong one in the wrong place can leave your users irritated, or slightly confused ("change dazed"). Using the right animations will improve user experience, and can even speed up their use of the application by giving them brief cues as to what they are expected to do next.

In this chapter, there are two primary types of animation which we will be looking at—widget animations and layout animations. We'll look at the standard animation structures provided by Android, and we'll look at how to create new animation types and extend the existing ones. We'll also be looking at timing and "good practice" use of animations, and keeping users happy without slowing them down or distracting them.

Using standard Android animations

Any `View` or `ViewGroup` object in Android can have an animation attached to it. Animations are generally defined as application resources in an XML file, and Android provides a few useful defaults in the `android` package. Android also includes several `View` classes which are designed specifically to handle animations. With these classes you will find that they have layout attributes which allow you to set a particular types of animations that will be used upon certain actions. However, animations are generally not specified in a layout file, instead they rely on the Java code to set and start `Animation` objects.

The main reason why animations are not normally specified as part of the layout XML is very simple—when should they run? Many animations can be used as a response to user input, letting the user know what's happening. Most animations will in some way or the other be triggered by a user's action (unless they are there to serve as a notification). Thus you will need to specify both—which animation to run on a widget, and the signal about when the animation should run. The default Android animations will begin animating immediately, while other animation structures may have a scheduled delay before they start.

Time for action – animating a news feed

We'll start off by creating a selector `Activity` and a simple `NewsFeedActivity`. In a news feed, we'll animate the latest headlines "in and out" using a timer. For this example we'll be working with some of the default animations provided by Android and driving the process mainly through the layout resources.

1. Create a new project to contain the animation examples from this chapter, with a main `Activity` named `AnimationSelectionActivity`:

   ```
   android create project -n AnimationExamples -p AnimationExamples
   -k com.packtpub.animations -a AnimationSelector -t 3
   ```

2. Open the `res/layout/main.xml` layout file in an editor or IDE.

3. Clear out the default content of the layout resource.

4. Declare a vertical `LinearLayout` consuming all the available screen space:

```
<LinearLayout
    xmlns:android="http://schemas.android.com/apk/res/android"
    android:orientation="vertical"
    android:layout_width="fill_parent"
    android:layout_height="fill_parent">
```

5. Create a `Button` labeled `News Feed` to link to the first animation example:

```
<Button android:id="@+id/news_feed"
        android:layout_width="fill_parent"
        android:layout_height="wrap_content"
        android:layout_marginBottom="10dip"
        android:text="News Feed"/>
```

6. Create a new layout resource file named `news.xml`.

7. Declare a vertical `LinearLayout` containing all of the available screen space:

```
<LinearLayout
    xmlns:android="http://schemas.android.com/apk/res/android"
    android:orientation="vertical"
    android:layout_width="fill_parent"
    android:layout_height="fill_parent">"
```

8. Add a `TextSwitcher` object to the `LinearLayout`, specifying the "in" and "out" animations to the default "slide" animations:

```
<TextSwitcher
        android:id="@+id/news_feed"
        android:inAnimation="@android:anim/slide_in_left"
        android:outAnimation="@android:anim/slide_out_right"
        android:layout_width="fill_parent"
        android:layout_height="wrap_content"
        android:text=""/>
```

9. Open the `res/values/strings.xml` file in an editor or IDE.

10. Declare a string-array named `headlines` with elements for some mock news headlines:

```
<string-array name="headlines">
    <item>Pwnies found to inhabit Mars</item>
    <item>Geeks invent \"atoms\"</item>
    <item>Politician found not lying!</item>
    <!-- add some more items here if you like -->
</string-array>
```

11. In the generated root package, declare a new Java source file named `NewsFeedActivity.java`.

12. Register the `NewsFeedActivity` class in your `AndroidManifest.xml` file:

```
<activity android:name=".NewsFeedActivity" android:label="News
Feed" />
```

13. The new class should extend the `Activity` class and implement `Runnable`:

```
public class NewsFeedActivity
        extends Activity implements Runnable {
```

14. Declare a `Handler` to be used as a timing structure for changing the headlines:

```
private final Handler handler = new Handler();
```

15. We need a reference to the `TextSwitcher` object:

```
private TextSwitcher newsFeed;
```

16. Declare a string-array to hold the mock headlines you added to the `strings.xml` file:

```
private String[] headlines;
```

17. You'll also need to keep track of which headline is currently being displayed:

```
private int headlineIndex;
```

18. Override the `onCreate` method:

```
protected void onCreate(final Bundle savedInstanceState) {
```

19. Invoke the `onCreate` method of `Activity`:

```
super.onCreate(savedInstanceState);
```

20. Set the content view to the `news` layout resource:

```
setContentView(R.layout.news);
```

21. Store a reference to the headline string-array from the `strings.xml` application resource file:

```
headlines = getResources().getStringArray(R.array.headlines);
```

22. Find the `TextSwitcher` widget and assign it to the field declared earlier:

```
newsFeed = (TextSwitcher)findViewById(R.id.news_feed);
```

23. Set the `ViewFactory` of the `TextSwitcher` to a new anonymous class that will create `TextView` objects when asked:

```
newsFeed.setFactory(new ViewFactory() {
    public View makeView() {
        return new TextView(NewsFeedActivity.this);
    }
});
```

24. Override the `onStart` method:

```
protected void onStart() {
```

25. Invoke the `onStart` method of the `Activity` class:

```
super.onStart();
```

26. Reset the `headlineIndex` so that we start from the first headline:

```
headlineIndex = 0;
```

27. Post the `NewsFeedActivity` as a delayed action using the `Handler`:

```
handler.postDelayed(this, 3000);
```

28. Override the `onStop` method:

```
protected void onStop() {
```

29. Invoke the `onStop` method of the `Activity` class:

```
super.onStop();
```

30. Remove any pending calls to the `NewsFeedActivity`:

```
handler.removeCallbacks(this);
```

31. Implement the `run` method which we'll use to swap to the next headline:

```
public void run() {
```

32. Open a `try` block to swap the headline inside.

33. Use the `TextSwitcher.setText` method to swap to the next headline:

```
newsFeed.setText(headlines[headlineIndex++]);
```

34. If the `headlineIndex` is past the total number of headlines, reset the `headlineIndex` to zero:

```
if(headlineIndex >= headlines.length) {
    headlineIndex = 0;
}
```

35. Close the `try` block, and add a `finally` block. In the `finally` block, post the `NewsFeedActivity` back onto the `Handler` queue:

```
finally {
    handler.postDelayed(this, 3000);
}
```

36. Open the auto generated `AnimationSelector` Java source in an editor or IDE.

37. The `AnimationSelector` class needs to implement `OnClickListener`:

```
public class AnimationSelector
            extends Activity implements OnClickListener {
```

38. In the `onCreate` method, ensure that the content view is set to the `main` layout resource created earlier:

```
setContentView(R.layout.main);
```

39. Find the declared `Button` and set its `OnClickListener` to `this`:

```
((Button)findViewById(R.id.news_feed)).
        setOnClickListener(this);
```

40. Declare the `onClick` method:

```
public void onClick(final View view) {
```

41. Use a switch to determine which `View` was clicked:

```
switch(view.getId()) {
```

42. If it's the news feed `Button`, then use the following `case`:

```
case R.id.news_feed:
```

43. Start the `NewsFeedActivity` using a new `Intent`:

```
startActivity(new Intent(this, NewsFeedActivity.class));
```

44. Break from the `switch` statement, thus finishing the `onClick` method.

What just happened?

The `TextSwitcher` is an example of an animation utility `View`. In this case it's the perfect structure to swap between the news headlines, displaying one headline at a time and animating a transition between each of the texts. The `TextSwitcher` object creates two `TextView` objects (using the anonymous `ViewFactory` class). When you use the `setText` method, the `TextSwitcher` changes the text of the "off screen" `TextView` and animates a transition between the "on screen" `TextView` and the "off screen" `TextView` (with the new text content displayed).

The `TextSwitcher` class requires that you specify two animation resources for it to work with, in order to create its transition effect:

- ◆ Animate text onto the screen
- ◆ Animate text off the screen

In the previous case, we made use of the default `slide_in_left` and `slide_out_right` animations. Both of these are examples of translation-based animations due to the fact that they actually alter the "on screen" position of the `TextView` objects in order to create their effect.

Using flipper and switcher widgets

The first example of this chapter made use of the `TextSwitcher` class, an animating `View` class in the standard Android API. There are several other animation utility classes, some of which you may have encountered before (such as `ImageSwitcher`). Both `TextSwitcher` and `ImageSwitcher` are related classes, and both inherit from the more generic `ViewSwitcher` class.

The `ViewSwitcher` class is a generic animation tool, and defines the `ViewFactory` interface that we implemented anonymously in the previous example. A `ViewSwitcher` is a `ViewGroup` with only two child `View` objects. One is displayed on the screen, while the other is hidden. The `getNext` utility method allows you to find out which is the "off screen" `View` object.

While you generally use a `ViewFactory` to populate a `ViewSwitcher`, you have the option to populate it manually. You could have populated the `TextSwitcher` in the example by using the `addView` method that is inherited from `ViewGroup`.

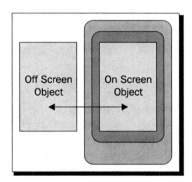

Using the ImageSwitcher and TextSwitcher implementations

The `ImageSwitcher` and `TextSwitcher` classes are specialized implementations of the `ViewSwitcher` that understand the type of `View` objects they contain. When you invoke the `setText` method of the `TextSwitcher` object, it's much like invoking the following code snippet on a `ViewSwitcher` containing two `TextView` children:

```
((TextView)switcher.getNext()).setText("Next text to display");
switcher.showNext();
```

`TextSwitcher` can be used to display content such as (as in the example) a news feed, or as with the Android notification area, to display text content that doesn't fit into a single line. Displaying multiple lines in a `TextSwitcher` is particularly effective when the animation runs the text upwards, causing the text to appear to scroll upwards behind the `TextSwitcher` object.

An `ImageSwitcher` is most commonly used in a gallery, slide show, or similar structure. You could also use an `ImageSwitcher` to allow the user to select from a small list of images, for example a short list of login avatars.

Have a go hero – populating the TextSwitcher

As an alternative to populating the `TextSwitcher` with a `ViewFactory` in the news feed example, try populating it in the XML layout resource. Remember that it requires exactly two `TextView` child widgets. If you get this right, try giving each of the two `TextView` objects different font colors and styles.

Animating layout widgets

Using the animation utility widgets such as `TextSwitcher` and `ImageSwitcher` can allow you to display much more information over time than you could fit on the screen at a time. `ViewGroup` objects can also be animated without any serious modification through the `LayoutAnimationController` class. However, in this case, animation needs to be added in your Java code.

A `LayoutAnimationController` is best used to create "entry" or "exit" effects on a `ViewGroup` as it appears or just before it disappears off the screen. The controller simply starts a specified animation on each of the `View` children of a specified `ViewGroup`. However, it doesn't have to do it all at the same time, or in a sequential order. You can easily configure a `LayoutAnimationController` to leave a slight delay between the starting of an animation on each child widget, creating a staggered effect.

If applied correctly to a `LinearLayout`, you could achieve a result similar to the one illustrated in the following diagram:

Time for action – animating a GridView

The `GridView` class has its own `LayoutAnimationController` specifically designed to animate it in terms of rows and columns, allowing more complex effects than can be achieved with a standard `LayoutAnimationController`. For this next part of the "animations" example we're going to build a lovely color selector out of a `GridView`. When the selector first appears on the screen, each color swatch will fade in, starting in the top left corner and ending on the bottom right corner.

1. Start by declaring a new Java source file in the root package of your project named `ColorAdapter.java`, which will generate the color swatches for the `GridView`.

2. The `ColorAdapter` needs to extend `BaseAdapter` to take care of the boiler plate `Adapter` requirements:

   ```
   public class ColorAdapter extends BaseAdapter {
   ```

3. The `ColorAdapter` will be created with a specified number of rows and columns, the same numbers which will be displayed on the `GridView`:

   ```
   private final int rows;
   private final int cols;

   public ColorAdapter(int rows, int cols) {
       this.rows = rows;
       this.cols = cols;
   }
   ```

4. The number of items that the `ColorAdapter` will provide is the number of rows multiplied by the number of columns:

   ```
   public int getCount()
       return rows * cols;
   }
   ```

5. The ID of a color is the position or index at which it's found:

```
public long getItemId(int pos) {
    return pos;
}
```

6. We use a utility method to compose the color from an index in the "list." For this function we make use of the HSVtoRGB method in the Android Color class:

```
private int getColor(int pos) {
    float h = (float)pos / (float)getCount();
    return Color.HSVToColor(new float[]{h * 360f, 1f, 1f});
}
```

7. The item at an index in the Adapter model is returned as it's color value:

```
public Object getItem(int pos) {
    return getColor(pos);
}
```

8. To create the color swatch View objects, we implement the getView method of Adapter as usual:

```
public View getView(int pos, View reuse, ViewGroup parent) {
```

9. The View we return is going to be an ImageView object, so we either re-use the one given by the parent widget, or create a new one:

```
ImageView view = reuse instanceof ImageView
        ? (ImageView)reuse
        : new ImageView(parent.getContext());
```

10. We make use of the ColorDrawable class to fill the ImageView with the color specified by our getColor utility method:

```
view.setImageDrawable(new ColorDrawable(getColor(pos)));
```

11. The ImageView needs to have its android.widget.AbsListView.LayoutParams set, and then it can be returned to the GridView for display:

```
view.setLayoutParams(new LayoutParams(16, 16));
return view;
```

12. Create a new XML layout resource file named res/layout/colors.xml to hold the declaration of the GridView that will act as the color selector.

13. The contents of the colors.xml layout file are just a single GridView widget:

```
<GridView
    xmlns:android="http://schemas.android.com/apk/res/android"
    android:id="@+id/colors"
```

```
android:verticalSpacing="5dip"
android:horizontalSpacing="5dip"
android:stretchMode="columnWidth"
android:gravity="center"
android:layout_width="fill_parent"
android:layout_height="fill_parent" />
```

14. Define another new Java source file in the root package of your `AnimationExamples` project. Name this one `ColorSelectorActivity.java`.

15. The new class declaration should extend `Activity`:

```
public class ColorSelectorActivity extends Activity {
```

16. Override the `onCreate` method as normal, and set the content view to the `colors` XML layout resource you just wrote:

```
protected void onCreate(Bundle savedInstanceState) {
    super.onCreate(savedInstanceState);
    setContentView(R.layout.colors);
```

17. Now you can load the default `Android` "fade in" animation using the handy `AnimationUtils` class from the `android.view.animation` package:

```
Animation animation = AnimationUtils.loadAnimation(
        this, android.R.anim.fade_in);
```

18. In order to animate the `GridView` correctly, you need to instantiate a new `GridLayoutAnimationController` object, passing it the "fade in" animation:

```
GridLayoutAnimationController animationController =
        new GridLayoutAnimationController(
        animation, 0.2f, 0.2f);
```

19. Now look for the `GridView` which you have declared in the `colors.xml` file:

```
GridView view = (GridView)findViewById(R.id.colors);
```

20. Set the number of columns in the `GridView` to `10` (note that we didn't do this in the XML layout resource as you normally would):

```
view.setNumColumns(10);
```

21. When you set the adapter of the `GridView` to a `ColorAdapter`, you also need to know the number of columns, and the easiest way to do this is to keep both in Java:

```
view.setAdapter(new ColorAdapter(10, 10));
```

22. The `view` object is now ready for the `GridLayoutAnimationController`:

```
view.setLayoutAnimation(animationController);
```

23. In order to start the animation when the screen is displayed, we override the onStart method. It is in here that we look up the GridView again and start the animation:

```
protected void onStart() {
    super.onStart();
    ((GridView)findViewById(R.id.colors)).
            getLayoutAnimation().start();
}
```

24. In order to integrate this new example with the other animation examples, you'll need to open the res/layout/main.xml file in an editor or IDE.

25. Add a new Button to the end of the LinearLayout, the one we'll use to start the color selection example:

```
<Button android:id="@+id/colors"
        android:layout_width="fill_parent"
        android:layout_height="wrap_content"
        android:layout_marginBottom="10dip"
        android:text="Color Selector" />
```

26. Open the AnimationSelector source file in your editor or IDE.

27. After setting the OnClickListener of the news_feed Button, find and set the OnClickListener of the new colors Button in the same way:

```
((Button)findViewById(R.id.colors)).setOnClickListener(this);
```

28. In the onClick method, after the switch case for the news_feed Button, add another switch case for the new colors Button, and start the ColorSelectorActivity:

```
case R.id.colors:
    startActivity(new Intent(this, ColorSelectorActivity.class));
    break;
```

29. Open the AndroidManifest.xml file in your editor or IDE.

30. At the bottom of the <application> section, register the new ColorSelectorActivity:

```
<activity android:name=".ColorSelectorActivity"
          android:label="Your Favorite Color" />
```

What just happened?

The new example makes use of the GridLayoutAnimationController to start each "fade in" animation a fraction of a second after the previous one started. This creates a fluid animation effect of the color swatches appearing from the top-left to the bottom-right of the screen.

When you instantiate a `GridLayoutAnimationController`, it requires you to provide the animation and two parameters which indicate the amount of time between starting animations for the next row, or the next column. The delay given is not specified in a "direct" time format, but instead by how long the given animation takes to complete. In our case, if the animation took one second to complete, the delay between each animation starting would be 200 milliseconds, since the delay is specified as `0.2`.

The fact that we animate the swatches just as this `Activity` becomes visible, effectively makes this a transition animation, introducing the user to this new screen. For these types of animations, it's imperative to take as little time as possible while still giving a pleasing introduction. When you run the new example you should get an animation similar to the ones illustrated in the following images:

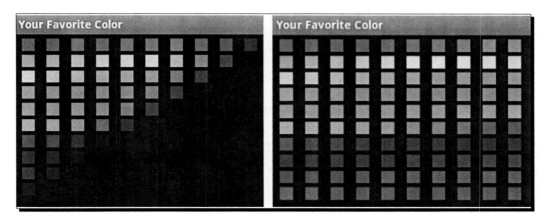

Creating Custom Animations

So far we've explored using Android's stock animations with the normal widgets, but what about applying a custom animation to a widget that isn't built for animations? Android includes support for four basic animation types that can be applied to `View` objects:

- Translate/Move
- Rotate
- Scale
- Alpha/Transparency

These different animation structures can be applied by themselves, or merged together in an animation set where any combination of the three can be run at the same time. By creating an animation with a delay time before it starts, you can create complex animations by having simple sets of animations follow each other.

Like so many things in Android, the easiest way to create your own custom animations is to define it in a resource XML file. The elements in the animation format used by Android correspond directly to the classes in the `android.animation.view` package. An animation file can also reference animations in other animation resources, which makes it much easier to compose complex animations and re-use simple animations.

Time for action – writing a custom animation

Writing a custom animation is very simple, but not entirely intuitive. For this section you'll define a custom animation which will increase the size of its animated widget by a factor of five, while at the same time fading it until its entirely transparent.

1. Create a new XML resource file named `res/anim/vanish.xml` and open it in an editor or IDE.

2. The root element of the animation file will be an animation `set` element:

   ```
   <set xmlns:android="http://schemas.android.com/apk/res/android">
   ```

3. In the `<set>` element, declare an element to define the scale up animation:

   ```
   <scale />
   ```

4. The duration of the scale up animation needs to be set as `300` milliseconds:

   ```
   android:duration="300"
   ```

5. The animation starts to scale from the original size:

   ```
   android:fromXScale="1.0"
   android:fromYScale="1.0"
   ```

6. The scale animation needs to increase the size by a factor of `5.0`:

   ```
   android:toXScale="5.0"
   android:toYScale="5.0"
   ```

7. We want the scale to expand from the center of the widget:

   ```
   android:pivotX="50%"
   android:pivotY="50%"
   ```

8. The last part of the `<scale>` element defines the acceleration curve of the animation. Here we want the scale up to decelerate as it runs:

   ```
   android:interpolator="@android:anim/decelerate_interpolator"
   ```

9. Next, define a new element to handle the fade out part of the animation:

   ```
   <alpha />
   ```

10. The duration of the fade out animation is also `300` milliseconds:

```
android:duration="300"
```

11. We start with no transparency:

```
android:fromAlpha="1.0"
```

12. The fade out ends with a completely invisible widget:

```
android:toAlpha="0.0"
```

13. The fade out should accelerate as it runs, so we use an accelerate interpolator:

```
android:interpolator="@android:anim/accelerate_interpolator"
```

What just happened?

This is a relatively simple animation set, but its effect is visually pleasing. Keeping the animation at `300` milliseconds is quick enough to not interfere with the user's interaction, but just long enough to be seen in full by the user.

When defining animations in an animation `<set>` element, each non-set sub animation needs to have its `duration` defined. The `<set>` element has no concept of its own `duration`. However, you can define a single `interpolator` for the entire set to share.

The `<scale>` animation will by default, scale the widget using the top-left corner as the "pivot" point, causing the widget to grow to the right and downward, but not left and upward. This causes a lopsided animation which is not very appealing. In the preceding example, the scale animation runs with the pivot at the center of the animated widget.

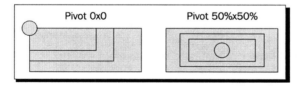

Time for action – making a Button vanish

So how can we apply the nice shiny animation to a `Button` object? The `Button` object doesn't have an animation attribute, and so you can't just reference it from the layout resource file. What we want, is the animation to run when the `Button` widget is clicked.

1. Create a new layout resource file named `res/layout/vanish.xml` and open in an editor or IDE.

2. At the root of the new layout, declare a `RelativeLayout` element:

```
<RelativeLayout
    xmlns:android="http://schemas.android.com/apk/res/android"
    android:layout_width="fill_parent"
    android:layout_height="fill_parent">
```

3. The `Button` needs to be nice and large, and centered on the screen. For this we give it some inner padding:

```
<Button android:id="@+id/vanish"
        android:paddingTop="20dip"
        android:paddingBottom="20dip"
        android:paddingLeft="60dip"
        android:paddingRight="60dip"
        android:layout_centerInParent="true"
        android:layout_width="wrap_content"
        android:layout_height="wrap_content"
        android:text="Vanish" />
```

4. Create a new Java source file in the root package of the `AnimationExamples` project named `VanishingButtonActivity.java`.

5. The new class needs to extend `Activity` and implement the `OnClickListener` interface:

```
public class VanishingButtonActivity extends Activity
        implements OnClickListener {
```

6. Override the `onCreate` method and invoke the `Activity.onCreate` method to perform the required Android setup:

```
protected void onCreate(Bundle savedInstanceState) {
    super.onCreate(savedInstanceState);
```

7. Set the content view to the new `vanish` layout resource:

```
setContentView(R.layout.vanish);
```

8. Find the `Button` widget declared in the XML layout resource and set its `OnClickListener`:

```
Button button = (Button)findViewById(R.id.vanish);
button.setOnClickListener(this);
```

9. Implement the `onClick` method of `OnClickListener`:

```
public void onClick(View clicked) {
```

10. Load the `Animation` from the resource file:

```
Animation vanish = AnimationUtils.loadAnimation(
        this, R.anim.vanish);
```

11. Start the `Animation` on the `Button` object:

```
findViewById(R.id.vanish).startAnimation(vanish);
```

12. Open the `AndroidManifest.xml` file in an editor or IDE.

13. Declare the `VanishingButtonActivity` at the end of the `<application>` section with a display label:

```
<activity android:name=".VanishingButtonActivity"
        android:label="Vanishing Button" />
```

14. Open the `res/layout/main.xml` layout resource in your editor or IDE.

15. Add a new `Button` to the end of `LinearLayout` to activate the `VanishingButtonActivity`:

```
<Button android:id="@+id/vanish"
        android:layout_width="fill_parent"
        android:layout_height="wrap_content"
        android:layout_marginBottom="10dip"
        android:text="Vanishing Button" />
```

16. Open the `AnimationSelector` Java source file in your editor or IDE.

17. At the end of the `onCreate` method, fetch the new `vanish` `Button` from the layout and set its `OnClickListener`:

```
((Button)findViewById(R.id.vanish)).setOnClickListener(this);
```

18. In the `onClick` method, add a new switch case to start the `VanishingButtonActivity`:

```
case R.id.vanish:
    startActivity(new Intent(
        this, VanishingButtonActivity.class));
    break;
```

What just happened?

The addition of the preceding example will display a single `Button` in the middle of the screen. When clicked, the `Button` will be mutated by the `vanish` animation for `300` milliseconds. When it is complete, the animation won't have any effect on the `Button` anymore. This is an important characteristic of animations—when they are complete, the widget they have animated is returned to its original state.

It's also important to note that it's not the widget itself that is modified by an animation, but rather the state of the `Canvas` it's painted on. This is much the same concept as modifying the state of `Graphics` or `Graphics2D` object in Java AWT, or Swing before a widget uses the `Graphics` object to paint itself.

In the following images you can see the effect that animation has on the `Button` when it's clicked. The `Button` is actually re-painted for each frame in the animation, and remains entirely active during that time.

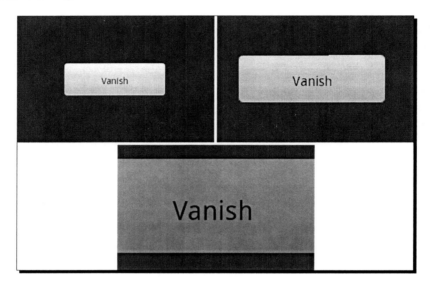

Summary

In this chapter, we explored the various methods by which you can apply animations to various parts of your user interface. We explored how some widgets are designed to animate themselves. Layouts can be animated for transitions in and out of an `Activity`.

Several simple animations are available by default in the Android resource, but ultimately creating your own animations and applying them to your user interface manually creates, by far, the most visually appealing and user-friendly experience for your users.

Many applications on a mobile device need to present a large amount of information on the screen, and present it in such a way that it can be easily absorbed. In the next chapter, we'll explore user interface design with regards to presenting information to the user in a friendly and useful manner. This allows users to access the information that they need as quickly as possible, in a swift and easy manner, while not limiting the information they have access to.

8
Designing Content-centric Activities

When you have a lot of data to display to the user, and you need a content presentation Activity*. Generally, such types of Activities turn out to be content-centric. The main purpose of a content-centric* Activity *is to give the user as much of the information as possible while not overwhelming them. This is a common requirement of applications that perform some sort of search, or present any type of specialized information.*

Shopping and related e-commerce applications are an ideal example of a content-centric application. Much of the effort in the design is dedicated to displaying information about the products on sale. If the users can't find the information about a product they are looking for, they will look somewhere else. For this reason, the product display must not only be attractive and easy to use, but also provide as much information as possible, without being cryptic or cluttered.

Another example of a content-centric layout is a user's profile page in a social-networking application. People generally have a lot to say about themselves, and if they don't, other people will often say a lot about them. These applications not only have a lot of information to present to the user, but the information varies widely in terms of quality and relevance. Just because one user thinks something is important, doesn't mean the next person will. In cases like these, it's also very important to have an interface that can be customized to the user's preferences (often just by re-organizing the order in which information is displayed), and is also able to draw the user's attention to new information or areas they may find interesting.

A great example of a good way to draw a user's attention is seen in a chat application. If the user has scrolled up, he/she is probably reading something that was said a few minutes ago. If a new message arrives, it's very rude to just scroll them to the new message, since they may well still be reading it. An audio tone to notify them of a new message is a common option, but will also draw others' attention to the user (this is a mobile device after all). The best option is a small animated icon at the bottom of the screen, possibly color-coded to tell the user the relevance of the message (if that is available). Such an icon could also be an interactive element, allowing the user to touch it in order to automatically scroll to the most recently posted message. This type of thinking is important when designing any application, but when building a content-centric `Activity,` putting some extra thought into your design is even more critical.

In this chapter, we'll be exploring the different aspects to consider when displaying content to the user, as well as different ways in which content screens can be developed. Specifically, we'll be exploring:

♦ Thought process when designing content displays on Android

♦ How users use and view content screens

♦ Using the `WebView` class to display content

♦ Building native layouts for displaying content

♦ Formatting and styling text in Android

♦ Drawing attention to specific areas of the screen

Considering design options when displaying content on an Android device

A content-centric `Activity` bears a strong resemblance to a web page, but has some key design considerations that people don't have in mind when creating a web page. For example, a touchscreen device generally doesn't have a software pointer, and so doesn't have any concept of a "roll over". However, many web pages are built using cursor roll over to drive everything from link highlighting to menus.

When designing a content-centric `Activity,` you'll want to consider carefully the aesthetics of your design. The screen should avoid clutter since many elements may be interactive, presenting the user with additional information when touched. At the same time, you should attempt to minimize the need to scroll, especially horizontal scrolling. The need to keep information concise is often the motivator to make more of the elements interactive. As mentioned in previous chapters, it's a good idea to consider using icons instead of text where you can, and to organize the information in order of importance to the user.

Also bear in mind that screen-sizes change. Some devices have a large number of pixels (such as the various Android Tablets), while others have tiny 3.5 inch screens. For this reason it's important to consider that while some people will be able to see all of the presented information on a single screen, others will be presented with three or four screens worth of content for the same amount of information.

A web page is a great way to quickly and easily put together a content-centric layout when working on an Android application. It has the advantage of having great HTML and CSS support from WebKit, and easy integration with the rest of your application. It can also be handled by an existing web-designer, or even just display a web page if your application is connected to a web-based system.

A web page is however constrained (to some degree) to the layout structures dictated in HTML and CSS. While these are extremely flexible at one level, HTML and CSS layout development can also be a tedious and frustrating process even when only targeting a single rendering engine (in Android's case: WebKit), if you are not used to building web-based systems. When it comes to animations and similar structures, you are further constrained by the performance of the HTML rendering engine, whether using JavaScript or CSS3 animations.

Considering user behavior

As with any type of user interface, it's important to understand your user behavior and how they will interact with the screens you provide them with. In the context of large amount of content information, it's important to understand both what information is important, and how users will read and absorb that information.

While you may want to draw attention to a selected piece of information (such as price), running a looping animation to change the color of that element will distract the user from the other information on the screen. However, simply changing the font, placing the data in a box, or changing the text color can also have the desired effect. It's also important to consider how a user will interact with the screen. On a touchscreen device, users can and will touch almost every part of the screen. They'll also drag items that look movable, and use scroll gestures if the content appears to run over the screen length.

Most people scan information in the same way. When a user is presented with a screen for the first time, or with lots of information on it, their minds approach reading the information in more-or-less the same way. The following are illustrations of the various movement patterns a user's eyes will follow when scanning for important information on the screen.

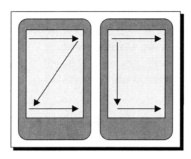

You'll generally want to make sure that important information is in the areas where one arrow meets another. The most important area is the corner in which your user normally starts reading. For most Western users, this is the top-left corner of the screen, while Asian and Arab users will often start at the top-right.

> When designing a content screen, consider making the information in these areas stand out a little more than normal. This will create a "linger" time where the users' eyes will generally focus on that area a little longer than normal. This is why we normally put a logo on the top-left of a web page.

Drawing user attention

Almost always, some information is more important than other information. You want your user to be able to pick-out the important information as quickly as possible, and get on with what they are doing. Once a person is familiar with your application, they may well stop reading the fine print altogether. This is a good thing, you're helping your users make better use of your application by letting them get on with their lives.

When you need to draw attention to specific information, such as a product's name or price, it's a good idea to make use of the extensive options provided by the `TextView` class. Simply changing an item's color can make it stand out for the user. If you need to go further, consider adding a shadow, or placing the content in a "highlight box". As we've already discussed in *Chapter 7, Animating Widgets and Layouts*, animations can also be used to draw attention to specific areas of the user interface. A simple "blink" animation (consisting of a fade-out followed by a fade-in animation) can be used to draw the users' attention to a change.

A more specific example: money

If you are selling something to your user, and allowing them to choose between different shipping methods and packaging options, the total price will change based on their selections. Make sure that the total amount stands out by rendering it in a bold font. When the price is updated, cycle through a series of "intermediate" prices so that the total is graphically "counted up" or "counted down" to its new value.

Think carefully about the widgets that you'll want to make use of in your user interface. Instead of using the normal `TextView`, you may well want to place a piece of what would normally be a single field in a `TextSwitcher` (or something similar) to allow you to animate a single word or value.

Displaying content with the WebView class

The `WebView` class (in the `android.webkit` package) is often a logical choice for content-centric designs and holds some very serious advantages over building the user interface and a normal Android XML layout resource. The `WebView` class offers you a single point at which you can place all of the content for a screen, and it handles all of its own history and scrolling, making your code very simple to write.

When displaying content that requires complex layout and/or lots of text content (which may require markup), the `WebView` class is a highly favorable option. Having built-in support for HTML and CSS mark up, it reduces the number of widgets that you'll need on the screen. Given that Android makes use of Web-Kit as a rendering engine, you also have many CSS3 structures available (such as CSS animations). Although the `WebView` is generally used for browser like networked applications where hyperlinks are very important, you can just as easily supply it with local content containing no links. You can also intercept link requests to allow navigation to other parts of your application.

Generally when working with a `WebView` structure, you'll need some method by which you can generate the content that you will be displaying. In contrast to building the user interface in a layout resource, where you can simply ID the various `View` objects that you need to inject dynamic content into. That said, a full template engine is often much easier to work with than a hybrid of XML layout and Java code, although the ease of implementation is strongly dependant on both the skills available to you and the type of information you need to display on the screen.

Using a WebView object

To work a bit with the `WebView` and give a more specific example on how it can be used to present large amounts of content, we'll be building an `Activity` to display a food recipe on the screen. For this example we'll be hard coding the actual recipe and the layout code to generate the HTML. In practice, you would want to make use of a template engine such as Velocity/FreeMarker or XSLT to generate the HTML code.

Time for action – creating a recipe viewer application

You'll notice that the following example doesn't use an XML layout resource, but rather creates the entire `Activity` in Java. In this example we use a `Recipe` object to generate HTML code into a `StringBuilder` for display. It's a simple but effective implementation. However, it requires that the Java code be modified if a change to the look and feel of the recipe is required.

1. Create a new project to contain the recipe reader application:

```
android create project -n RecipeViewer -p RecipeViewer -k com.
packtpub.viewrecipe -a ViewRecipeActivity -t 3
```

2. Create a new `Ingredient.java` source file in the root package of the new application to hold information for a single required ingredient, and open this new file in your editor or IDE.

3. Declare fields for the `name`, `amount`, and `unit` required for a recipe:

```
private final String name;
private final double amount;
private final String unit;
```

4. Create a constructor to take the parameters and assign them to the fields:

```
public Ingredient(
        String name,
        double amount,
        String unit) {
    this.name = name;
    this.amount = amount;
    this.unit = unit;
}
```

5. Create a getter method for each of fields:

```
public double getAmount() {
    return amount;
}

// . . .
```

6. In the root package of the project, create a new source file named `Recipe.java` to contain a single recipe, and open it in your editor or IDE.

7. Declare a field for the name of the `Recipe` object:

```
private final String name;
```

8. Declare another field to contain the list of ingredients required for this `Recipe`. We store these as an array of `Ingredient` objects:

```
private final Ingredient[] ingredients;
```

9. Then declare an array of `String` objects that will contain the list of instructions that need to be followed for the `Recipe`:

```
private final String[] instructions;
```

10. Create a constructor to accept the field data and assign it for storage:

```
public Recipe(
        String name,
        Ingredient[] ingredients,
        String[] instructions) {
    this.name = name;
    this.ingredients = ingredients;
    this.instructions = instructions;
}
```

11. Create a getter method for each of the three fields:

```
public Ingredient[] getIngredients() {
    return ingredients;
}

// . . .
```

12. In this example the `Recipe` class is responsible for generating the HTML. Declare a new method named `toHtml`:

```
public String toHtml() {
```

13. Create a `DecimalFormat` object to handle the formatting of the volumes:

```
DecimalFormat format = new DecimalFormat("0.##");
```

14. Create a new `StringBuilder` object to build the HTML into:

```
StringBuilder s = new StringBuilder();
```

15. Append the HTML headers:

```
s.append("<html>").append("<body>");
```

16. Append a first-level header element with the name of the recipe:

```
s.append("<h1>").append(getName()).append("</h1>");
```

17. Append a second-level header element to open the `ingredients` section:

```
s.append("<h2>You will need:</h2>");
```

18. Open an unordered list to list the ingredients required for the recipe:

```
s.append("<ul class=\"ingredients\">");
```

19. For each `Ingredient` object open a list item for the new ingredient:

```
for(Ingredient i : getIngredients()) {
    s.append("<li>");
```

20. Append the amount of the ingredient to the `StringBuilder` after formatting it with the `DecimalFormat` declared:

```
s.append(format.format(i.getAmount()));
```

21. Then append the measurement unit for the ingredient:

```
s.append(i.getUnit());
```

22. Now append the name of the ingredient to the `StringBuilder`, and close the `ingredient` list item:

```
s.append(" - ").append(i.getName());
s.append("</li>");
```

23. After closing the for loop, close the unordered list:

```
s.append("</ul>");
```

24. Create a second-lever header opening the `Instructions` section of the recipe:

```
s.append("<h2>Instructions:</h2>");
```

25. Open another unordered list to render the recipe instructions into:

```
s.append("<ul class=\"instructions\">");
```

26. Use a for-each loop over the array of instructions to render them into the unordered list structure in the `StringBuilder`:

```
for(String i : getInstructions()) {
    s.append("<li>").append(i).append("</li>");
}
```

27. Close the unordered list, and HTML headers, returning the `String` contents of the `StringBuilder` object:

```
s.append("</ul>");
s.append("</body>").append("</html>");
return s.toString();
```

28. Open the `ViewRecipeActivity` Java source code in your editor or IDE.

29. In the `onCreate` method, directly after invoking `super.onCreate`, create a new `WebView` object passing `this` to it as its `Context`:

```
WebView view = new WebView(this);
```

30. Set the `WebView` `LayoutParams` to take up all available screen space, since the `WebView` (much like a `ListView`) has built-in scrolling capabilities:

```
view.setLayoutParams(new LayoutParams(
        LayoutParams.FILL_PARENT,
        LayoutParams.FILL_PARENT));
```

31. Create a `Recipe` object to display in the `WebView`, the full recipe is at the end of this example section:

```
Recipe recipe = new Recipe(
        "Microwave Fudge",
        // . . .
```

32. Load the HTML content generated by the `Recipe` object into the `WebView`:

```
view.loadData(recipe.toHtml(), "text/html", "UTF-8");
```

33. Set the content view of the `Activity` to the `WebView` object we created:

```
setContentView(view);
```

What just happened?

The recipe viewer example shows a simple structure which can be extended in many different ways to present large amounts of information to the user in an easy-to-use format. Thanks to the fact that `WebView` works with HTML, it makes presenting non-interactive lists of information more appealing than working with a `ListView` or similar structures.

The `loadData` method used previously is limited in that it doesn't allow for your page to easily reference external structures such as style sheets or images. You can work around this limitation by using the `loadDataWithBaseURL` method which works in much the same way, but renders the page relative to a specified URL, which may be online or local on the device.

The `Recipe` object is considered responsible for rendering its HTML, which works well in a pure Java situation. You could also pass the `Recipe` to a template engine, or use something like a visitor pattern to render the `Recipe` object as HTML code. The full code for the `Recipe` object in the previous example is as follows:

```
Recipe recipe = new Recipe(
    "Microwave Fudge",
    new Ingredient[]{
        new Ingredient("Condensed Milk", 385, "grams"),
        new Ingredient("Sugar", 500, "grams"),
        new Ingredient("Margarine", 125, "grams"),
        new Ingredient("Vanilla Essence", 5, "ml")
    },
    new String[]{
        "Combine the condensed milk, sugar and margarine "
        + "in a large microwave-proof bowl",
        "Microwave for 2 minutes on full power",
        "Remove from microwave and stir well",
        "Microwave for additional 5 minutes on full power",
        "Add the Vanilla essence and stir",
        "Pour into a greased dish",
        "Allow to cool",
        "Cut into small squares"
    });
```

An unfortunate side effect of using the `WebView` object is that it doesn't conform to the look and feel of other widgets. It is for this reason it doesn't work well when you place it with other widgets on the same screen. The end effect of the previous example is effectively a non-interactive web page which looks as follows:

Microwave Fudge

You will need:

- 385grams - Condensed Milk
- 500grams - Sugar
- 125grams - Margarine
- 5ml - Vanilla Essence

Have a go hero – improving the look of the recipe viewer

The previous example generates a very simple HTML page and doesn't include any styling. Including an inline CSS is a very simple operation, and could even be done by reading the styling content from an application resource. Create a CSS, include it inline in the HTML page, with rules such as:

- Color the background of first-level header and second-level header elements
- Change the font-color of the first and second-level headers to white
- Round the corners of the header elements by five pixels
- Change the list bullet to a square instead of a circle

Taking WebView further

The `WebView` class has significant functionality that can be very useful when dealing with content screens, for example, using hyperlinks to provide a **show/hide** disclosure section for less important content. This requires the use of JavaScript in the HTML page, at which point it's strongly advisable that your application use a template engine to produce the HTML pages instead of generating them in Java code (as the Java code will quickly become difficult to maintain).

The `WebView` class also allows your application to interact with the JavaScript code on the page using a very simple mechanism by which you can expose Java objects to the JavaScript code. This is done with the `addJavascriptInterface` method. This allows the HTML page to invoke actions on a Java object that you provide, effectively allowing the page to take control of a part of your application. If your content screen needs to take a business action, such as **Buy** or **Cancel**, the required functionality can be exposed in a JavaScript interface object. When the **Book** HTML element is selected by the user, the JavaScript in the page can invoke the `appInterface.buy();` method which you defined.

Another important feature to consider with the `WebView` class is the "zoom" controls. When presenting your user with lots of information, it may be useful for the user to be able to zoom in or out in order to make some elements easier to read. To enable the built-in zoom controls of the `WebView`, you'll need to access the `WebSettings` object:

```
webView.getWebSettings().setBuiltInZoomControls(true);
```

The `WebSettings` object can be used to enable and disable a large number of other features that are available in the WebKit browser component, and it's well worth reading through the available documentation.

The primary problem with the `WebView` class is its look and feel. Where an Android application with the default theme is light grey on a black background, the `WebView` class is black on a white background, which makes the screens driven by a `WebView` stand out to the user as though they are a separate application.

The simplest way around the styling problem would appear to be to style the HTML pages to look just like the rest of the application. The problem is that some device manufacturers have their own Android application styling, so you can't really be sure what the rest of your application is going to look like. Changing the background and foreground of the HTML page to be in line with the standard Android theme could well make it stand out against the rest of your application when run on manufacturer-themed devices.

Pop quiz

1. What is the best way to render large object graphs to HTML for rendering in a `WebView`?

    a. Convert them to XML and run them through XSLT

    b. Send them to an external web service to be rendered

    c. Hard code the HTML generation

    d. With a simple template engine

2. How can you access external CSS and images with a `WebView`?

    a. Use the `loadDataWithBaseURL` method

    b. Specify the full URL path in the HTML page

    c. Generate HTML code that includes the in line data

3. What rendering engine does Android use for `WebView`?

    a. Gecko

    b. MSIE/Trident

    c. KHTML

    d. WebKit

Creating relative layouts for content display

The `WebView` offers an easy way by which large amount of content can be displayed to the user in an easy-to-read format. It also has many built-in features designed specifically for viewing content. However, it doesn't always offer the easy way out and often doesn't allow for functionality that other widgets provide out-of-the-box. The `RelativeLayout` class provides much of the same layout functionality that the `WebView` class provides you with.

As we just discussed, the `WebView` stands out almost as though it were a separate application. Working with a `RelativeLayout`, you'll be populating your screen with standard Android widgets, which in turn means that there will be no change in the look and feel from one screen to the next. While `WebView` requires some form of template engine (whether it be in an API or simply a `StringBuilder` as in the example), a `RelativeLayout` can be declared in an application resource as an XML file. Using a layout file also means that the screen layout will be selected through the resource selection process, allowing for sophisticated customizations that are difficult to achieve with the `WebView` class and HTML code.

Using a `RelativeLayout` in a way provides a form of template engine. By only giving IDs to `View` objects that you will need to populate with data, you can populate the screen by injecting the relevant content into these exposed objects. When we built the HTML-based view, we needed to create header elements for the ingredients list and list of instructions, with a coded layout structure those headers would be loaded from within the layout file, or from a string bundle resource.

When dealing with lists of information, which is a common requirement of a content layout, you can provide the data in several different ways. You could use a `ListView` object, or you could use an embedded `LinearLayout` to act as a list. When working with either of them, it's advisable to have a layout resource that can be reused for each of the items in the list. Making use of a `ListView` means you have an `Adapter` through which you can convert your data objects into `View` objects that can be displayed on the screen. However, `ListView` objects have various other constraints (such as the size of the contained items) and are best used when the items they display are interactive in some way. If you need a non-interactive list (or grid) of items, it's a good idea to follow the `Adapter` mechanism by creating a separate class that is responsible for creating `View` objects based on your data objects.

Taking full advantage of RelativeLayout

`RelativeLayout` structures have the major advantage that they offer direct integration with the rest of your application. They can also be more easily localized than an HTML page. The event structures provided by a direct `ViewGroup` structure are more versatile than those provided by a `WebView` object via its specialized event listeners and JavaScript.

The XML layout structures also provide much the same effect as a template engine, avoiding the need to import an external API such as an XSLT engine, a Java template engine, or hard coding the HTML generation. Standard Android `Activity` classes also have the built-in Android animation structures to work with. While the `WebView` class allows for CSS animations or could run JavaScript animations, this requires re-layout of the HTML structure for each frame in the animation.

An Android `Activity` class implementing the entire content screen also has the advantage that it can load its external resources from the application resource structure. This not only allows you to do things such as localize your images more easily, but also means that all of the resources are run through the resource compiler and as such can be optimized by the Android tool chain. With a `WebView` you would need a base URL to load such resources from, or be able to encode them inline in the HTML page.

Considering Android layout constraints

There are some drawbacks to developing the entire content view as an Android layout. From a skills point-of-view, only a developer can build and maintain the user interface. It also means that any styling done to individual widgets must be managed by a developer. With a `WebView` based layout, much of the creation work on the layout could be handled by a web developer and graphic designer.

 Adding more widgets to your screen comes with another problem—performance. Not only can larger, more complex layouts lead to a very slow user experience, it can cause your `Activity` to crash entirely.

Keeping fewer widgets on the screen means that the interface will have less information for the user to absorb in one hit, and will be easier to work with.

Layouts with either too much length, or too much depth will cause an application to crash. If you need to animate a single word in the middle of a sentence, you'll have to define two additional `TextView` widgets that will display the non-animated text on either side of the animated word. This increases the length of your layout. If you also needed a horizontal `LinearLayout` in which to place these three `TextView` objects, you would be increasing the depth of your layout structure. By factoring in both of these constraints, you can imagine how quickly you can run out of memory or processing power when it comes to layout rendering. Each of the widgets must be measured for layout before being rendered. Each measurement, layout step, or rendering step makes use of the language stack (by recursively invoking methods) in order to make sure all of the widgets are correctly rendered at the correct point on the screen (or not rendered if they are off screen). The software stack size in Android is limited, and each method call requires each of its parameters to be pushed onto the stack for the invocation. On top of that, all of the measurement information needs to be stored in the heap space, which is another seriously limited resource on the Android platform (by default the Dalvik VM only allocates 8 MB of heap space to begin with).

The following diagram illustrates the difference between the length and depth of a layout structure. The left screen illustrates a long layout, while the right screen illustrates a deep layout:

Styling TextView objects

At this point it's rather concerning to think about how you might make a single word in a sentence bold, or give it a shadow. In the `WebView` it's as easy as adding a `<span>` element with some special styling on it, but in a native layout, wouldn't you need to add separate `TextView` objects for each section of the text? If this were so, you would be dramatically limited in the amount of text you would be able to display to the user, since you would be creating thousands of almost useless objects.

Fortunately, Android makes it very easy to mark up the text in all of its default widgets. Any class that extends from `TextView` can handle text with style information or even images. Generally the classes available in the `android.text.style` package can be used to style sub-segments of the text strings you want to display.

In order to use these different styling structures, you will need to use a `SpannableString` object. A `SpannableString` is a specialized type of Android string that keeps track of styling information in relation to a normal `CharSequence` of text that needs to be displayed. There are several other similar classes (such as `SpannableStringBuilder`) which handle easy modification of the text, and are thus suited to text that will be edited. For our current purposes, a `SpannableString` is perfect, and much simpler to work with. A `SpannableString` has a method that it's required to implement, based on the `Spannable` interface—`setSpan`. The `setSpan` method allows you to add markup structures to the `SpannableString`, which affect how a specific part of the text is rendered.

If we simply wanted to write the text **There is nothing to fear!** on the screen, you would normally just use a `TextView` object with the specified string. What if we wanted to strike the **nothing** out of that string? The way forward now is to use a `StrikethroughSpan` object for characters 9 through 16. In this case, the string can't just be defined in the layout file anymore, a `SpannableString` needs to be created in the Java code. The following is a simple example of how this can be done, and what the resulting `TextView` would look like:

```
TextView fear = new TextView(this);
SpannableString string = new SpannableString(
        "There is nothing to fear!");
string.setSpan(new StrikethroughSpan(), 9, 16, 0);
fear.setText(string);
```

The result of this little snippet of Java code is a `TextView` widget displaying styled content instead of a plain `String`, as shown in the following screenshot:

There is ~~nothing~~ to fear!

As you can see, using this type of markup is brilliantly effective, and really quite easy to work with. This sample is also very quick to execute when compared to the `WebView` rendering, since it doesn't include any form of parsing.

There are a few problems with the mechanism though. The most important one being the index handling. In order to know when to start or stop a `Span` of markup rendering, you need to specify the first and last character that needs to be rendered with the given `Span`. Not a problem unless you plan on changing your text, or even worse—internationalizing it.

Fortunately, once again Android already has a built-in solution, although it comes at the expense of performance. You can convert almost any HTML text into a `Spannable` object which can in turn be passed directly to any `TextView` object for rendering. The class to use is the `android.text.Html` class, which includes utility methods for parsing HTML code into a `Spannable` object, and also for converting a `Spannable` object into a HTML code.

If you need to internationalize strings that you plan on rendering with additional style attributes, the `Html` class is probably the only sensible way to do it. It also has the added advantage that the loading of images can be handled by your application (through use of the `Html.ImageGetter` interface). Additionally, the `TextView` will still look and feel like a normal Android widget, which enhances the users' experience.

Most HTML tags are handled by the `Html` class, but not quite all of them. For one thing—CSS styles are ignored, so colors and borders are out of the question. However, great styling is still possible, and at least you don't need to record the character index values somewhere in an application resource so that all of the styling lines up.

If you wanted to format some text in a `Button` label as bold, it's really easy to do with the `Html` class. It's much quicker to just pass the result of the `fromHtml` method directly to the `TextView` object. For example, the following code snippet would yield a `Button` object with the word **Hello** in italic script, while the word **World** would have a bold weight to it:

```
Button button = new Button(this);
button.setText(Html.fromHtml("<i>Hello</i> <b>World!</b>"));
```

You can also specify HTML content in a layout resource XML file, and it will be parsed with the `Html` class before being passed into the `TextView` object's `setText` method.

The above Java snippet creates a `Button` widget that would look as follows:

HTML tags can also be used to render mini-documents into a `TextView` object, and while they carry their own styling, they also adhere to the styling of the `TextView` object. This means that if you're looking for a solution that's quicker to work with than a `WebView` for carrying some static text (and no hyperlinks), then a `TextView` can actually serve as a good alternative. For example, consider the following code snippet:

```
TextView text = new TextView(this);
text.setTextColor(0xff000000);
text.setBackgroundColor(0xffffffff);
text.setText(Html.fromHtml(
        "<h1>Cows Love to Eat Grass</h1>"
        + "<p>Do not fear the Cow</p>"));
```

This will render the `TextView` with a first-level header and a single-lined paragraph element. Both of which will include some padding in order to space them apart from the other elements on the screen. The resulting image should look quite familiar:

As you can see, a correctly styled `TextView` makes a great alternative to a `WebView`, especially if you are fitting it inline with a series of native widgets. However, the black-on-white styling does bring back the inconsistency problem. So unless you entire application follows this model, it's a better idea to leave the styling as default.

If you are planning on using a `TextView` for longer content, it's important to consider some additional factors:

- ◆ Make sure that the user will be able to scroll if the text runs longer than the size of their screen. This is easily done by placing the `TextView` in a `ScrollView` object.

- ◆ If your text is very long, consider styling the content, either making the text brighter white or working with a black on white background. While it is very inconsistent with other Android applications, and other screens in your own application, it is much easier on the eyes and your users will thank you for that.

- ◆ Consider allowing the user to change the font size with a long touch or a menu. If their screen is low density, or they don't have perfect vision, you may be making their lives a little easier.

Pop quiz

1. If you need to display a non-interactive bullet point list, which of these is preferable?

    a. A `WebView` with an unordered list

    b. A specially styled `ListView` object

    c. A `TextView` object with HTML content

2. With regards to hyperlinks, you might use a `WebView` instead of a `TextView` because:

   a. `TextView` cannot handle hyper links

   b. They look better in a `WebView`

   c. A `WebView` has built-in history management

3. A native interface works better for animation intensive applications because:

   a. You can use Android animation resource files

   b. The `WebView` class doesn't handle animations

   c. HTML animations are more expensive to run

Time for action – developing specialized content views

In many situations, you'll need a specific type of interactive logic that you would want to reuse in many parts of your application. On a content screen, some parts of the display will need to be updated, driven by changes that are made to other parts of the display. This is often because while some area of the screen is giving the user information, the other parts are capturing new data from them. Next, we'll build a simple widget responsible for displaying an amount of money to the user. Its main reason for its existence is the fact that it not only animates between changes, but also feeds back to the user whether the amount has gone up or down by changing its color.

1. Create a new Java source file named `AmountBox.java` for the new class, and open the new file in an editor or IDE.

2. The new class should extend the `TextSwitcher` class and implement the `ViewSwitcher.ViewFactory` interface:

   ```
   public class AmountBox extends TextSwitcher
           implements ViewSwitcher.ViewFactory {
   ```

3. Declare a field for the `DecimalFormat` to be used to render the amount:

   ```
   private DecimalFormat format = new DecimalFormat("0.##");
   ```

   Also declare a field to store the current numeric value displayed:

   ```
   private double amount;
   ```

4. Declare copies of the two constructors made available from the `TextSwitcher` class in order to allow the `LayoutInflator` class to instantiate the `AmountBox` class from resource files:

   ```
   public AmountBox(Context context, AttributeSet attrs) {
       super(context, attrs);
   ```

```
        init();
    }
    public AmountBox(Context context) {
        super(context);
        init();
    }
```

5. Declare the `init()` method to take care of "common constructor" requirements:

```
private void init() {
```

6. Set the "in" and "out" animations to the fade animations provided by Android:

```
setOutAnimation(getContext(), android.R.anim.fade_out);
setInAnimation(getContext(), android.R.anim.fade_in);
```

7. Next, set the `ViewFactory` to the `AmountBox`:

```
setFactory(this);
```

8. Finally, invoke `setAmount(0)` to ensure the displayed amount is specified:

```
setAmount(0);
```

9. Declare a setter method to allow overriding of the default `DecimalFormat`:

```
public void setFormat(DecimalFormat format) {
    this.format = format;
}
```

10. Declare a getter method to allow easy access to the current numeric value:

```
public double getAmount() {
    return amount;
}
```

11. Override the `makeView()` method from `ViewFactory`:

```
public View makeView() {
```

12. Create a new `TextView` object with the context given to this `AmountBox`:

```
TextView view = new TextView(getContext());
```

13. Specify a large text size since the amount will represent money, and then return the `TextView` object for display:

```
view.setTextSize(18);
return view;
```

14. Now declare a setter method to allow the amount value to be changed:

```
public void setAmount(double value) {
```

15. This method will change the color of the text, so declare a variable for the new text `color` that will be displayed:

```
int color;
```

16. First check to see what `color` we should change the text to:

```
if(value < amount) {
    color = 0xff00ff00;
} else if(value > amount) {
    color = 0xffff0000;
} else {
    return;
}
```

17. Fetch the off screen `TextView` object:

```
TextView offscreen = (TextView)getNextView();
```

18. Set the font color based on the change to the numeric value:

```
offscreen.setTextColor(color);
```

19. Render a shadow around the text in order to create a "halo" effect:

```
offscreen.setShadowLayer(3, 0, 0, color);
```

20. Set the text of the `TextView` to the new value:

```
offscreen.setText(format.format(value));
```

21. Display the off screen `TextView` and remember the new value:

```
showNext();
amount = value;
```

What just happened?

The `AmountBox` class is a great example of a small unit of content that needs to be updated. This class provides information to the user, but also provides a form of feedback. When the user does something which affects the amount displayed, the `AmountBox` reacts by updating the font color to reflect the direction of the change—green for the amount going down, and red for an amount going up.

The example makes use of the standard Android fade through animations as discussed in *Chapter 7, Animating Widgets and Layouts*. The speed of the animations provides a great cross fade effect between the two amounts. Notice that in the `setAmount` method, the updating of the text content and switching the `View` objects is handled manually.

You could potentially replace the `offscreen.setText` and `showNext` method calls with a call to `setText`, but it's nice to see how it works under the hood. This method is also not subject to future implementation changes that may occur.

Developing an online music store

A great example of a content-centric layout is a music store built into a media player application. The ability to buy music directly from the media player is a massively user-friendly feature, and also fits nicely with the way Android applications behave as "connected" applications instead of purely offline systems. Android also makes it very easy to truly include the shop as part of the application instead of simply providing a link to an appropriate website. Generally, users are more inclined to feel a sense of trust if they pick the **Buy Music** button and are not suddenly whisked off to their web browser. Having both online and offline parts of your application properly integrated can also go a long way for your sales statistics.

Buying music online is very different to purchasing it in a store. The availability of additional information about the songs, artists, or albums the user is looking at is part of the appeal. For this reason, an online music store for a mobile device must be carefully designed to provide as much information as possible without either cluttering the screen, or detracting from the fact that the user is there to purchase music. The feeling of integration with the application also helps build trust with the user, so the look and feel is very important. Another advantage of buying music online is you pay only for what you want to purchase. For this the user interface needs to allow the user to select which tracks from an album the users would like to purchase, and which they either don't want or plan to buy later. Also, how do they know which ones they like? They also need to be able to play a sample (whether it be time limited, or just a lower quality) of each track.

Designing the music store

To really illustrate how a content-centric design fits together, you need to build one. For this example we'll be working through the design process, and then the implementation of that design. Since the design and its implementation are the important parts here, we won't go into building a functional example. It'll really just be a pretty screen.

To begin with, we need to have a basic user interface design. I find it best to start with a whiteboard or a piece of paper and a pen. While there are plenty of tools for drawing mock screens out there, none of them really approach the user interface of a paper and pen. To start off, we draw a high level wireframe of the overall screen design. This is simply a series of boxes that will tell us what type of information to show in what parts of the screen.

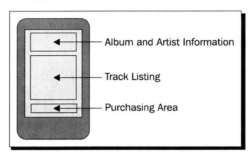

In the diagram, we've divided the user interface into three parts:

- Album and Artist Information area: This area displays the name and cover art of the album the user is looking to buy
- Track List area: In this area, users can listen to samples and select which tracks they want to purchase
- Purchasing Area: This area displays the total amount users will be paying, and also a button to buy their selected tracks

In the previous diagram, I've stuck to the size of the screen, but depending on the screen size and number of tracks available, the user interface may need a scrollbar to be fully accessible.

The next bit of work is to look at each of the sections of the user interface that we've defined and decide what widgets will go into each of them. Firstly we'll need to look at the album and artist information. The album information will be displayed as the album cover artwork and the album name. We'll include an image area for an artist logo, and also include a text block with the name of the recording label.

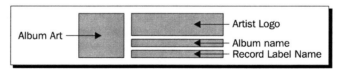

A simple block diagram like this lets you visually consider the various elements. It also allows you to start thinking about things such as font size, borders, and spacing. In the previous diagram, we want the three elements on the right to be roughly the same size as the cover art on the left. Unfortunately the Android `RelativeLayout` class doesn't currently allow us to directly stipulate this as a contract. The next element of the design we need to consider is the track listing box. For this, instead of drawing everything in the box, we'll focus on what a single line will look like and what information it will contain.

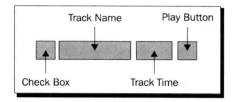

The preceding structure is a very simple one line structure for displaying the details of a single track. The `CheckBox` on the left can be used to select those tracks that the user wants to purchase, while the button on the right side can be used to play a sample of the given track. The two button-like elements on either side create a kind of framing for the plain text elements in the middle of the line.

Finally, we need to consider how we plan on asking the user to send their money. This is a very important part of the user interface, it needs to be obvious—the amount of money they will be expected to pay. We also need to make it really easy for the user to actually make the transaction, so a single **Purchase** or **Buy Selected Tracks** button is needed.

The final section of the user interface simply has two widgets in it, one on the left for purchasing, and the total amount the user is expected to pay on the right. For the left side button, we'll work with a simple Android `Button` widget, while on the right side we'll make use of the new `AmountBox` written in the previous part of this chapter.

Developing the music store

We'll start with the new example by building a new series of model classes, but first you'll need to create a new project for our conceptual media player. To do this, run the following command on a command line or console:

```
android create project -n PacktTunes -p PacktTunes -k com.packtpub.
packttunes -a ShopActivity -t 3
```

After creating the new project, copy the `AmountBox` source code into the root package of the new project. You then need to create a class to contain the data for a single track. This simply needs to have the name of the track and the duration of the track stored as the number of seconds. We'll also include utility methods to calculate the minutes:seconds values that we can use to display the duration data.

```
public class Track {
    private final String name;
    private final int length;
```

```
        public Track(final String name, final int length) {
            this.name = name;
            this.length = length;
        }

        public String getName() {
            return name;
        }

        public int getLength() {
            return length;
        }

        public int getMinutes() {
            return length / 60;
        }

        public int getSeconds() {
            return length % 60;
        }
    }
```

The Track class is a very simple structure which could easily be parsed from XML or deserialized from a binary stream. We also need another class to hold the information about a single artist. While the following class is really nothing more than a form of data store, it could easily be extended to store things like biography information if needed:

```
public class Artist {
    private final Drawable logo;
    private final String description;
    public Artist(
            final Drawable logo,
            final String description) {
        this.logo = logo;
        this.description = description;
    }

    public String getDescription() {
        return description;
    }

    public Drawable getLogo() {
        return logo;
    }
}
```

Finally, on the data class front, we'll need a class for linking the two previous classes to a single album. This class will be used as a single point which can be handed to an `Activity`. Copy the following code into a new file named `Album.java` in the root package of your project:

```java
public class Album {
    private final Drawable cover;
    private final String name;
    private final Artist artist;
    private final String label;
    private final Track[] tracks;

    public Album(
            final Drawable cover,
            final String name,
            final Artist artist,
            final String label,
            final Track... tracks) {
        this.cover = cover;
        this.name = name;
        this.artist = artist;
        this.label = label;
        this.tracks = tracks;
    }
    public Drawable getCover() {
        return cover;
    }
    public Artist getArtist() {
        return artist;
    }
    public String getLabel() {
        return label;
    }
    public String getName() {
        return name;
    }
    public Track[] getTracks() {
        return tracks;
    }
}
```

Time for action – building a track item

To get working on the new user interface, you'll need a few images. For this next section, you'll need an image for the play buttons. The play image should be a simple "play" arrow, the button we place it in will provide a background and border. The lines in the list structure will be placed into a `TableLayout` in order to align all of the sub-structures.

1. Create a new layout resource file in the `res/layouts` directory of the project, and name the new file `track.xml`.

2. Declare the root element of the new file as a `TableRow` element consuming all of the available width and only the required height:

```
<TableRow
    xmlns:android="http://schemas.android.com/apk/res/android"
    android:layout_width="fill_parent"
    android:layout_height="wrap_content">
```

3. As the first element of the `TableRow`, create a `CheckBox` the user can use to select and unselect the tracks they want to buy:

```
<CheckBox android:id="@+id/selected"
        android:checked="true"
        android:layout_width="wrap_content"
        android:layout_height="wrap_content"/>
```

4. Declare a `TextView` element to display the name of the track with a larger-than-usual font, and a pure-white font color:

```
<TextView android:id="@+id/track_name"
        android:textSize="16sp"
        android:textColor="#ffffff"
        android:layout_width="wrap_content"
        android:layout_height="wrap_content"/>
```

5. Follow the track name `TextView` with another right-aligned `TextView` object to be used to display the duration of the track:

```
<TextView android:id="@+id/track_time"
        android:gravity="right"
        android:layout_width="wrap_content"
        android:layout_height="wrap_content"/>
```

6. End the `TableRow` element with an `ImageButton` element, which can be used by the user to sample the track before buying it:

```
<ImageButton android:id="@+id/play"
            android:src="@drawable/play"
            android:layout_width="wrap_content"
            android:layout_height="wrap_content"/>
```

What just happened

The above layout resource file will handle the layout of the track list items for the second part of the user interface. We need to be able to create several of these structures to handle all of the tracks available in an album. We wrap them in a `TableRow` element which when placed in a `TableLayout` object, will automatically align each of its sub-elements with those in the other rows.

Later, in the Java code we'll use the `LayoutInflator` to load this resource, populate it with the name and duration of a track, and then add it to a `TableLayout` object that we will declare as part of the main user interface. Once this new item has been populated with some data, it'll look something like the following screenshot:

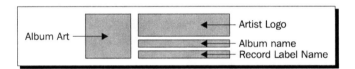

Time for action – developing the main user interface layout

Having built the layout resource file that will become track items in a list later, we now need to define the remaining elements of this user interface. While this structure is relatively simple, it's also very easily extended and has a few minor details that keep it looking really good. It also needs some Java code in order to be correctly populated, but we'll get into that after we've finished with the resource file.

1. Create or open the `res/layout/main.xml` file in the new project.

2. The root element of the main layout needs to be a `ScrollView` in order to handle the possibility that the interface runs longer than the available screen space. The `ScrollView` should take up all available screen space:

    ```
    <ScrollView
        xmlns:android="http://schemas.android.com/apk/res/android"
        android:layout_width="fill_parent"
        android:layout_height="fill_parent">
    ```

3. As the only element to the `ScrollView`, declare a `RelativeLayout` which consumes the available width, but only the required height. The `RelativeLayout` should include some padding at the top and bottom to provide a little "breathing room" so that its contents don't look to cramped:

```
<RelativeLayout android:layout_width="fill_parent"
                android:layout_height="wrap_content"
                android:paddingTop="10dip"
                android:paddingBottom="10dip">
```

4. The first element of the `RelativeLayout` is the album art, a fixed size `ImageView` object that will fit the album cover art in the available space:

```
<ImageView android:id="@+id/artwork"
           android:scaleType="fitCenter"
           android:gravity="left"
           android:layout_alignParentTop="true"
           android:layout_alignParentLeft="true"
           android:layout_width="84dip"
           android:layout_height="84dip"/>
```

5. The second element after the album art is the artist's logo image, also an `ImageView`. This element is required to center the logo in the available space:

```
<ImageView android:id="@+id/artist_logo"
           android:adjustViewBounds="true"
           android:scaleType="center"
           android:layout_alignParentTop="true"
           android:layout_toRightOf="@id/artwork"
           android:layout_width="fill_parent"
           android:layout_height="wrap_content"/>
```

6. After the artist's logo, we need a plain `TextView` object with some font styling to hold the name of the album we're trying to sell. We'll place this below the artist's logo in the user interface as per the image we saw earlier:

```
<TextView android:id="@+id/album_label"
          android:gravity="center"
          android:textSize="22dip"
          android:textColor="#ffffff"
          android:textStyle="bold"
          android:layout_below="@id/artist_logo"
          android:layout_toRightOf="@id/artwork"
          android:layout_width="fill_parent"
          android:layout_height="wrap_content"/>
```

7. Below the `TextView` with the album name, we have a small non-styled `TextView` to hold the name of the record label under which the album is released:

```
<TextView android:id="@+id/record_label"
          android:gravity="center"
          android:layout_below="@id/album_label"
          android:layout_toRightOf="@id/artwork"
          android:layout_width="fill_parent"
          android:layout_height="wrap_content"/>
```

8. As promised, we follow these elements with a `TableLayout` which will hold the available track information. We layout the `TableLayout` element against the album art rather than the record label `TextView`:

```
<TableLayout android:id="@+id/track_listing"
             android:stretchColumns="1"
             android:layout_below="@id/artwork"
             android:layout_width="fill_parent"
             android:layout_height="wrap_content"/>
```

9. Underneath the track list, we start by placing the **Buy Selected Tracks** button element on the left side of the screen:

```
<Button android:id="@+id/purchase"
        android:text="Buy Selected Tracks"
        android:layout_below="@id/track_listing"
        android:layout_alignParentLeft="true"
        android:layout_width="wrap_content"
        android:layout_height="wrap_content"/>
```

10. Finally, on the right side of the screen, we add our custom `AmountBox` widget where we will tell the user how much they will be paying:

```
<com.packtpub.packttunes.AmountBox
    android:id="@+id/purchase_amount"
    android:layout_alignBaseline="@id/purchase"
    android:layout_alignParentRight="true"
    android:layout_width="wrap_content"
    android:layout_height="wrap_content
```

What just happened?

In the preceding layout, each of the specified widgets has an important part to play by either providing the user with information, or gathering new information from them. As far as possible, we have given the user only the information that is important to them. The cover art and artist's logo are often the first way people recognize a specific album, while the name may well be a secondary recognition. The colors and shapes in the album cover art are generally recognized faster by a person's brain than the text indicating the album's name.

All of the top elements: Cover art, artist logo, album name, and record label, could be made into interactive elements, taking the user to screens with more information about the selected element. The linked information could include reviews, discussion forums, and rating widgets. Another great addition would be linking to music videos from the selected album or artist (if there are some available).

Also notice at the bottom in our purchasing area. The `AmountBox` has been aligned with the "baseline" of the `purchase Button` widget. In this case, it aligns the baseline of the text in these two widgets, making them looked centered in relation to each other, although it's an aesthetic centering rather than an exact computation.

Time for action – developing the main user interface Java code

In order to put this example together entirely and have a working content-centric screen (although only in the example sense), we need some Java code. This code will handle populating the user interface layout with an `Album` object. For this next piece of code, you'll need images for the cover art and for the artist's logo.

1. Open the `ShopActivity` Java source file in an editor or IDE.

2. In the `onCreate` method, ensure that the `main.xml` layout resource is being set as the content view for the `ShopActivity`:

```
setContentView(R.layout.main);
```

3. Fetch the application resources and invoke a new `setAlbum` method with the contents of your favorite music album:

```
Resources resources = getResources();
setAlbum(new Album(
        resources.getDrawable(R.drawable.album_art),
        "The Android Quartet",
        new Artist(resources.getDrawable(R.drawable.sherlock),
        "Sherlock Peterson"),
        "Green Records",
        new Track("I was a robot", 208),
        new Track("Long is not enough time", 243),
        new Track("The rocket robot reel", 143),
        new Track("I love by bits", 188)));
```

4. Declare the `setAlbum` method to accept an `Album` object:

```
private void setAlbum(Album album) {
```

5. Fetch the `track_listing` part of the user interface and use a new `addTrackView` method to add each of the tracks to the display:

```
ViewGroup tracks = (ViewGroup)findViewById(R.id.track_listing);
for(Track t : album.getTracks()) {
    addTrackView(tracks, t);
}
```

6. Fetch the album cover art widget and set its content:

```
ImageView albumArt = (ImageView)findViewById(R.id.artwork);
albumArt.setImageDrawable(album.getCover());
```

7. Fetch the artist's logo widget and set its content:

```
ImageView artistLogo = (ImageView)findViewById(R.id.artist_logo);
artistLogo.setImageDrawable(album.getArtist().getLogo());
```

8. Fetch the album name widget and set its content:

```
TextView albumLabel = (TextView)findViewById(R.id.album_label);
albumLabel.setText(album.getName());
```

9. Fetch the record label widget and set its content:

```
TextView recordLabel =
        (TextView)findViewById(R.id.record_label);
recordLabel.setText(album.getLabel());
```

10. Fetch the `AmountBox` widget and set its format to a money format before setting its value to `1.99` multiplied by the number of tracks:

```
AmountBox amount =
        (AmountBox)findViewById(R.id.purchase_amount);
amount.setFormat(new DecimalFormat("$ 0.##"));
```

11. Declare the `addTrackView` method and use it as it was used previously:

```
private void addTrackView(ViewGroup tracks, Track track) {
```

12. Use a `LayoutInflator` to inflate the `track` layout resource:

```
LayoutInflater inflater = getLayoutInflater();
ViewGroup line = (ViewGroup)inflater.inflate(
        R.layout.track,
        tracks,
        false);
```

13. Fetch the track name widget from the new `ViewGroup` and set its content:

```
TextView trackName =
        (TextView)line.findViewById(R.id.track_name);
trackName.setText(track.getName());
```

14. Fetch the track duration widget from the new `ViewGroup`, and create a `StringBuilder` with which to display the track duration:

```
TextView trackTime =
        (TextView)line.findViewById(R.id.track_time);
StringBuilder builder = new StringBuilder();
```

15. Append the minutes and a separator to the `StringBuilder`:

```
builder.append(track.getMinutes());
builder.append(':');
```

16. If the number of seconds is less than `10`, we need a prefix `'0'` character:

```
if(track.getSeconds() < 10) {
    builder.append('0');
}
```

17. Append the number of seconds in the duration:

```
builder.append(track.getSeconds());
```

18. Set the text of the duration widget and add the new line to the "tracks" list:

```
trackTime.setText(builder.toString());
tracks.addView(line);
```

What just happened?

The preceding Java code is enough to copy the data given in the `Album` object into the user interface. Once on the screen, it looks like a simple music store page, but themed as an Android application. This provides much of the benefit of a web page in terms of layout structures and the easy maintenance that comes with an XML layout and at the same time integrates entirely with whatever branding and styling may exist on the end user's device. Once on the screen, the previous example will present you with something looking like the following screenshot:

Have a go hero – updating the total price

To really make the previous example feel more real, it needs to update the total amount at the bottom of the screen when the user selects or unselects tracks from the album listing. It should also disable the **Buy Selected Tracks** button if there are no tracks selected.

Try adding an event listener to each of the CheckBox elements in the track layouts, and keep a track of which are selected. For the total amount to display, multiply 1.99 with the number of selected tracks.

Summary

In this chapter, we've delved into many important areas and techniques used when presenting the user with lots of information or content. It's important to think through your interfaces carefully before you start building them, but also try not to take up too much time before you put fingers to the keyboard and start coding. Sometimes having a simple user interface up and running can tell you far more than your diagrams and mock-ups ever will about how users will work with the screen.

We've completed an example of displaying recipes to the user with the WebView class, demonstrating how easy it is to use HTML on the Android platform. We've also looked at the native alternative to an HTML view by building an online music store using a RelativeLayout to display the content. With these two examples, we've compared the differences between the two mechanisms giving insight into where each can best be used.

Always consider your performance and user experience when deciding on how to display your content. While a WebView may be more flexible in some regards, allowing you to change the content view depending on what content you are displaying, it may also lead to inconsistencies and an irritated user. A RelativeLayout provides a more rigid structure, and will also ensure a more consistent code base.

In the next chapter, we'll be looking in more detail at how you can go about adding more style to your Android application. We'll also look at how best to go about handling changes to the device and configuration (such as the changing language or a change from portrait to landscape mode).

9
Styling Android Applications

Up to this point we've been working with the standard Android themes and styling. From a consistency point of view, this is a very good thing, since the application will blend properly with the device's theming (if it has any). However, there are times when you need to be able to define your own styling. This styling may only apply to a single widget, or it may apply to the entire application. In any of these cases, you'll need to know what tools you have available from Android in order to decide how best to approach the problem at hand.

There is more to styling than just making your application look good. Also, what you think would look good, another person may hate. It's also about making the application more useful to your users. This may involve making sure that your application looks right no matter which language the user chooses. It may involve additional colors for some chosen widgets, or it may simply involve implementing a landscape layout for some key screens.

In the previous chapter, we looked at the overall choices that can be made when designing certain screens of an application. The chapter also looked at the idea of using `WebView` as a container for content and widgets. One of the advantages of using a `WebView` is the fact that you then have CSS at your disposal. As any web developer will tell you, using CSS makes advanced styling very easy to do. However, Android has a collection of styling tools built in as well, with the ability to achieve many of the same effects as CSS and in some cases the ability to do much more.

Making a single button on the screen appear to be different makes it stand out against all of the other widgets. This helps draw attention to the fact that it does something different than anything else on the screen; it does something special. You may also want a rendered line between two groups of widgets in order to inform the user that they have a logical separation. Much like trying to understand someone else's source code, getting to grips with a new application is getting to understand someone else's logic. Correctly styling your application can go a long way to helping the user understand what your thinking was when building the application, while also providing them with cues as to what they are expected to do. If you need to provide instructions on how the application should be used, you have failed in your effort to design and style the application.

In this chapter, we'll be exploring how Android allows you to style the various widgets it provides, and therefore how to adopt your own styles and themes. We'll also work through examples where custom styling can be used to make the application easier to use for the user. We'll cover topics such as:

- Defining styling resources
- The different types of graphical resources that can be used for styling
- Creating and using nine-patch images
- Handling changes in the device configuration at runtime
- Defining styles that are portable across different devices and screens

Working with style resources

The first point of attack when dealing with Android styling is to understand how the style values work. An application has the ability to define any number of styles, much like the ability to define strings and string arrays as resources. The style resources are used to define a series of defaults for certain user interface elements, in much the same way as a CSS rule can define styling attributes. The main difference is that in Android, the styles can override any XML attribute defined for a given widget class.

The following table gives a quick comparison of Android style resources and CSS stylesheets. They have many common features, but behave quite differently.

Android style resources	CSS stylesheets
May apply to any XML attribute	Have a purpose-defined set of attributes they can define or alter
May inherit from a parent style	Cascade together in order of definition to form complex styles
Must be explicitly applied to a `View`, `Activity`, or `Application`	Are matched to document elements by their selector
Are defined as plain XML	Defined using specialized grammar

Android styles cascade in a manner similar to the way CSS rules do. However, the definition of this cascading owes more to a Java class hierarchy. Each style may declare a parent style from which it will inherit parameters. Once inherited, these parameters may be selectively overridden by the new style. It's always a good idea to have a parent style, as the device manufacturer may have modified the defaults, allowing you to continue to fit-in with the first-party software installed on the users device while creating your own new styles.

A style declaration cannot simply override the styles of all the available `TextView` objects. Instead you must either import the style for a specified widget on the widget declaration, or reference the style in your manifest file as a theme, in order to apply either to a single `Activity` or to your entire application. For starters, we'll focus on simply building styles and applying them to single widgets.

Styles, like dimensions, strings and string-arrays, are value resources. When creating a styling element, you can place it in any XML file in the `res/values` directory (although it's best to keep your resources separate and place the styles in a `styles.xml` file). Like all XML resources in the `values` directory, the root element is expected to be `<resources>`, after which you will list your `<style>` elements. The following is a simple style that can be used to style any `TextView` as a header:

```
<resources>
    <style name="TitleStyle" parent="@android:style/TextAppearance">
        <item name="android:textSize">25dip</item>
        <item name="android:textColor">#ffffffff</item>
        <item name="android:textStyle">bold</item>
        <item name="android:gravity">center</item>
    </style>
</resources>
```

The name attribute in the above `<style>` element is mandatory, while the parent attribute optionally determines which style to use for the default items (in this case, the default appearance of a `TextView` object). The following code snippet declares a `TextView` with the `TitleStyle` we declared above as its style:

```
<TextView
    style="@style/TitleStyle"
    android:layout_width="fill_parent"
    android:layout_height="wrap_content"
    android:text="Header"/>
```

Notice the lack of the `android` namespace prefix in the preceding example. Applying a style effectively happens at compile time, when the resources are converted into binary data for packaging. When applying the additional attributes, any items declared on the `<style>` element that are not available on the widget the style is being applied to, are simply ignored. This, in theory, allows you to create more abstract styles and apply them to many different widgets.

The `TextView` along with the `TitleStyle` applied, will render as follows:

Header

Who Overrides Whom?

When applying a style to a widget, Activity, or application, it's important to know the order of overrides. Each style overrides the style information of its parent (if it has one), while each widget will override any style information from any styles applied to it. This means that while you can apply an `android:text` style item to a `TextView` object, it's generally not very useful since any `android:text` attribute on the `TextView` will override the value specified in the style.

Using shape resources

It's all very fine and well being able to change the size and color of the fonts in a widget, but what about fundamentally changing the way in which that widget is rendered? We've already worked a little bit with XML drawable objects, but there is much more that can be done with them.

The work done so far with the XML drawable structures has been confined to putting default images in widgets designed to have an image. However, all widgets in Android are designed to have images. The `background` attribute of the `View` class allows you to pass in any `drawable` resource, combined with style resources. This becomes a very powerful tool. When a shape resource is loaded in Java code, it's returned as a `Drawable` object.

The shapes that are available to you are in the `android.graphics.drawable.shapes` package, other than the `Shape` class which is the abstract class from which the other classes in the package inherit. You reference these classes through XML files in the `res/drawable` directory. However, unlike the layout XML resources, shapes are more limited:

* You don't have direct access to the class attributes
* You can only create a single shape per shape file
* You cannot paint arbitrary paths (that is diagonal lines or bezier curves)

For all their limitations however, shapes are extremely useful and important because:

* They scale to the dimensions of the widget they are attached to
* This makes them perfectly suited for creating borders and/or background structures
* They also differentiate between the outline and fill of the shape

How shapes behave

Each shape structure that you can define behaves slightly differently to each of the others, not just in the way it's rendered, but also in what attributes apply to it. Since shape resources are fairly limited in how complex they can become, they are also somewhat limited in their use.

Rendering lines

The line shape in Android is always a straight horizontal line, vertically centered in the widget. Earlier we used the line shape as a placeholder image in the memory game. However, a much more common use of the line shape is as a vertical separator. The line shape is common when used with a `ListView`. A line shape doesn't allow for gradient fills, so it is always a solid color (defaulting to black). However, the line shape does allow for the full set of attributes in the `stroke` element to be used.

A simple white line can be defined in just a few lines, and will generally serve well as a separator in a `ListView` or similar structure. The following code snippet is such a line definition:

```
<shape xmlns:android="http://schemas.android.com/apk/res/android"
    android:shape="line">
  <stroke android:width="1sp" android:color="#ffffffff"/>
</shape>
```

Time for action – drawing a broken line

All of the shapes defined in Android allow you to use the `<stroke>` element to define a dotted or dashed line structure, but it's really best shown-off on the line element. If we increase the width of the line and define a dash pattern with dash segments double the size of the spacing, we get a line that looks much like a "cut" or "tear" line on a printed page. This is a great way to make harder separators on a user-interface.

1. Create a new shape resource XML file in the `res/drawable` directory named `line.xml` and open this file in an editor or IDE.

2. Declare the root element of the file as a `line` shape:

    ```
    <shape xmlns:android="http://schemas.android.com/apk/res/android"
        android:shape="line">
    ```

3. Declare a stroke element for the new line with a `width` of `3sp`, a white color, a `dashGap` of `5sp`, and a `dashWidth` of `10sp`:

    ```
    <stroke android:width="3sp"
            android:color="#ffffffff"
            android:dashGap="5sp"
            android:dashWidth="10sp" />
    ```

4. Close the shape declaration:

```
</shape>
```

What just happened?

The `shape` resource you just created will display a dashed line. The dashes in the line have a spacing of exactly half the length of the dashes themselves. The sizes are set relative to the user's preferred font size, so the dashes will grow and shrink according to the users preferences.

The following is a screenshot of this line running with the default emulator settings:

Rendering rectangles

Rectangles are the most commonly used shape resource since `View` objects take up a rectangular space on the screen (even if they don't use every pixel of that space). The rectangle shape includes the ability to have rounded corners, where each corner may optionally have a different radius.

With no additional style information, a basic rectangle declaration will render a filled black box with no visible outline. However, rectangles are better suited to creating outlines which can be used to either draw attention to a single widget, or isolate a group of widgets from all of the others on the screen. A simple white rectangle border can be built copying the following code-snippet into a file named `res/drawable/border.xml`:

```
<shape xmlns:android="http://schemas.android.com/apk/res/android"
        android:shape="rectangle">

    <stroke android:width="2dip" android:color="#ffffffff" />
    <padding android:top="8dip"
             android:left="8dip"
             android:bottom="8dip"
             android:right="8dip" />
</shape>
```

The padding element in this shape will cause any `View` object it's used in to increase the size of it's padding by `8dip`. This will stop the contents of the widget from intersecting the border rendered by the shape resource.

Time for action – creating a rounded border

A rectangular shape may also have its corners curved in order to make a rounded rectangle. A rounded rectangle is useful for styling buttons, or creating cleaner looking borders.

1. Create a new shape resource XML file in the `res/drawable` directory named `rounded_border.xml` and open this file in an editor or IDE.

2. Declare the root element of the file as a `rectangle shape`:

   ```
   <shape xmlns:android="http://schemas.android.com/apk/res/android"
          android:shape="rectangle">
   ```

3. Set the rectangle stroke to `2dip` wide and white in color:

   ```
   <stroke android:width="2dip" android:color="#ffffffff" />
   ```

4. Pad the rectangle with `8dip` of empty space:

   ```
   <padding android:top="8dip"
            android:left="8dip"
            android:bottom="8dip"
            android:right="8dip" />
   ```

5. Curve the corners by `4dip`:

   ```
   <corners android:radius="4dip"/>
   ```

6. Close the shape declaration:

   ```
   </shape>
   ```

What just happened?

To apply the rounded border you just created to a `View` object, you have several different options available to you, the most simple of which is to apply it directly as a background. For this, you would reference the shape as though it were any other image file in the drawable directory. Earlier, we declared a `TitleStyle` and applied it to a `TextView` with the word `Header` as its content. If you applied the new `rounded_border` to this `TextView`, the `TextView` declaration in the layout resource would look something more like this:

```
<TextView
        style="@style/TitleStyle"
        android:background="@drawable/rounded_border"
        android:layout_width="fill_parent"
        android:layout_height="wrap_content"
        android:text="Header"/>
```

Alternatively, you could apply this border to the `TitleStyle`, which would then apply the new border to every widget assigned the `TitleStyle`, which is rather fitting for headers and title widgets:

```
<style name="TitleStyle" parent="@android:style/TextAppearance">
    <item name="android:background">@drawable/rounded_border</item>
```

```
        <item name="android:textSize">25dip</item>
        <item name="android:textColor">#ffffffff</item>
        <item name="android:textStyle">bold</item>
        <item name="android:gravity">center</item>
    </style>
```

Either of these will result in the exact same rendering of the new widget. The implementation decision is really a matter of what you are trying to achieve. Styles are the best way to keep commonality between different widgets that are used for the same purpose.

Using the above style on a `TextView` will result in a nice header widget that looks as follows:

Rendering ovals

The oval shape is exactly what the name implies—an ellipse. An oval is more limited in its use than a rectangle, unless the widget drawing on top of it is best bordered by a circle or ellipse, such as an analogue clock. That said, an oval, or rather a circle is a very useful shape to use as an image in your user-interfaces. A perfect example is a symbol to inform the user whether they are connected to the Internet or not, or whether a widget is valid or not. Using an oval shape for such a purpose is exactly the same as using a bitmap. However, the oval can be scaled according the users' preferences without any loss of quality, while you would need several differently-sized bitmap images to achieve a similar effect (even then, some of the bitmaps would require scaling).

If we wanted an oval shape to represent an invalid widget (for example, to show that two password entries don't match when the user is selecting a password), then it would be best to color the oval in red. In the following code-snippet, we declare an oval shape as XML with a grey border and a red fill:

```
<shape xmlns:android="http://schemas.android.com/apk/res/android"
        android:shape="oval">

    <solid android:color="#ffff0000"/>
    <stroke android:width="1sp" android:color="#ffaaaaaa"/>
</shape>
```

In the preceding case, we use the `<solid>` element to fill the oval with a plain red color, while using the `<stroke>` element to surround it with a thin grey outline. Also, notice the lack of sizing on the `shape` elements. As previously stated, their dimensions are inherited from the width they are placed in, either as a background, or in the case of an `ImageView`, as the content of the widget. If you want to place this oval shape into an `ImageView`, you would specify it in the `src` attribute, as follows:

```
<ImageView
        android:src="@drawable/oval"
        android:layout_width="8dip"
        android:layout_height="8dip"/>
```

The preceding code is about the right size for a validation icon to sit next to a widget, while scaling the icon up or down is as easy as changing the width and height of the `ImageView`. If you use `wrap_content` as the size of the `ImageView`, it will be sized as zero-by-zero pixels, and will effectively vanish off the screen.

Following is a screenshot of four different sizes of the same oval, each scaled to double the size of the previous (starting off with the 8x8 dip on the left):

Time for action – applying a gradient to an oval shape

The previous screenshot shows that while the oval looks okay, it's not going to be very visually appealing when surrounded by the gradient painted widgets which make up the default Android toolkit. In order to get the little oval to fit in nicely, it needs to look more like a ball, which requires a simple radial gradient to be applied.

1. Create a new shape resource XML file in the `res/drawable` directory named `ball.xml` and open this file in an editor or IDE.

2. Declare the root element of the file as an `oval`:

    ```
    <shape xmlns:android="http://schemas.android.com/apk/res/android"
            android:shape="oval">
    ```

3. Instead of declaring a `solid` color as the fill, declare a `gradient` fill starting with a light grey and ending in red:

    ```
    <gradient android:type="radial"
                android:centerX="0.5"
                android:centerY="0.25"
                android:startColor="#ffff9999"
                android:endColor="#ffff0000"
                android:gradientRadius="8" />
    ```

4. Define the thin light grey outline of the oval in a `stroke` element:

```
<stroke android:width="1sp" android:color="#ffaaaaaa"/>
```

5. Close the shape declaration:

```
</shape>
```

What just happened?

Unfortunately, the affected radius of a radial gradient doesn't scale with the rest of the image, leaving a very small gradient area when you scale the image to large sizes. The effect in this case is that while the smallest version of the image looks great, the larger versions look terrible. At the time of writing this book, there is no direct way to work around this limitation. Instead, you will need to tie the size of your oval shape to the size of the `ImageView` if you want to use a radial gradient.

Rendering rings

The ring shape is also circular in its rendering, but serves a very different purpose to the oval shape. While the oval shape's content area is everything inside the outline space, a ring shape's content area is a circle.

The following diagram illustrates the logical difference between the two shapes:

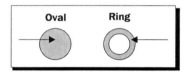

The ring shape also how two outlines, one on the outside and another on the inside (as shown in the preceding diagram). Combine this with the ability to fill the ring's content area with a gradient and you have the perfect shape to use for progress spinners (the default Android indeterminate progress spinner it built with a ring).

Time for action – rendering a spinner ring

By default, a shape will assume that it's being used as part of a `LevelListDrawable`, and may not appear unless you disable this behavior. You do this by specifying the `useLevel` attribute as `false` on the shape element. If you don't disable this functionality, the ring will not render correctly, or at all.

1. Create a new shape resource XML file in the `res/drawable` directory named `spinner.xml` and open this file in an editor or IDE.

2. Start the root element of the file as a `ring` shape:

```
<shape xmlns:android="http://schemas.android.com/apk/res/android"
       android:shape="ring"
```

3. The `ring` shape requires its relative thickness to be set on the `shape` declaration:

```
       android:innerRadiusRatio="3.2"
       android:thicknessRatio="5.333"
```

4. Finish the `shape` declaration by turning off the `useLevel` functionality:

```
       android:useLevel="false">
```

5. Declare a `sweep` gradient centered in the oval:

```
<gradient android:type="sweep"
          android:useLevel="false"
          android:startColor="#ffaaffff"
          android:centerColor="#ff0000ff"
          android:centerY="0.50"
          android:endColor="#ff0000ff"/>
```

6. Outline the `ring` with a thin white border:

```
<stroke android:width="1sp" android:color="#ffffffff"/>
```

7. End the `shape` declaration:

```
</shape>
```

What just happened

The sweep gradient is another form of radial gradient. Instead of extending out from the center of the image, it sweeps in a circle like the hands of a clock.

The image on the left-hand side is a rectangle filled with the sweep gradient; while the image on the right-hand side is the ring shape. As you can see, the two effects are quite different. The image on the right-hand side is based on the image used by Android 1.6 for the indeterminate spinner.

Defining layers

So far, we've only defined shapes as single-element images. It's possible to combine these shapes into more complex images. These images are combined together in layers, which is a commonly used graphics structure. In Android, this is done with a layer-list structure. A layer-list is not a type of shape, but it is a Drawable structure which means it can be used in place of a normal bitmap image.

Layered image resources are not confined to being used with vector Drawable structures such as the shapes we've already talked about. A layered Drawable object may also include some layers that are bitmap images, or any other Drawable type that can be defined.

For each layer in a layer-list, you need to define an <item> element. The item element is used to declare optional meta-information such as an ID for the layer (which can be used to retrieve the Drawable object for that layer in your Java code). You can also declare location offsets or padding for the layer in the item element. While you can reference a layer as an external Drawable resource, you are also able to inline the Drawable object inside the <item> element, allowing you to compose various different Drawable structures in a single file.

Sizing your layers

Only the first <item> of a layer-list will be sized according to the widget it's placed in. All other layers will be sized to their "natural" size. For a bitmap image, this is the size it is rendered in. For a <shape> element, the natural size is 0x0. In order to specify a natural size for a <shape>, you'll need to give the <shape> a <size> child-element with an android:width and android:height attribute.

If you wanted a two-layer image to act as a large green button, you would probably declare a layer for a grey rounded rectangle as a background, and another layer for a green oval to look something like a light, or ball on top of the grey background. Such a layer-list could look something similar to the following code-snippet:

```
<layer-list xmlns:android="http://schemas.android.com/apk/res/
android">
    <item>
        <shape android:shape="rectangle" android:useLevel="false">
            <stroke android:width="1dip" android:color="#ffffffff" />
            <gradient android:type="linear"
                    android:angle="90"
                    android:startColor="#ffaaaaaa"
                    android:endColor="#ffcdcdcd" />
            <padding android:top="8dip"
                    android:left="8dip"
                    android:bottom="8dip"
                    android:right="8dip" />
            <corners android:radius="4dip" />
        </shape>
    </item>
    <item>
        <shape android:shape="oval" android:useLevel="false">
            <size android:width="32dip" android:height="32dip" />
            <gradient android:type="radial"
              android:centerX="0.45"
              android:centerY="0.25"
              android:startColor="#ff1a4e1a"
              android:endColor="#ff1ad049"
              android:gradientRadius="32" />
        </shape>
    </item>
</layer-list>
```

In the preceding snippet, there are only shape layers, but you could easily add in a bitmap layer by referencing the bitmap resource on the <item> element, as in the following code snippet:

```
<item android:drawable="@drawable/checkmark"/>
```

Stretching using nine-patch images

There are times when you want a border that is more than a simple line, for example, if you want to add a shadow. On a web-page, you'll commonly find various HTML tricks used to insert eight or nine images into a box so that the content can be scaled while the border remains intact. In Android, this technique is called a "nine-patch" image because it consists of nine different parts. A nine-patch image in Android is handled specially when it's rendered at sizes larger than its original size. In order to identify these images as special, they have a .9.png extension (and must be valid PNG files).

A nine-patch image combines a border and a background in a single image. The background area will grow when the content becomes too large for the image, and the border areas of the image will be scaled up so that no "holes" are left.

Conceptually, you can start off by thinking about a nine-patch image as shown in the following diagram:

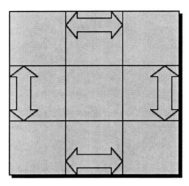

The arrows in the diagram indicate the conceptual "border" areas that will grow in size according to the size of the center "content" area. The corners of a nine-patch image will be entirely unaffected by any scaling that takes place.

Creating nine-patch images

In order to create a nine-patch image, you'll need a decent image editing application. I personally make use of the **GIMP** application (available for free at http://www.gimp. org), although you may prefer to use another application. Whatever application you use, it must be able to write out **Portable Network Graphics** (**PNG**) files, and should also be able to zoom to fairly extreme levels. The entire data in a nine-patch image is actually encoded into the image file, meaning there is no need for an XML file to tell Android what parts of the image are border areas, and what parts must not be affected by scaling.

Unlike CSS boxes that appear on web pages, the size manipulation done on a nine-patch image in Android is nearest-neighbor scaling. **Nearest-neighbor scaling** doesn't attempt to improve the quality of the scaled image in any way, the pixels simply become larger solid blocks of color. While this works excellently for gradient content backgrounds (provided they aren't forced to grow too large), it may cause your image to have some strange artifacts to it. Since currently there is no color interpolation performed during the scaling, some effects may look rather strange when they are scaled. Scaling also takes longer than simple image copying, so bear this in mind when sizing the image, it may need to get a lot larger than you think. However, this also means that nine-patch images are far more flexible than those you might know from the Web.

The following two images are scaled-up versions of the same 32x32 pixel nine-patch image:

The image on the left-hand side is the raw PNG file that can be used as a nine-patch image. The image on the right-hand side is the same image with a part of it highlighted to show which areas will be scaled. The top, bottom-left, and right areas will be scaled only horizontally or vertically, while the center area will be stretched to fit the size of the content. The following image is the same image being used as the background of a TextView object:

So, the black lines on the left-hand side and top of the image tell Android what parts of the image to scale, but what do the lines on the right and bottom signify? These two lines determine where to place the content of the widget, much like the <padding> element in a <shape> resource.

To get to grips with how your nine-patch image will be rendered and the possible ways it can be scaled, Android provides you with a utility in the tools directory of an Android SDK installation. The draw9patch utility renders your nine-patch scaled to various shapes and sizes, and allows you to effectively debug the image before using it in your application.

Using bitmap images in Android

Images are a major part of styling your application. They are used for icons, borders, backgrounds, logos, and many other purposes. Android does its best to make sure the images you use as resources render as well as possible across the different types of screens used on Android devices.

Android's automatic handling of images if far from perfect. However, there are times when you will need several different variations of the same image for your application to look right on all of the different devices.

Handling different screen sizes

When working with any bitmap image in Android, it's very important to consider that your application will be run on a variety of different screens, both different sizes and densities. When working on very large screens (such as those found on a laptop or tablet), you will want to use larger images than you use on an extremely small screen. While nine-patch images go a long way to keep things simple, they are still scaled with a nearest-neighbor algorithm, and this may start to show on a large screen with a larger font-size than you anticipated.

You can provide images of different sizes in your resources directory. For each screen size, you can provide a different `drawable` directory. The resource loading tools will automatically pick files from the directory that most closely matches the current device configuration. You don't need a copy of every resource in each of these directories, but only the ones you want to provide a more suitable alternative for. The resource loader will fall back on looser matching directories when it attempts to find a resource file to load.

Android recognizes five important parameters with regards to the size of a screen. While you can specify parameters that relate to the exact number of pixels on the screen, this is not a good idea as you won't easily be able to cater to all of the different screen sizes. Instead, it's best to stick to the five parameters that Android provides:

- `small`
- `medium`
- `large`
- `long`
- `notlong`

The first three parameters are directly related to the size of the screen, while the last two are related to whether the screen is "traditional" (such as VGA) or has a "wide" (such as WVGA) format. These parameters can be mixed together in various combinations such as:

- `/res/drawable-small/`
- `/res/drawable-medium-long/`
- `/res/drawable-large-notlong/`

The preceding examples are all valid resource directories that can be used to override file in the normal `drawable` directory. You can't combine parameters that contradict each other, such as:

- `/res/drawable-small-large/`
- `/res/drawable-long-notlong/`

In the preceding cases, you will receive an error from the resource packaging tool. Whenever you work with bitmap images, it's important to consider these size parameters, since some devices have screens very different from the one that the emulator shows by default.

Handling different screen densities

Screen density generally refers to the number of pixels packed into a given physical space (that is, dots-per-inch or DPI). It also has a relationship to the size of the pixels on the screen. While most Android devices have medium or high-density screens, a large number of cheaper devices make use of a relatively low-density screen.

Why does this affect nine-patch and bitmap images? The same reason it affects font rendering—the lower the density, the worse anti-aliasing and shadows look. The best way to explain this is with images. In the following images, the one on the left is a simple rounded-rectangle as it would appear on a high-density screen. The image on the right is similar to how the same image would render on a low-density screen:

Although both are the same source image rendered at the same physical size, a reduction in the number of pixels available makes the image look blocky on a low-density screen.

The following two images are taken from the bottom-right corner, and enlarged to illustrate in better detail what happens:

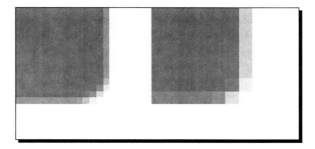

Again, these images are configured to take up the same amount of physical space. If an image's size is specified in screen-pixels, it will take up much more physical space on a low-density screen. This is one of the reasons it's recommended that you size images in Android using the "density-independent-pixels" (dp or dip) unit instead of the normal pixels (px) unit.

As with screen sizes, Android provides a series of configuration parameters that can be used to provide different resources for different screen densities. The parameters available for selecting a screen-density can be mixed with those selecting based on the screen-size. The following is a list of parameters Android makes available for resources to be provided based on the screen-density of the current device:

- `ldpi`: Low-density screens (~120dpi)
- `mdpi`: Medium-density screens (~160dpi)
- `hdpi`: High-density screens (~260dpi)
- `nodpi`: Special case

The final "special case" can be used when you have a nine-patch image, or a bitmap image, that you don't want scaled according to device density. Android, by default, will re-scale an image in an attempt to keep the image's physical size as close to the intended size as possible. An image in a `nodpi` directory will not be scaled automatically by Android, and will be rendered on a pixel-for-pixel basis.

> **Different density icons**
>
> There are times when a large high-resolution icon does not scale down very well. In these cases, it's often a good idea to design entirely different icons for low-density screens.

Handling configuration changes

When you provide Android with different resource directories relating to various possible hardware configurations, the resource loader will attempt to match the best resource files for the device that your application is running on. However, not all of the configuration parameters relate directly to the hardware, but instead describe the device state or some software configuration parameter. Examples of these types of parameters are the device language, network IDs, and device orientation. These parameters may change while your application is running. The most common example being the device orientation. Android has a built-in mechanism to handle such changes for you, and for the most part you won't need any special Java code to handle these changes. However, it is strongly desirable to at least provide resource files for some of these parameters.

When a configuration parameter changes, Android will store any of your `Activity` state in a `Bundle` object, and then shut down the `Activity`. It will then start up a new instance of the `Activity` object with the new configuration parameters, and restore the state from the `Bundle` object. All of the default Android widgets will store their current state before your `Activity` is shut down by the system. This means you don't generally need to perform any special handling for the configuration changes.

Providing landscape layouts

So far through the book, we've only built portrait layouts. Unlike a desktop or web system, a mobile application's orientation by default is portrait (hence the configuration parameters `long` and `notlong` as opposed to `wide` and `narrow`). One of the great things about having the Android platform is that an accelerometer is a required piece of hardware, which means that your application can respond to the orientation of the device. Thanks to Android's configuration handling (as mentioned previously), you, as a developer, don't need to do anything except provide alternative landscape layout resources, assuming you don't build major parts of your user interface in Java. In order to provide layouts which are specific to either a portrait or a landscape orientation, you place the specific versions of your layout's XML resources in directories configured with the following resource configuration parameters:

- `port`: Portrait-specific layouts
- `land`: Landscape-specific layouts

When the screen is longer vertically than horizontally (that is, portrait orientation), using a simple vertically-oriented `LinearLayout` to layout an input form makes quite a lot of sense. Any input widgets you make use of will be positioned below their labels and so have more horizontal space to display their data. The additional horizontal space allows for labels to include more information as well.

The following diagram illustrates the difference between these two layout concepts:

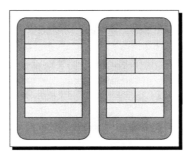

The layout method used on the right is very common in a web or desktop system, and will work well on a mobile device if the size of the labels and input widgets are small enough.

When switching to a landscape orientation, the dramatic increase in horizontal space coupled with the massive loss in vertical space makes the vertical `LinearLayout` a terrible choice. If you are working with a simple input form, then a landscape layout should use `TableLayout` or `RelativeLayout` to position the labels on the same lines as the input widgets they relate to.

Providing text input on a landscape layout

When building your landscape layouts, you need to carefully consider what parts of the user interface are most important. If your screen is being used to compose an e-mail or a document, your landscape layout could be almost identical to the portrait layout. However, such a layout has a mostly hidden enemy: the software keyboard. On a portrait layout, the software keyboard will confine itself to the bottom of the screen and consume a relatively small amount of space (about a quarter to one-third of the available screen space). On a landscape layout however, the software keyboard can consume as much as half of your vertical screen space, making it very hard to build content-centric landscape layouts. If your layout is strongly input-driven, it may make sense to either remove parts of your user-interface when the orientation is landscape, re-working your user interface so that the software keyboard won't get in the way.

Android does provide a series of configuration parameters which will tell you about the keyboard on the device on which your application is running. It's a good idea to take all of the possibilities into account when building your application. The following is a short list of the possible keyboard situations that your application may be faced with:

- Software Keyboard only
- Hardware Keyboard
- Hardware Keyboard available; Software Keyboard in use

On top of these possibilities, devices with smaller screens will often make use of a 12-key keyboard instead of a full QWERTY keyboard. If this is a software keyboard (which it often is), the keyboard may take as much as 80 percent of your available screen space. This problem if often handled by Android opening a "text input" screen when a text-input box is activated by the user. You can determine the different states of keyboard availability, and the type of keyboard used, with the following configuration parameters:

- `nokeys`: Software keyboard only
- `qwerty`: A full hardware keyboard is available
- `12key`: A 12-key hardware phone-keyboard is available
- `keysexposed`: The user has a keyboard visible, whether it's hardware or software
- `keyshidden`: There isn't any keyboard currently visible
- `keyssoft`: The user will use a software keyboard (though it may not be visible)

When designing your screens, consider that the software keyboard may take up to half of your vertical space. Ensure that content areas will scroll, while vital widgets will always remain visible on the screen. If a chat application is simply wrapped in `ScrollView`, the input `EditView` object may become invisible when the software keyboard is visible. It's important not just to consider how the screen will look, but how it will react to the changes that your users will throw at it. Finally, it's vital to test how your screen will look and behave with and without a software keyboard.

Altering screen content

One of the great advantages of the Android XML layout format is the decoupling it provides. Portrait and landscape layouts are often quite different from each other, and users may individually find a preferred orientation from which to use your application. A not-very-common, but useful trick when designing the new layouts, is the ability to add or remove "non-functional" elements from the two different layouts.

In a simple example, you may want to abbreviate the text in labels for the portrait layout and include some icons as graphical hints, while for the landscape layout, you may want icons double the size and two-line labels, all on the same line as your input field.

The following diagram illustrates this concept:

On the landscape layout in the preceding diagram, you could make use of an additional TextView element for the sub-text on the label. Assuming your Java code doesn't look for the additional TextView object, your application will run perfectly. The ability to alter the actual structure of the user interface, and not just its layout, is a very important consideration when designing alternative layouts for an Activity.

Summary

The look and feel of an application is vital. A single change to color or font can make or break a screen's usability. At the same time, over-styling an application can make it feel out-of-place on the user's device. An alien look and feel will drive users away from the application towards those that look and feel more familiar and comfortable to them.

Android provides an extremely powerful set of capabilities with the style resource structure. When combined with the ability to place your graphics in resource files and override the defaults, you can effectively re-style any widget. Using styles also helps with the maintenance of your application as you will only need to change styling in the style resources and not on each widget declaration of a particular style.

Keeping most of your widget graphics as <shape> resources will ensure the most consistent look and feel possible for your application. However, this is not always practical. When you need to provide bitmap resources, it's vital to provide different images for the various screen sizes and densities the user may be working with.

Styling an application also includes the layout and the ability for the application to adapt to the device it's running on. Having a great idea is only half of an application's appeal, its styling and execution are critical to its survival in the "wild". Attention to detail is a powerful tool that will draw users to your application. Applications that "just work" are always favored over those that require time and effort to work with.

Make use of the various screen-sizes and densities provided to you by the Android emulator to ensure that your application will look good on as many devices as possible. Don't forget that many devices don't have hardware keyboards and that the software keyboard can take as much as half of your screen space.

In the next chapter, we'll be extending this styling knowledge into the overall design and theming of an application. We'll be building a styled application with many of the provided layouts and will be performing fairly extensive styling.

10
Building an Application Theme

Whether graphical styling or not, every application has a theme. The theme of an application is what gives it a distinct appearance and logic.

When a person uses a mobile application (which accounts for most Android devices), there are some fundamental differences in their behavior when compared to a desktop or laptop:

- They often have less time for the application, and therefore less patience
- They are often focused entirely on a single application at a time
- Touchscreen devices encourage an almost tactile response

Android devices are diverse and run on almost everything including common mobile phones, tablets, laptops, and a few desktop machines. An Android application is expected to function well in all of these environments, and the theme of the application should be carefully constructed to allow the user the best possible access to each of these devices.

The device interface forms a part of your application theme. When using a mouse on a desktop or laptop device, a user interface designed with only touchscreen in mind may feel over-sized to a user (since all widgets need to be finger-sized). Contrary to this, an application designed for a mouse-driven system will normally include rollover effects, which won't work properly on a touchscreen device. The only way to make sure your application works on all these different devices is to consider all of these environments when building the screens of your application.

Android itself defines a theme of sorts and as far as possible, applications built for the Android platform should attempt to conform or extend this theme, rather than redefine it. This doesn't mean your application must look and behave exactly the same way as all other Android applications, but rather that your application should be based on the underlying principles that Android lays down.

Keep in mind that many of the device manufacturers define additional parts to the basic Android theme, and your application should do the same.

In this chapter, we will examine the building of an application, including the design of the screens, their construction, and their styling. We'll also examine how this application will interact with various different devices, making sure it looks right and functions as the user would expect it to. The application we're going to build is a calculator, having both a standard and a scientific calculator. The calculator will be styled to look more like a physical calculator than a generic Android application, and will change its functionality according to the capabilities of the device it's running on. Overall, we'll be defining an application with its own, consistent theme.

Creating a basic calculator layout

The first thing we need in order to build this project is a basic portrait layout for a standard calculator. This basic layout will serve as the screen that the user will look at when they first start the application. Given the nature of a calculator application and how the user perceives it, it's very important that the screen be simple and that the application starts as quickly as possible.

 It's important that the calculator screen takes up all available space with functional components, in order to make itself as quick to use as possible (bigger buttons equals easier usage).

Pop quiz

1. When do layout resources become Java classes?

    a. When the resource-processor is run

    b. When the application package is built

    c. When the layout resource is loaded

    d. Never

2. How do you reference widgets that are not defined by default in Android?

    a. By using the full class name as an element name

    b. By defining an XML namespace for the Java package

    c. It's currently impossible

    d. By specifying the Java package name in the the `android:package` attribute

3. What is the default width and height of a `View` object?

   a. The size of it's content

   b. Zero-by-zero pixels

   c. It depends on the `ViewGroup` it's placed in

   d. The width of its parent and the height of its content

4. You write a layout resource as XML, what format is it stored in?

   a. As raw XML text

   b. Android binary XML

   c. Layout specific binary format

   d. Java classes

Designing a standard calculator

Before starting to build the calculator application, it's a good idea to sketch out what it's going to look like. This will also help you to decide how exactly to construct the screens. Since a calculator is something that is both, a rather old invention as well as something people are very familiar with, it's important to stick to the most common design. If you introduce a calculator that is too foreign to people, they may well not have the patience to "get to know" your application. New ideas are good (that is, slide keyboards), but the most successful are those that are extensions of existing ideas. Also, make it obvious to the user how they work. The following is a block diagram of the standard calculator screen that we will start building:

It's important that we maximize the use of the screen space, so we'll do our best to make the buttons as large as possible. Also, we want to space the buttons slightly apart in order to avoid the undesired button from being pressed by the user. Since we only have a single output area, we'll make sure that the display area is also sufficiently large.

The arrow in the display area will be an icon which will act as a *Backspace* button, allowing the user to delete unwanted content. It's always important to give the user a way to undo what they have done. We'll use an icon similar to the one used in the dialer application, which will keep a feeling of overall consistency with the rest of the system. This also effectively gives us space for an additional button. This user interface doesn't include the normal "memory" functions associated with many calculators. The basic screen is designed to be as simple as possible, and we'll introduce more functionality as we develop the application.

Time for action – building the standard calculator

The first layout for the calculator will consist of a normal series of **0** to **9** buttons with a button for the various basic arithmetic operations—add, subtract, multiply, and divide. It will also have buttons for equals and a button for the decimal point. While this would be a very easy screen to build in Java code, we'll build this example entirely as an XML resource. Since this application will have several different permutations of the same screen, using layout resource files with no Java code will make your life much easier.

1. Start by creating a new project for the calculator:

```
android create project -n Calculator -p Calculator -k com.
packtpub.calculator -a CalculatorActivity -t 3
```

2. Open the standard main layout file `/res/layout/main.xml`.

3. Remove the generated layout structure from the file.

4. Start by declaring a vertical `LinearLayout` as a root element to consume all the available space on the screen:

```
<LinearLayout
    xmlns:android="http://schemas.android.com/apk/res/android"
    android:orientation="vertical"
    android:layout_width="fill_parent"
    android:layout_height="fill_parent">
```

5. Declare a `RelativeLayout` that will compose the display with the **Delete** or **Cancel** button that the user can use to remove unwanted input:

```
<RelativeLayout android:layout_width="fill_parent"
                android:layout_height="wrap_content">
```

6. Use the standard Android input delete icon in an `ImageView` on the right side of the `RelativeLayout`:

```
<ImageView android:id="@+id/delete"
           android:src="@android:drawable/ic_input_delete"
           android:layout_centerInParent="true"
           android:layout_alignParentRight="true"
```

```
           android:layout_width="wrap_content"
           android:layout_height="wrap_content"/>
```

7. On the left side of the `RelativeLayout,` create a `TextView` that will actually display the numeric status of the calculator:

```
<TextView android:id="@+id/display"
          android:text="0"
          android:layout_alignParentTop="true"
          android:layout_toLeftOf="@id/delete"
          android:layout_width="fill_parent"
          android:layout_height="wrap_content"/>
```

8. Inside the `LinearLayout,` declare a `TableLayout` that will be used to contain the button inputs for the simple calculator:

```
<TableLayout android:id="@+id/standard_functions"
             android:layout_width="fill_parent"
             android:layout_height="fill_parent"
             android:layout_margin="0px"
             android:stretchColumns="0,1,2,3">
```

9. The `TableLayout` will be made up of four `TableRow` objects. Declare the first of these with no margin and a `layout_weight` of 1:

```
<TableRow android:layout_margin="0px"
          android:layout_weight="1">
```

10. The top-right `Button` object needs to be the `plus` sign, which we also use as the name for the `Button` ID:

```
<Button android:id="@+id/plus"
        android:text="+"/>
```

11. The next three `Button` objects on the first row will be the numbers **1**, **2**, and **3**. These all need IDs as well:

```
<Button android:id="@+id/one"
        android:text="1"/>
<Button android:id="@+id/two"
        android:text="2"/>
<Button android:id="@+id/three"
        android:text="3"/>
```

12. Continue to declare `TableRow` objects with buttons in the order defined in the block-diagram.

13. Open the `CalculatorActivity.java` source file in an editor or IDE.

14. In the `onCreate` method, ensure that the content view of the `Activity` is set to the `main` layout you've just defined:

```
setContentView(R.layout.main);
```

What just happened?

You should now have a basic user interface for a calculator; although it still looks like a very generic Android application, but it's a start at the basic level. The user interface will need styling work, including colorization and some font changes, but the basic structure is now complete. The use of the `RelativeLayout` is to ensure that we can correctly position the delete icon to the right of the `TextView`, no matter what the size of the screen is.

In order for the buttons to consume as much of the available space as possible, we tell the `TableLayout` to stretch all of its columns. If the `TableLayout` doesn't stretch its columns, then it will only consume as much horizontal space as its children require (effectively the same as `wrap_content` width). Although the `TableLayout` is told to consume all of the vertical space as well, its children will be sized according to the amount of space they need, which is why the buttons don't take up all of the available screen space. The following image is a screenshot of the basic calculator running in the emulator:

Building the calculator styling

We really want this calculator to look more like a real calculator, and for that we need to apply some styling. The current theme of the calculator is entirely the standard Android theme, and while it looks exactly like the rest of the Android system, it doesn't really suit this application. We want to style both the buttons and the display area of the application. We'll define style values in a resource file and relate to these in the layout XML file.

To start with, we'll define a series of nine-patch images to create our own button designs. We need three different images for this purpose. The first image is the "normal" state of the button, the second will be the "pressed" state of the button, and finally, a "focused" state of the button.

Pop Quiz

1. What are the black lines around the border of a nine-patch image for?

    a. Hints to the system as to what parts of the image to copy

    b. To indicate what parts of the image to scale and where to put the widget content

    c. Defines what parts of the image contain meta-information

2. What formats may a nine-patch image be stored as?

    a. JPEG, GIF, or PNG image file

    b. An XML file with an embedded TIFF

    c. A portable-network-graphic image

3. What does the `draw9patch` application do?

    a. Renders a nine-patch image in various shapes and sizes

    b. It's an application for drawing nine-patch images

    c. Generates the meta-data for a nine-patch image as an XML file

Time for action – creating the button images

In order to build the button images in this section you will need to download "The GIMP" (available at `http://www.gimp.org`). It's perfect for this sort of image creation or manipulation and has the added advantage that it's open source.

1. Open "The Gimp", and select **File | New** to create a new image.

2. Change the width and height to `38x38` pixels.

3. Open the **Advanced Options** and change the **Fill With** option to **Transparency** so that there is no background color.

4. To help with sizing, zoom in to about **800%**.

5. Select the **Rectangle** tool in the top-left of the toolbox (the default keyboard shortcut key is *R*).

6. Enable the **Rounded Corners** option and set it to `5`.

7. Enable the **Fixed** option and select **Size** in the drop-down list.

8. Enter `36x36` as the fixed size of the rectangle selection.

9. Place the selection box at the center of the image canvas and there should be a one-pixel border between the selection box and the edge of the image.

10. Double-click on the "Foreground color" (black by default) in the toolbox.

11. Enter 444444 in the **Hex Notation** box of the color selector.

12. Close the color selector dialog box.

13. Select the **Bucket Fill** tool in the toolbox (the default keyboard shortcut is *Shift-B*).

14. Click inside the selection box to fill it with the selected color.

15. Use the **Select** menu and click the **None** option to remove the selection box.

16. Select **Filter | Decor | Add Bevel**.

17. Change the **Thickness** option to 3.

18. Uncheck the **Work on Copy** option and select the **Ok** button.

19. Select the **Rectangle** tool from the toolbox again.

20. Uncheck the **Rounded Corners** and **Fixed** options.

21. Use the selection tool to select a single pixel wide vertical box on the inside of the "button" shape, being careful to only select part of the content area of the button, avoiding the beveled border space:

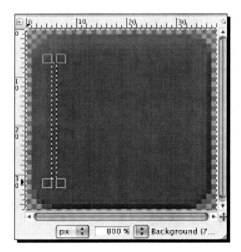

22. By placing the cursor in the middle of the selection box, drag the selection horizontally to the very edge of the of the image canvas (inside the one-pixel border).

23. Double-click on the "Foreground" rectangle again.

24. Reset the color to pure black.

25. Select the **Bucket Fill** option.

26. Click inside the selection box to create a single pixel wide, black vertical line down the left-side of the image.

27. Create a similar vertical line on the right side of the image.

28. Create a horizontal single-pixel high black line at the top and bottom of the image.

29. Save the image in your `res/drawable` directory as `button.9.png`, leaving the PNG Options as their defaults.

30. Repeat this exact process, changing the `444444` foreground color, as done in step 11, to `c16400` and save the new image as `button_focus.9.png`.

By inverting the image with the **Flip Tool** (default keyboard shortcut *Shift + F*), you will create the `button_down.9.png` image.

What just happened?

While there are many steps to building images, they are fundamentally very easy to create with the right tool and a bit of experimentation. If all you need is a simple button or something similar, then it's well worth finding a few tutorials on how to use "The GIMP" or a similar tool. There are great tutorials online at the following links:

- http://www.gimp.org/tutorials/
- http://gimp-tutorials.net/

The images you have saved in the last section should look like the following images that I have created for my calculator application:

Time for action – styling the calculator buttons

The next thing we need to do is use a selector-list and the nine-patch images you've just created to style the calculator buttons. We'll also be defining the button styling in a resource file so that we don't have to specify all of the styling for each of the buttons. In order to replace the standard button with our image, we only need to replace its background with the one we create for the purpose.

1. In the `res/drawable` directory, create a new XML file named `button.xml` and open it in an editor.

2. Define the root element of the file as a fixed-size selector:

```
<selector
    xmlns:android="http://schemas.android.com/apk/res/android"
    android:constantSize="true"
    android:variablePadding="false">
```

3. Create the pressed button state, as the first child of the selector:

```
<item android:state_pressed="true"
    android:drawable="@drawable/button_down"/>
```

4. The second child of the selector should be the focused state:

```
<item android:state_focused="true"
    android:drawable="@drawable/button_focus"/>
```

5. The final selector child is generic, and is the normal state:

```
<item android:drawable="@drawable/button"/>
```

6. Create a new file named `styles.xml` in the `res/values` directory and open it in an editor.

7. The root element of the `styles.xml` file should be a resources element with no namespace declaration (it's not needed in this file):

```
<resources>
```

8. Define the first style in the file as `CalculatorButton` with a parent style of the default Android `Button` widget style:

```
<style name="CalculatorButton"
        parent="@android:style/Widget.Button">
```

9. Set the text size to a nice large font and a light grey color:

```
<item name="android:textSize">30sp</item>
<item name="android:textColor">#ffcacaca</item>
```

10. Specify the background of the style as the new `button` drawable resource:

```
<item name="android:background">@drawable/button</item>
```

11. Create a two-pixel border around each of the `Button` widgets to create a little bit of spacing:

```
<item name="android:layout_margin">2dp</item>
```

12. Make sure the `Button` widgets consume all their available vertical space:

```
<item name="android:layout_height">fill_parent</item>
```

13. Open the `main.xml` layout resource in an editor.

14. On each of the `Button` elements, add a style attribute to give them the styling you just defined in the `styles.xml` file:

```
<Button style="@style/CalculatorButton"
        android:id="@+id/multiply"
        android:text="*"/>
```

What just happened?

We've just re-styled the `Button` objects for the calculator screen. The style is the child of the standard Android `Button` widget. The new styling is mostly driven by the change of the background image to the nine-patch image we created earlier. To work with the new background image, we also specify a font color and size. The new calculator user interface will look like the following screenshot when run:

In the original code, there was no margin around the buttons specified, but in the new code, we've added an explicit margin in the custom styling. Our nine-patch images have no padding around the content area.

You'll notice that we style each of the `Button` widgets in the layout. As already mentioned in the previous chapter, the style attribute is not part of the Android resources namespace. Unfortunately, Android doesn't currently allow us to style all widgets of a particular class. Instead, we are forced to either style each of the widgets individually, or style every widget in an `Activity` or application with the same styles. As part of the new `Button` styling, we declared a drawable resource as a `<selector>` resource. As with the tab structures, `Button` objects can be styled to use different drawable resources for their different states. In this case, we specify background images for instances when the `Button` is focused, pressed, or is in normal state. The styling only applies to the background image, since the background of the new `Button` objects is the `<selector>` resource.

Time for action – styling the display

Currently, the numeric display really looks quite awful. That's mostly because we just don't have any styling for it, and currently it's just a plain `TextView` object. We want the styling to encompass both the `TextView` object and the `ImageView`. The display currently looks like the following screenshot:

In order to fix this display and bring its styling inline with our new `Button` styling, we'll create two different styles. One to create a border and background around the `TextView` and `ImageView` objects, and another to style the `TextView` widget with a more suitable font.

1. Create a new drawable resource file named `display_background.xml` and open it in your editor or IDE.

2. The root of the display background needs to be a rectangle shape:

```
<shape
    xmlns:android="http://schemas.android.com/apk/res/android"
    android:shape="rectangle">
```

3. Declare some padding to inset the text and image:

```
<padding
    android:top="5sp"
    android:bottom="5sp"
    android:left="15sp"
    android:right="15sp"/>
```

4. Create a solid-grey background color for the rectangle:

```
<solid android:color="#ffcccccc"/>
```

5. Specify the stroke size and set its color to white:

```
<stroke android:width="2px"
        android:color="#ffffffff"/>
```

6. Open the `res/values/styles.xml` file in your editor or IDE.

7. Add a new `<style>` item for the display wrapper, and name the new style `CalculatorDisplay` with no parent style:

```
<style name="CalculatorDisplay">
Set the background as the display_background:<item
name="android:background">
```

```
    @drawable/display_background
</item>
```

8. Create a small margin underneath the display wrapper:

```
<item name="android:layout_marginBottom">25sp</item>
```

9. Add some padding above the display:

```
<item name="android:layout_marginTop">50sp</item>
```

10. Start a new `<style>` element with the name `CalculatorTextDisplay`, and the parent style should be the standard `TextView` styling:

```
<style name="CalculatorTextDisplay"
        parent="@android:style/TextAppearance">
```

11. In the new style, set font to `45` pixels, with black monospaced font:

```
<item name="android:typeface">monospace</item>
<item name="android:textSize">45sp</item>
<item name="android:textColor">#ff000000</item>
```

12. The text of the calculator display should be right-aligned, so we'll also specify the gravity to apply to the `TextView`:

```
<item name="android:gravity">right</item>
```

13. Open the `res/layout/main.xml` file in your editor or IDE.

14. Specify the style of the `RelativeLayout` as `CalculatorDisplay`:

```
<RelativeLayout style="@style/CalculatorDisplay"
                android:layout_width="fill_parent"
                android:layout_height="wrap_content">
```

15. Set the style of the `TextView` for the display:

```
<TextView android:id="@+id/display"
        style="@style/CalculatorTextDisplay"
        android:text="0"
        android:layout_alignParentTop="true"
        android:layout_toLeftOf="@id/delete"
        android:layout_width="fill_parent"
        android:layout_height="wrap_content"/>
```

What just happened?

The new styling applies to the `RelativeLayout` that wraps around the `TextView` object and the `ImageView` object. By styling this `RelativeLayout`, you effectively join the `TextView` and `ImageView` together as a single widget. If you look at the following screenshot, you'll see how this works for your user:

The margin on top and below the `TextView` object will shrink the amount of available space that can be used by the buttons. On a long vertical space, the buttons would normally become long and look disproportionate, so by adding a margin to the display area, we help keep the buttons a more square shape.

Have a go hero – Adding calculator logic

Right now, what we've got is a great user interface for a simple calculator. However, it's nothing more than a nice looking user interface. The next thing to do is to add some logic to the works.

Here are the steps that need to be completed to have a functional calculator:

1. Implement the `OnClickListener` interface and register it with each of the `Button` widgets on the user interface.

2. Create a new `Calculator` class to handle the actual calculations and store the non-user-interface state of the calculator.

3. Use the `StringBuilder` class to implement the construction and display of the currently entered value.

4. Implement the basic calculations using the `double` datatype in order to cater for numbers with a decimal place.

Pop quiz

1. When selecting a resource string from a layout, how is the string selected?

   a. Directly from the root `values` strings resources

   b. From a `strings.xml` file in the same directory as the layout

   c. From the `values` directory that is the closest match to the current configuration, and contains a string with the requested name

    d.   From a `values` directory with the same selectors as the directory the layout resource file was selected from

2.   What is the correct filename to place a style resource in?

    a.   Any file in the `values` directory

    b.   `styles.xml`

    c.   `values.xml`

    d.   `theme.xml`

3.   How is resource selection in Java code different to resource selection from an XML resource file?

    a.   The Java resource selection is faster

    b.   XML resources can only reference other resources with the same set of configuration qualifiers as themselves

    c.   There are no significant differences

    d.   XML resources can only reference a subset of all the resource types.

Scientific landscape layout

The scientific layout for the calculator is not simply a case of more buttons, because we want this layout to be used when the device is in a landscape orientation. This means we have significantly less vertical space, something the standard layout consumes lots of. To build this new user interface, we'll not just be defining a new layout resource, but also additional styling for the new layout.

The scientific layout also makes use of more complex text on its new buttons. Some mathematic functions such as square root, or inverse cosine have a specific notation that should be used. In these cases, we'll need to make use of either HTML styling or special characters. Fortunately, Android fully supports the UTF-8 character set, both in functionality and font-rendering, making this process much easier.

Defining string resources for the scientific layout

For the scientific functions, we'll define the string content of each as a resource string. This is partially in order to make them an independent part of the resource selection process (which is always recommended), but it's also to allow us to leverage the automatic HTML processing. If you make use of HTML in a string resource, that HTML will automatically be parsed by the resource processor if accessed with the `Resources.getText` method, instead of the usual `Resources.getString` method. This is exactly the way that the `TextView` class loads its string resources, making it even more attractive to place your text-content in a `values` resource file.

The following is the content of my `strings.xml` file in the `values` directory. You'll notice that the HTML markup is HTML 3.2, and not HTML 4 based. This is because the Android `Html` class doesn't handle HTML 4 markup, and the `Html` class is effectively what is used to load and string resource containing markup. Create a new resource file in the `res/values` directory named `strings.xml` and copy the following code snippet into the new file:

```xml
<resources>
    <string name="inverse">1/x</string>
    <string name="square">
        x<sup><font size="10">2</font></sup>
    </string>
    <string name="cube">
        x<sup><font size="10">3</font></sup>
    </string>
    <string name="pow">
        y<sup><font size="10">x</font></sup>
    </string>
    <string name="percent">%</string>

    <string name="cos">cos</string>
    <string name="sin">sin</string>
    <string name="tan">tan</string>
    <string name="log2">
        log<sub><font size="10">2</font></sub>
    </string>
    <string name="log10">
        log<sub><font size="10">10</font></sub>
    </string>

    <string name="acos">
        cos<sup><font size="10">-1</font></sup>
    </string>
    <string name="asin">
        sin<sup><font size="10">-1</font></sup>
    </string>
    <string name="atan">
        tan<sup><font size="10">-1</font></sup>
    </string>
    <string name="log">log</string>
    <string name="log1p">log1p</string>

    <string name="e"><i>e</i></string>
    <string name="pi">&#x03c0;</string>
    <string name="random">rnd</string>
    <string name="sqrt">&#x221a;</string>
    <string name="hyp">hyp</string>
</resources>
```

The unicode hex values in the `pi` and `sqrt` string values are used to reference the unicode characters for a lower case Greek Pi symbol, and the standard square root symbol.

Styling the scientific layout

The styles used in the standard calculator layout don't work very well for the scientific layout. In order to change the styles for the scientific layout, you can add the new styling to a new `values` directory for the landscape layout. Copy the following code snippet to a new file named `res/values-land/styles.xml`:

```
<resources>
    <style name="CalculatorDisplay">
        <item name="android:background">
            @drawable/display_background
        </item>
    </style>
    <style name="ScientificButton" parent="style/CalculatorButton">
        <item name="android:textSize">12sp</item>
    </style>
</resources>
```

The first style resource in the preceding snippet is used for the display area of the calculator. As with the standard calculator, we use the `display_background` shape written earlier in this chapter. We also define a new style for the scientific buttons. The scientific buttons will be exactly the same as the standard calculator buttons, except with a much smaller font. Since there are many more scientific buttons than standard buttons, the smaller font allows us to comfortably fit more of them on the screen.

Building the scientific layout

The scientific layout is comprised of the standard calculator buttons on the right side of the screen, with twenty additional buttons on the left side of the screen. The additional buttons represent mathematical functions and constants, most of which can be found in the `java.lang.Math` and `java.lang.StrictMath` classes. The following figure illustrates how we want to layout the scientific calculator:

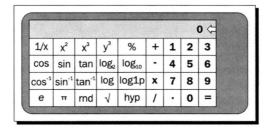

The effect of the new styles for the landscape layout on the calculator display will "remove" the margin between the display and the buttons. Since the landscape layout has less vertical space, such padding is nothing more than a waste of space that should be used for the buttons in order to maintain a reasonable size.

Time for action – coding the scientific layout

The landscape layout is broken into various sub-layouts in order to maintain IDs for the two individual functional areas: Scientific functions and standard functions. Maintaining these with their own ID values allows much easier detection of the available functionality from the Java code. Instead of the Java code deciding on the available functionality based on the configuration, it can use findViewById and test for null to check if the scientific functionality is available. This is not unlike "capability testing" in JavaScript (as apposed to inspection).

1. Create a new resource directory named res/layout-land.

2. Create a new layout resource XML file in the layout-land directory named main.xml and open this file in an editor or IDE.

3. Declare the root element of the new layout as a vertical LinearLayout consuming all of the available screen space:

```
<LinearLayout
    xmlns:android="http://schemas.android.com/apk/res/android"
    android:orientation="vertical"
    android:layout_width="fill_parent"
    android:layout_height="fill_parent">
```

4. The first element of the new layout is a RelativeLayout element to wrap the TextView and ImageView that are used as the calculator display:

```
<RelativeLayout style="@style/CalculatorDisplay"
                android:layout_width="fill_parent"
                android:layout_height="wrap_content">
```

5. Copy the TextView and ImageView elements from the standard calculator layout (res/layout/main.xml) as the two child elements of the RelativeLayout declared previously:

```
<ImageView android:id="@+id/delete"
           android:src="@android:drawable/ic_input_delete"
           android:layout_centerInParent="true"
           android:layout_alignParentRight="true"
           android:layout_width="wrap_content"
           android:layout_height="wrap_content"/>
<TextView android:id="@+id/display"
          style="@style/CalculatorTextDisplay"
          android:text="0"
```

```
            android:layout_alignParentTop="true"
            android:layout_toLeftOf="@id/delete"
            android:layout_width="fill_parent"
            android:layout_height="wrap_content"/>
```

6. The second child element of the root `LinearLayout` is a horizontally-oriented `LinearLayout` consuming the remainder of the screen space:

```
<LinearLayout android:orientation="horizontal"
            android:layout_width="fill_parent"
            android:layout_height="fill_parent">
```

7. Inside the new `LinearLayout` child, declare a new `TableLayout` to fill with the scientific buttons:

```
<TableLayout android:id="@+id/scientific_functions"
            android:layout_width="wrap_content"
            android:layout_height="fill_parent"
            android:layout_marginRight="10dip">
```

8. Create a `TableRow` element inside the `scientific_functions TableLayout`, to contain the first row of scientific `Button` elements:

```
<TableRow android:layout_margin="0px"
            android:layout_weight="1">
```

9. Declare the first five scientific functions as `Button` elements inside the new `TableRow`. The `Button` ID should be the same as the name of the resource string to be used as the `Button` label:

```
<Button style="@style/ScientificButton"
        android:id="@+id/inverse"
        android:text="@string/inverse"/>
```

10. The first row of scientific `Button` widgets contains `inverse`, `square`, `cube`, `pow`, and `percent`.

11. Create a `TableRow` with the second row of scientific `Button` widgets containing `cos`, `sin`, `tan`, `log2`, and `log10`.

12. The third scientific `Button` widgets in the third `TableRow` should be `acos`, `asin`, `atan`, `log`, and `log1p`.

13. The fourth and final `TableRow` of `Button` widgets should be `e`, `pi`, `random`, `sqrt`, and `hyp`.

14. That is all of the scientific functions, now create another `TableLayout` in the `LinearLayout` child element for the standard functions:

```
<TableLayout android:id="@+id/standard_functions"
             android:layout_width="fill_parent"
             android:layout_height="fill_parent"
             android:layout_margin="0px"
             android:stretchColumns="0,1,2,3">
```

15. Copy the contents of the `standard_functions TableLayout` in `res/layout/main.xml` into the new `TableLayout` element.

What just happened?

In the preceding layout, we reuse much of the basics that we created in the standard calculator layout, with the addition of a new `TableLayout` structure to contain the scientific functions. The new `TableLayout` is sized to a width of `wrap_content` and will only consume the amount of horizontal space needed to fit all of the `Button` widgets. The other main difference between the two `TableLayout` elements is that the scientific table doesn't stretch its columns, since this would effectively be the same as sizing it as `fill_parent` and leaving no space for the standard functions.

You'll also notice that among the string resources used to create the scientific `Button` labels, those that use HTML markup, do so without using XML escape entities (such as `&lt;` and `&gt;`). This is the main indicator to the resource compiler that a string resource contains markup and should be consumed differently. This usage requires that all HTML markup that is placed into a string resource must both conform to the HTML 3.2 specification, and remain valid XML content.

In order to test the new landscape layout, you'll either need to define an emulator device with a landscape screen size, or run the application on a physical device. Creating a virtual device in the emulator can be done with the **android** application in the **tools** directory of your Android SDK installation, the same tool used to create skeleton projects. The following is a screenshot of the new layout running on a physical Android device:

Have a go hero – using include in existing layouts

The preceding layout has several elements of the standard layout that it reuses. This is a good time to extract these elements into their own layout files and then make use of the include element to place them into the two specific layout resources. Information on layout includes can be found in *Chapter 5, Developing Non-Linear Layouts*.

1. Create a display.xml layout resource to contain the RelativeLayout with the calculator display, and include this at the appropriate point in the main.xml layout resource files.

2. Create a standard_buttons.xml layout resource to contain the TableLayout named standard_functions, and include this at the appropriate point in the main.xml layout resource files.

Handling the Activity restart

When the device changes orientation, the CalculatorActivity object on the screen is restarted with the new orientation. In this application, the restart leads to a serious problem: the state of the calculator is lost. As discussed in *Chapter 4, Leveraging Activities and Intents*, there are times when you need to take control of your application state in Android—saving it before shutdown and restoring it when the Activity is started again.

You'll need to override the Activity.onSaveInstanceState method to store the current state of your calculator in the provided Bundle. This Bundle object will be provided to you in the onCreate method when being restarted due to a configuration change. In your onCreate method, check to make sure that the provided Bundle object is non-null before restoring the save parameters from it.

Have a go hero – implementing the scientific calculation logic

The calculator should currently be able to function from the standard calculation buttons. However, the new scientific functions don't have any backing structures. Further, if you re-orient your device to change between scientific and standard layouts, any "in-progress" calculation will be lost.

The steps that need to be completed for the scientific calculations to function as expected, are as follows:

1. Implement the onSaveInstanceState to save the calculation state to the provided Bundle object.
2. Implement the onCreate method to restore the saved state from its provided Bundle object (assuming one is given).
3. Add the functionality required to make the scientific Button widgets function as expected, to the Calculator class you wrote earlier.

Supporting hardware keyboards

The calculator we developed here is now a great on-screen Android calculator application, with both the simple and scientific functionality you'd expect. However, if a device has a hardware keyboard, the user will probably expect to be able to use it, which currently they can't. Further, if the device lacks a touchscreen, clicking on-screen buttons will quickly become frustrating. We need to implement hardware keyboard support for the application.

Implementing the hardware keyboard handling code is only useful to you if you've done the "Have a go Hero" sections and built a `Calculator` class to perform the required functions. In order to handle hardware keyboard events, you'll use the methods declared in the `KeyEvent.Callback` interface. The `Activity` class implements the `KeyEvent.Callback` interface already, and provides default handling for all of the methods. For our handling of these key-events, we only need to override the `onKeyDown` method.

For this `onKeyDown` implementation, it's a good idea to make sure that the key events are coming from a hardware keyboard by checking the flags of the `KeyEvent`. It's also a good idea to pass it to your parent class before processing it yourself. Finally, if you're working on Android 2.0 (API-Level 5) or higher, you should check that the `KeyEvent` is not cancelled before processing it (again this is one of the `KeyEvent` flags). The following is a code snippet from my implementation of the `onKeyDown` method:

```java
@Override
public boolean onKeyDown(
        final int keyCode,
        final KeyEvent event) {
    super.onKeyDown(keyCode, event);
    boolean handled = false;
    if((event.getFlags() & KeyEvent.FLAG_SOFT_KEYBOARD) == 0) {
        switch(keyCode) {
            case KeyEvent.KEYCODE_0:
                calculator.zero();
                handled = true;
                break;
            case KeyEvent.KEYCODE_1:
                calculator.one();
                handled = true;
                break;
            // Cases for each of the handles keys
        }
        display.setText(calculator.getCurrentDisplay());
    }
```

```
        return handled;
    }
```

The preceding code snippet invokes a method for each one of the different keys that can be pressed on a hardware keyboard.

 If your Android device doesn't have a hardware keyboard, you can test this code using the emulator—your PC's keyboard, and the on-screen keyboard to the right of the emulator display, are both classified as hardware keyboards by the emulator.

Adding in display animations

Currently, the application has all the makings of a great calculator application. However, the display is currently just a simple `TextView` object. In order to improve the user experience, we should make use of a `ViewSwitcher` object to swap the `TextView` out when the calculator operation is changed, or when the "equals" `Button` is pressed.

Time for action – animating the display

In order to build a nice slide-out-slide-in animation for the calculator display, we'll need to define our own animations and bind them to a `ViewSwitcher` object. This will also require us to make changes to the Java code in order to handle the new mechanism. Since we don't want the view to animate each time a new digit is typed, we will make direct changes to the `TextView` currently on the screen.

1. Create a new XML resource file in the `res/anim` directory named `slide_out_top.xml`, and open this in an editor or IDE.

2. Declare a y-translate animation from `0%` to `100%` as the only element in the animation resource:

```
<translate
    xmlns:android="http://schemas.android.com/apk/res/android"
    android:fromYDelta="0%"
    android:toYDelta="-100%"
    android:duration="300"/>
```

3. Create a new XML resource file in the `res/anim` directory named `slide_in_bottom.xml`, and open this file in an editor or IDE.

4. Declare a y-translate animation from `100%` to `0%` as the only element in the animation resource:

```
<translate
    xmlns:android="http://schemas.android.com/apk/res/android"
    android:fromYDelta="100%"
    android:toYDelta="0%"
    android:duration="300"/>
```

5. Open either your `display.xml` file, or both of the `main.xml` files in your editor of IDE, and which among them you should open will depend on whether you have completed the "Have a go Hero – Layout Includes".

6. In the `RelativeLayout` used for the display, replace the `TextView` named `display` with a `ViewSwitcher` element using the two new animation resources:

```
<ViewSwitcher android:id="@+id/display"
              android:inAnimation="@anim/slide_in_bottom"
              android:outAnimation="@anim/slide_out_top"
              android:layout_alignParentTop="true"
              android:layout_toLeftOf="@id/delete"
              android:layout_width="fill_parent"
              android:layout_height="wrap_content">
```

7. As child elements to the `ViewSwitcher`, declare two `TextView` elements with the `CalculatorTextDisplay` style:

```
<TextView style="@style/CalculatorTextDisplay"
          android:text="0"
          android:layout_width="fill_parent"
          android:layout_height="wrap_content"/>
```

8. Both of the `TextView` elements will be identical to each other.

What just happened?

The use of the `ViewSwitcher` for the display will cause any existing Java code to crash, since the Java code will be expecting the object to be a `TextView` of some sort. What you need to do instead is update the display using the `ViewSwitcher.getCurrentView`, instead of the `ViewSwitcher` itself.

When an operation `Button` is used, for example, the multiply or equals `Button`, you'll want to place the next display content on the `ViewSwitcher.getNextView` widget, and then invoke the `ViewSwitcher.showNext()` method. The animation of the number disappearing upwards with the new content appearing from the bottom of the display is a simple, but explanatory animation. It's also quite commonly used in calculator applications, meaning the user will usually be comfortable with it.

In this application's case, the animation is more eye-candy than useful. However, if you implemented a history-stack in the calculator, the animation could be reversed when the user presses the "back" `Button`. A history-stack in a calculator is a very useful structure because it allows slight variations of the same calculations to be run over and over again.

Have a go hero – rounding off

This calculator application is quite complete at this point. It's been styled, and has some nice eye-candy and functions as expected. It does have a few caveats, however—the scientific calculation layout doesn't work very well on small-screen devices. The following screenshot is the application running in scientific layout on a small-screen phone:

The preceding image also demonstrates how some devices theme applications. In order to make sure the application works well on all devices:

1. Define a new `values` directory for small-screen devices.

2. Create a new `styles.xml` file in the directory with styles that have less margin and padding than the defaults.

3. Reduce the size of the `display` font when on a small-screen device that has a landscape orientation.

This sort of rounding-off process will follow most successful Android application projects. It's a matter of trying the application out on various different emulator configurations and devices, and then leveraging the resource-loaders to ensure the application works well on as many devices as possible.

Summary

Creating an application theme is a key part of the success of a new application, whether running on Android, the desktop, or on the Web. We've explored how to make use of the various tools that Android provides in order to keep an application consistent in order to keep it user-friendly.

An application's theme, and its look and feel go far beyond the simple styling. The more you personally use you application, the more you will see places where a slightly different color, or a transition animation will make a difference. Each of those small differences is what makes an application truly user-friendly, because it makes the application feel polished.

While running on hundreds of wildly different devices, Android makes it easy for developers to keep their applications running as though they were built specifically for that hardware. The resource-loader system is one of the most key structures in Android, and not to leverage it, can be suicidal to the application.

I strongly recommend familiarizing yourself with existing Android applications, as well as applications on other mobile devices. Knowing how to drive a decent image-manipulation application also goes a long way. Draw a diagram of each of your screens before your start building them, and pencil and paper is often the best way to get an idea about the user interface, before you start coding.

Think carefully about where you can use the existing Android icons and styles, and where you will want to replace or extend them. You always want to keep your application consistent, but adding some flashy eye-candy is often what makes an application stand out from the crowd.

With the combination of XML resources and the Java language, Android is a highly compelling platform to design and code for. It's widely deployed and has excellent developer support. There are dozens of hardware manufacturers producing Android devices, in all shapes and sizes, and thousands of developers making applications.

In this book, we've worked on leveraging the Android platform to build applications that are user-focused, easy to use, and good looking. The Android platform and the Android Markets allow for a captive audience and great exposure for new ideas. From here on, you should be able to add your own unique ideas and work to the Android ecosystem. Anything that has been done can always be done better, and anything that hasn't been done, has people waiting for it. Whether you're part of a team, or hacking away on the-next-big-thing in your attic at night, the key to a successful application is a great user-interface.

Pop quiz answers

Chapter 1

Layouts as XML files

Question number	Answers
1	b
2	d
3	c

Populating an activity

Question number	Answers
1	b
2	c
3	c

Chapter 2

List views and adapters

Question number	Answers
1	c
2	a
3	c

Chapter 3

Gallery objects and ImageViews

Question number	Answers
1	c
2	b
3	a

Chapter 4

Intents & Activities

Question number	Answers
1	c
2	b
3	a

Chapter 5.

Custom layouts

Question number	Answers
1	d
2	b
3	c

Chapter 6

Text input

Question number	Answers
1	c
2	c
3	a

Chapter 8

The WebView widget

Question number	Answers
1	d
2	b
3	d

WebView versus native layouts

Question number	Answers
1	a
2	c
3	c

Chapter 10

Layout resources

Question number	Answers
1	d *Hint:(they are loaded as objects, not compiled to classes)*
2	d
3	c

Nine-Patch Images

Question number	Answers
1	b
2	c
3	a

Android resources

Question number	Answers
1	c
2	a
3	c

Index

C

calculator
button images, creating for 255-257
numeric display, styling 260, 262
styling 254
CalculatorActivity object 269
calculator buttons
styling 257-259
calculator display
slide-out-slide-in animation, building
for 271, 272
calculator logic
adding 262
CardLayout 121
CHOICE_MODE_MULTIPLE 40
CHOICE_MODE_NONE 38, 42
CHOICE_MODE_SINGLE 39
choice modes, ListView class
about 38
CHOICE_MODE_MULTIPLE 40
CHOICE_MODE_NONE 38
CHOICE_MODE_SINGLE 39
CircleLayout
example 137, 138
using 137
CircleLayout class 136
ColorAdapter 183
common dimensions
defining 25
complex layouts
creating, with include tag 97
creating, with ViewStub 99
configuration changes, handling
about 244
landscape layouts, providing 245
screen content, altering 247
text input, providing on landscape layout 246
consistency 67
contact editor
creating 141-143
content
displaying, relative layouts used 204, 205
displaying, with WebView class 197
content-centric Activity
about 193, 194
user attention, drawing for
information 196, 197

content-centric layout
about 193
online music store, developing 213-217
content display
design options, considering for 194, 195
user behavior, considering for 195, 196
CSS style resources
and Android style resources,
differences 228, 229
CursorAdapter
creating 165-168
custom adapters
creating 47
menu, creating for restaurant 47
custom animation
creating 187
writing 188, 189
customized pizzas
ordering example 57, 58
custom layout
creating 134-136

D

data
getting, back from Intent 113, 114
listing 38
passing, in Intent 112
selecting 38
data set
modifying 159
date
capturing 156-158
DatePickerDialog 156
DatePicker widget 67, 156
design options
considering, for content display 194, 195
Dialog widgets 162
dots-per-inch. *See* DPI
DPI 243
draw9patch utility 241
drawable directory 242
Drawable object 230

Thank you for buying
Android User Interface Development Beginner's Guide

About Packt Publishing

Packt, pronounced 'packed', published its first book "*Mastering phpMyAdmin for Effective MySQL Management*" in April 2004 and subsequently continued to specialize in publishing highly focused books on specific technologies and solutions.

Our books and publications share the experiences of your fellow IT professionals in adapting and customizing today's systems, applications, and frameworks. Our solution based books give you the knowledge and power to customize the software and technologies you're using to get the job done. Packt books are more specific and less general than the IT books you have seen in the past. Our unique business model allows us to bring you more focused information, giving you more of what you need to know, and less of what you don't.

Packt is a modern, yet unique publishing company, which focuses on producing quality, cutting-edge books for communities of developers, administrators, and newbies alike. For more information, please visit our website: www.packtpub.com.

About Packt Open Source

In 2010, Packt launched two new brands, Packt Open Source and Packt Enterprise, in order to continue its focus on specialization. This book is part of the Packt Open Source brand, home to books published on software built around Open Source licences, and offering information to anybody from advanced developers to budding web designers. The Open Source brand also runs Packt's Open Source Royalty Scheme, by which Packt gives a royalty to each Open Source project about whose software a book is sold.

Writing for Packt

We welcome all inquiries from people who are interested in authoring. Book proposals should be sent to author@packtpub.com. If your book idea is still at an early stage and you would like to discuss it first before writing a formal book proposal, contact us; one of our commissioning editors will get in touch with you.

We're not just looking for published authors; if you have strong technical skills but no writing experience, our experienced editors can help you develop a writing career, or simply get some additional reward for your expertise.

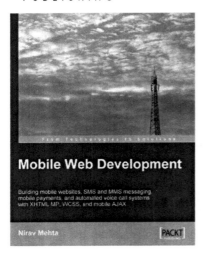

Silverlight 4 User Interface Cookbook

ISBN: 978-1-847198-86-0   Paperback: 280 pages

Build and implement rich, standard-friendly user interfaces with Silverlight and Expression Blend

1. The first and only book to focus exclusively on Silverlight UI development.

2. Have your applications stand out from the crowd with leading, innovative, and friendly user interfaces.

3. Detailed instructions on how to implement specific user interface patterns together with XAML and C# (where needed) code, and explanations that are easy-to-understand and follow..

4. Real world projects which you can explore in detail and make modifications as you go.

jQuery UI 1.6: The User Interface Library for jQuery

ISBN: 978-1-847195-12-8   Paperback: 440 pages

Build highly interactive web applications with ready-to-use widgets of the jQuery user interface library

1. Packed with examples and clear explanations to easily design elegant and powerful front-end interfaces for your web applications

2. Organize your interfaces with reusable widgets like accordions, date pickers, dialogs, sliders, tabs, and more

3. Enhance the interactivity of your pages by making elements drag and droppable, sortable, selectable, and resizable

4. No experience of jQuery UI expected, but familiarity with jQuery is required

Please check **www.PacktPub.com** for information on our titles

Breinigsville, PA USA
30 March 2011
258773BV00002B/73/P